Journeys in Complexity

In this book, fascinating autobiographical accounts by leading scholars in a variety of fields and disciplines provide a rich introduction to the art and science of complexity and systems thinking. We learn how the authors' interest in complexity thinking developed, the key figures and texts they encountered along the way, the experiences that shaped their path, their major works, and their personal journeys. This volume serves as an introduction to complexity as well as a vivid account of the personal and intellectual development of important scholars.

This book was originally published as a special issue of *World Futures*.

Alfonso Montuori is an educator, consultant, and musician. He is currently a Professor at the California Institute of Integral Studies, USA. He has been a Distinguished Professor in the School of Fine Arts at Miami University, in Oxford, Ohio, USA, and in 1985–1986 he taught at the Central South University in Hunan, China.

Journeys in Complexity

Autobiographical Accounts by Leading
Systems and Complexity Thinkers

Edited by
Alfonso Montuori

Routledge
Taylor & Francis Group

LONDON AND NEW YORK

First published 2015
by Routledge
2 Park Square, Milton Park, Abingdon, Oxon, OX14 4RN, UK

and by Routledge
711 Third Avenue, New York, NY 10017, USA

Routledge is an imprint of the Taylor & Francis Group, an informa business

British Library Cataloguing in Publication Data
A catalogue record for this book is available from the British Library

ISBN 13: 978-1-138-78847-3

Typeset in Times New Roman
by Taylor & Francis Books

Publisher's Note
The publisher accepts responsibility for any inconsistencies that may have arisen during the conversion of this book from journal articles to book chapters, namely the possible inclusion of journal terminology.

Disclaimer
Every effort has been made to contact copyright holders for their permission to reprint material in this book. The publishers would be grateful to hear from any copyright holder who is not here acknowledged and will undertake to rectify any errors or omissions in future editions of this book.

Contents

Citation Information

The chapters in this book were originally published in *World Futures*, volume 69, issues 4–6 (July 2013). When citing this material, please use the original page numbering for each article, as follows:

Chapter 1
Introduction to the Special Issue: The complexity of life and lives of complexity
Alfonso Montuori
World Futures, volume 69, issues 4–6 (July 2013) pp. 197–199

Chapter 2
Systems theory, arrogant and humble
Jay Ogilvy
World Futures, volume 69, issues 4–6 (July 2013) pp. 332–344

Chapter 3
Systems patterns and possibilities
Linda E. Olds
World Futures, volume 69, issues 4–6 (July 2013) pp. 382–396

Chapter 4
The starry night sky
Guy Burneko
World Futures, volume 69, issues 4–6 (July 2013) pp. 231–247

Chapter 5
A passion for pushing the limits
Elisabct Sahtouris
World Futures, volume 69, issues 4–6 (July 2013) pp. 359–381

Chapter 6
My life in chaos
Allan Leslie Combs
World Futures, volume 69, issues 4–6 (July 2013) pp. 248–268

Chapter 7

Human possibilities: An integrated systems approach
Riane Eisler
World Futures, volume 69, issues 4–6 (July 2013) pp. 269–289

Chapter 8

Encounter with a wizard
Stanley Krippner
World Futures, volume 69, issues 4–6 (July 2013) pp. 290–310

Chapter 9

A cigarette is sometimes just a cigarette
Albert Low
World Futures, volume 69, issues 4–6 (July 2013) pp. 311–331

Chapter 10

*Bringing forth that which is within: How an invisible hand led me
to a life that "feels like my own"*
S. J. Goerner
World Futures, volume 69, issues 4–6 (July 2013) pp. 345–358

Chapter 11

Complexity and transdisciplinarity: Reflections on theory and practice
Alfonso Montuori
World Futures, volume 69, issues 4–6 (July 2013) pp. 200–230

Please direct any queries you may have about the citations to
clsuk.permissions@cengage.com

Notes on Contributors

Guy Burneko, The Institute for Contemporary Ancient Learning, Seattle, Washington, USA

Allan Leslie Combs, Center for Consciousness Studies, California Institute of Integral Studies, San Francisco, California, USA

Riane Eisler, Center for Partnership Studies, Pacific Grove, California, USA

S. J. Goerner, The Integral Science Institute, Chapel Hill, North Carolina, USA

Stanley Krippner, Saybrook University, San Francisco, California, USA

Albert Low, Montreal Zen Center, Montreal, Canada

Alfonso Montuori, California Institute of Integral Studies, San Francisco, California, USA

Jay Ogilvy, Independent Scholar, Castle Valley, Utah, USA

Linda E. Olds, Professor Emerita, Linfield College, McMinnville, Oregon, USA

Elisabet Sahtouris, Independent Scholar, Mallorca, Spain

INTRODUCTION

THE COMPLEXITY OF LIFE AND LIVES OF COMPLEXITY

ALFONSO MONTUORI

California Institute of Integral Studies, San Francisco, California, USA

INTRODUCTION

Everything is said by an observer, Humberto Maturana (1987) tells us. In this collection of articles, I have invited one set of "observers" to tell us more about themselves. I have asked them to tell us who they are, why they went down the particular roads they chose and have become identified with, what they found, and how and what they have observed. The observers are all scholars who have, to a greater or lesser extent, expressed an interest in and drawn on systems and complexity theories. As we can see from the rich variety of their articles, they interpret these theories in different ways, emphasizing different aspects in different contexts and disciplines, exploring different issues.

We are slowly coming out of many years in which scholarly inquiry meant completely eliminating the inquirer, the researcher, the writer, sacrificed on the altar of objectivity. In the process, we never really knew much about who we were reading or listening to, and how they really developed their ideas. It was mostly easy enough to situate an author's ideas in the discourse, in the larger ecology of ideas. But we never really had a sense of the personal journey, of how the ideas and concerns and passions emerged from very real events, from a history, from connections, interactions, exchanges, dialogues. And we certainly never had any idea of who the people behind the ideas where.

It's usually biographies and autobiographies that tell us about the lives and experiences of the thinkers we read and whose ideas we work with. In the worlds of systems theory and cybernetics, we have biographies of Ludwig von Berta-lanffy (Davidson 1983), Norbert Wiener (Conway and Siegelman 2005), and more recently Ervin Laszlo's autobiography (2011). We also have accounts of the interactions between various founders of systems theory and cybernetics (Bateson 2004; Heims 1991; Pickering 2010), Gleick's best-selling account of the birth of chaos theory (1988) and Waldrop's account of complexity (1992). In France we have a number of biographies of Edgar Morin, who, with his work on complex thought, spans all the "transversal" approaches like systems theory and cybernetics (Bianchi 2001; Lemieux 2009). It seems to me these accounts are necessary in order to contextualize these approaches, to make the thinkers' trajectories somewhat more transparent, to make their efforts more human, so that they do not appear like some deterministic inevitability that follows from simply applying the scientific method.

The authors in this issue will be discussing that strange family of interrelated approaches, General System Theory, cybernetics, chaos, and complexity theories, in many of their permutations. These different approaches have certainly spawned a large number of interpretations. Already in the early 1990s, systems theory–oriented management textbooks offered a wide range of approach with at times truly radically different assumptions, epistemologies, implications, and applications (Cavaleri and Obloj 1993; Jackson 1991). I still continue to be amazed by the multiple and often contradictory ways in which the approaches are understood and interpreted.

Our contributors come to systems and complexity theories from a wide range of interests. In each case they were seeking a more systemic, complex way of approaching their inquiry. It is interesting that they probably all trace their interest to experiences with different topics, with different precursors and disciplines. We do find references to Chinese philosophy, key figures in Western philosophy such as Kant, Hegel, and Whitehead, and "homeless" thinkers like Bateson. The recurrence of spiritual and feminist concerns is likely more due to the choice of contributors. It reflects an interesting and potentially very promising direction, and one that is navigated by our contributors skillfully and with considerable care.

Of course, these articles do not attempt to pretend to provide us with the "one right way," *the* correct interpretation of systemic/complex approaches. They offer insights into how eminent scholars have interpreted and applied this family of approaches to make sense of the world, and specifically to go beyond the limitations of more reductionist approaches. They lead by example.

REFERENCES

Bateson, M. C. 2004. *Our own metaphor: A personal account of a conference on the effects of conscious purpose on human adaptation.* Cresskill, NJ: Hampton Press.

Bianchi, F. 2001. *Le fil des idées. Une éco-biographie intellectuelle d'Edgar Morin. [The thread of ideas. An intellectual eco-biography of Edgar Morin].* Paris: Seuil.

Cavaleri, S. and K. Obloj. 1993. *Management systems.* Belmont, CA: Wadsworth.

Conway, F. and J. Siegelman. 2005. *Dark hero of the information age: In search of Norbert Wiener, the father of cybernetics.* New York: Basic Books.

Davidson, M. 1983. *Uncommon sense: The life and thought of Ludwig von Bertalanffy (1901–1972), father of general systems theory* (1st ed.). Los Angeles: J. P. Tarcher.

Gleick, J. 1988. *Chaos: Making a new science.* New York: Penguin.

Heims, S. J. 1991. *The cybernetics group.* Cambridge, MA: MIT Press.

Jackson, M. 1991. *Systems methodology for management sciences.* New York: Springer.

Laszlo, E. 2011. *Simply genius!: And other tales from my life: An informal autobiography* (1st ed.). Carlsbad: Hay House.

Lemieux, E. 2009. *Edgar Morin l'indiscipliné.* Paris: Seuil.

Maturana, H. 1987. Everything is said by an observer. In *Gaia, A way of knowing*, Ed. W. I. Thompson, 65–82. Great Barrington, MA: Lindisfarne Press.

Pickering, A. 2010. *The cybernetic brain: Sketches of another future*. Chicago and London: University of Chicago Press.

Waldrop, M. M. 1992. *Complexity: The emerging science at the edge of order and chaos*. New York: Simon & Schuster.

SYSTEMS THEORY, ARROGANT AND HUMBLE

JAY OGILVY

Independent Scholar, Castle Valley, Utah, USA

Systems Theory has multiple lineages: From Hegel's System, through General Systems Theory, to Systems Dynamics, cybernetics, and various approaches to various complex systems like healthcare. This article develops a distinction between those approaches to complex systems that stem from a common trunk: the insight that all things are interconnected. Arrogant systems thinkers aspire to a totalizing grasp of the whole. Humble systems thinkers start from the same premise of interconnectedness, but recoil from totalization and become pessimistic about the possibility of avoiding unintended side effects of any intervention in complex systems.

First I would like to thank our esteemed editor, Alfonso Montuori, for his invitation to contribute to this issue. I have learned from my attempt to answer his call. What is systems/complexity/cybernetic theory? How did I come to it? What drew me? The nature of the call itself invites a kind of reflection that is appropriate to the subject matter, namely, to place the discipline in the context of a larger whole, a life of inquiry and all the various subjects to which these tools might be applied.

In his initial letter of invitation, Montuori notes that he can find no text that adequately introduces the new student to the subject matter he has in mind, and that the challenge may indeed lie in some confusion located somewhere between his own mind and the subject matter itself. Is there a there *there*? Or is there some confusion *in here*, in one's own understanding of something that is in itself quite clear?

I sympathize. I remember well an invitation from Fritjof Capra[1] who asked me to address a conference on the subject of systems theory. He knew my work and he seemed quite confident that I was up to the task. At first I agreed. Of course I knew about systems theory. But then as the date approached, I realized that, a little like Augustine, who wrote that he knew perfectly well what *time* was until someone asked him about it, so likewise, when asked to talk about systems theory, I was at something of a loss. Yes, I knew a lot about various systems, from Hegel's System (as capitalized by Kierkegaard in his rejection of it) to Norbert Wiener and Gregory Bateson on cybernetic systems, to the contemporary public education and healthcare *systems* ... but when it came to explicating "systems theory," I suddenly found myself aware of all of the works of Heinz von Foerster, Theodor Dhobzhansky, or Jay Forrester and his school that I had *not* read.

What *is* systems theory? I suddenly realized that I had hardly a clue. And that was 29 years ago. So when Monty's letter of invitation arrived, I decided to take it seriously and to fill in some of the gaps in my boundless ignorance. I hunted through my library for an unread book whose title had mocked me for years: *Systems Thinking* edited by F. E. Emery (1969), a name I had admired from afar after once meeting his colleague, Eric Trist. It's a wonderful anthology that pulls together under Emery's authoritative editorship many of the classic papers by Wolfgang Köhler, "Closed and Open Systems" (1938), Ludwig von Bertalanffy, "The Theory of Open Systems in Physics and Biology" (1950), W. Ross Ashby, "Self-Regulation and Requisite Variety" (1956), and Russ Ackoff, "Systems, Organizations, and Interdisciplinary Research" (1960). These are my people, I said to myself, and I dove in with relish and delight.

After reading and appreciating most of the chapters, I came to the very last paper in the volume, "The Road to 1977," by M. Ways, a paper published in *Fortune* magazine in 1967. This paper, read in retrospect in the year 2003, is extremely instructive with respect to the pretensions of what I will call *arrogant* systems theory, and therefore suggestive of why I usually (but not always) prefer *humble* systems theory. I will review this paper, and then explain more about what I mean by *arrogant* and *humble* systems theory.

ARROGANT SYSTEMS THEORY

The paper by Ways is built around the device of addressing a high school graduate in the year 1967. What can we tell him about the decade ahead? "By 1977, college and graduate school behind him, he will become a full-fledged member of American society, contributing his trained skills and using his informed values to shape its future." M. Ways—a name I have not heard before or since—then shares with the readers of *Fortune* the great achievements of systems theory that will help this young man and those around him, "a new style of private and public planning, problem solving, and choosing. This new style promises to add a missing ingredient to the quality of American life."

A few paragraphs later, he breaks into italics for emphasis:

> *The further advance of this new style is the most significant prediction that can be made about the next ten years. By 1977 this new way of dealing with the future will be recognized at home and abroad as a salient American characteristic. Compared to this development, the argument between the liberals and the conservatives, while it will retain a certain atavistic fascination, will come to seem about as relevant to the main proceedings as a fistfight in the grandstand during a tense innings of a World Series game* (372–388).

Our author then acknowledges, not unlike the editor of this present issue, that, "The new style of dealing with the future has no accepted, inclusive name." But, "the techniques themselves, which are apt to be called 'systems analysis,' or 'systems planning', are now widely used." He lists a series of characteristics of this way of thinking, all of which will be familiar to the writers and readers of this issue, and concludes his list with:

5. An emphasis on information, prediction, and persuasion, rather than on coercive or authoritarian power, as the main agents of coordinating the separate elements of an effort.
6. An increased capability of predicting the combined effect of several lines of simultaneous action on one another; this can modify policy so as to reduce unwanted consequences or it can generate other *lines* of action to correct or compensate for such predicted consequences (Ways 1967, 375)

Again I said to myself, this is my kind of thinking. For the past 30 years I have been practicing strategic planning using alternative scenarios, "modifying policy so as to reduce unwanted consequences," generating different "*lines* of action to correct or compensate for such predicted consequences." So *this* is where scenario planning came from: From the systems thinkers of the 1940s, 1950s, and 1960s! I had often suspected as much. I read further with interest and curiosity, only to find that, as his crowning example of the strength and power of this new way of thinking, M. Ways, writing in 1967, offers up the work of Robert McNamara's system of planning for the Vietnam War. "True, there have been shortages of specific materials and underestimations of cost. Nevertheless, the Vietnam war thus far has been the best-calculated military supply effort in twentieth-century U. S. history."

Oh my! If our high school graduate of 1967 puts his faith in this new way of thinking, by 1977, rather than having graduated from high school and graduate school as an expert in systems thinking, he is just as likely to have come home in a body bag with the honor of having his name inscribed in the Vietnam War Memorial.

Hindsight, as they say, is 20/20. Surely it is unfair to brand all of systems theory with this one dreadful failure, but it gives one pause: What is it about systems theory that might lead to such dreadful miscalculations? Reflecting on the great range of systems theorists and the consequences of their ideas, it occurs to me that the great temptation of systems thinkers is *totalizing too quickly.* Because you know that you cannot understand the part apart from an understanding of its place in a larger whole, and you also know that every so-called "whole" is always but a part of some greater whole, you then come to believe that you cannot understand *anything* unless you understand *everything.* You therefore become a generalist in the fine tradition of thinkers from Hegel to Gregory Bateson, thinkers who refused to remain confined to some narrow specialty.

Think of some examples: Watzlawick and Weakland, R.D. Laing, all that takes-a-village campaigning about education—you can never locate a pathology in just one place. Not in the single individual, because you have to understand the individual in the context of the family (cf. R. D. Laing's *The Politics of the Family*, 1969). But you cannot really understand the family without understanding its place in a larger society, and now you are into mastering the disciplines of sociology and anthropology. And if you follow the trail further, as members of the Frankfurt School did, from psychology through sociology to politics, you will be drawn inexorably, as they were, to something like Marxism (or, as they called it to gain safer cover during their exile to the United States during the Second World War, "*critical theory*"). Once you come to understand the linkages between psychology, sociology, aesthetics, and politics, you will think you have to have an answer for *everything* before you feel prepared to say *anything.*

You become victim to see-sawing back and forth between the sins of the specialist, who learns more and more about less and less until he knows everything about nothing, and the sins of the generalist, who knows less and less about more and more until she knows nothing about everything. It's possible to break this see-saw by denying the tradeoff. Just because you learn as much as you can about *more* different subjects, from the sciences to the humanities, it does not follow that you learn less about each. It *is* possible to be master of several disciplines, not just one. If you want to follow a hyper-quantified way of doing the math to prove the point, imagine that the 80/20 rule applies to knowledge acquisition of a *field* of knowledge, where the definition of a "field" follows very closely the departmental structures of our major universities as represented in their course catalogs. They all have fairly similar taxonomies of the *fields* of knowledge. If you agree that the 80/20 rule applies (such that you achieve 80% of your goal with the first 20% of your effort, while it will take another four times as much effort to cover the last 20% of total mastery), then if you want to know virtually *everything* about *something* you are going to spend *five times* as much time as it would take someone else to gain 80% mastery of that field.

If a dilettante generalist, who thought that 80% was quite *good enough* used the rest of his time to acquire a mere 80% command of four other fields in the time he saved *not* acquiring 100% mastery of just one, would that so-called dilettante not tend to find instructive isomorphisms, memes, and tropes that repeat themselves across different fields? A certain value would accrue to these unpredictable combinatorial effects. Ideas would emerge that might never have occurred to the specialist in any one field. Thus did Bateson's studies of evolution inform his ideas about education, and so did his ideas about psychology influence his thinking about anthropology, and vice versa. If you think of these combinatorial effects as following successive cycles, you see how thoughts proliferate, how the trunk of one idea branches into several, which then break out into countless leaves. They did not call it "the tree of knowledge" for nothing.

You can observe a kind of broad gauge brilliance in people we all know. There are some who possess so vast a command of so many disciplines that, rather than being masters of none, they are hyper-masters of many. Their minds dart so quickly and with such relish from information theory to music, from cybernetics to Bach. Douglas Hofstadter comes immediately to mind.

The playfulness exhibited by Hofstadter—the incredible inventiveness of the sheer varieties of sketches—shows a mind in which the combinatorial effects of many cycles of recombination self-multiply until the number of interactions goes exponential and begins to soar on the logic of compound interest, and the multiples keep multiplying on a much larger base. You can see this range, this capaciousness, in the writings of Dan Dennett and Nick Humphrey where you find throwaway quotes revealing a depth of knowledge in many different fields.

There is an *Aw shucks* trope often evident in systems theorists as they oscillate between the humble and the arrogant. It comes out with a twinkle of the eye behind nerdy glasses. You see it in Bateson's chats with his then very young daughter, Mary Catherine, who clearly benefited from their Louis Carroll–like whimsicality (see Bateson 1972). By putting certain thoughts in the form of child's play, systems thinkers can disarm critics who might otherwise be able to identify an amazing arrogance and pomposity in the very idea that anyone could ever master *the whole system!* You see this *aw shucks* rhetoric in the writings of Russ Ackoff from time to time.

You see it in Marvin Minsky and Ray Kurzweil in its arrogant form; you see it in Bill Joy in its humble form. Bill Joy, the brains behind Sun Microsystems, wrote in a cover story for *WIRED* magazine entitled, "The Future Doesn't Need Us" 2000, a very scary scenario about what could happen if garage technicians mixed and matched information theory and software with nano-technology and biotechnology to produce a witch's brew, a green slime or gray goo that could choke out the entire ecosystem in no time. The logic that inspires Joy's humble and fearful *not* knowing is precisely the combinatorial logic so prevalent in biotechnology, nano-technology, and information theory—the three fields whose combinations could produce unpredictable monsters as well as medical miracles.

The distinction between arrogant and humble forms of systems theory goes way back. You can see it in the difference between Socrates's self-effacing claim that he knew nothing about the things that really matter, and Aristotle's authoritative grasp of absolutely everything. You can see the distinction again in Kierkegaard's reaction against Hegel's System, his existential cry for the individual's freedom in the face of all the determinative forces exerted in and through Hegel's System. You can see it in the late Wittgenstein's rejection of his own earlier positivism in the youthful and rectilinear *Tractatus Logico Philosophicus* (1961). You can see it in feminism's rejection of hyper-masculine systems theory. Look at Evelyn Fox-Keller's work as opposed to E. O. Wilson's. Evelyn's is all about how the system of pheromone trails dictates the movement of all of the parts—the individual ants—and (as a combinatorial effect) the behavior of the whole, the entire ant colony. It took her years to convince her male colleagues that no one, least of all the so-called Queen, was *in charge.* In E. O. Wilson's work on the other hand, despite the rightness of intentions to save species and seek "consilience" among the sciences and humanities, once you get down to precisely *how* he would like to reduce sociology to evolutionary biology, you find him repeatedly guilty of what I like to call *the phallusy of misplaced physics*—the distortion of biological or social phenomena by treating them as if they were composed of "atoms" whose mass and momenta could be calculated with deterministic precision.

Hegel is an ambiguous case. On the one hand his chutzpah in even entertaining the idea of "absolute knowledge" is nothing short of terrifying, especially if you see it, as Popper did in his two-volume *Open Society and its Enemies* (1945), as an enemy to open society precisely to the extent that it paved the way for

Marxist totalitarianism. On the other hand, if you really get into the way Hegel approaches his so-called absolute (which was really just his hook into the systems theoretical trope of always seeking for the larger context), then you see, as Judith Butler (1987) does, that Hegel's so-called "absolute" is a never ending process of successive sublations (*Aufhebungen*) that never come to rest in any ultimate telos (for a similar argument see Ogilvy 1975). Or you see with Adorno (1979) that the dialectic is finally negative, not positivistic, and never finds closure in any final destination.

CLOSE FRIENDS MAKE THE BEST ENEMIES

Arrogant and humble systems theories remain locked in a lovers' quarrel because, like many dialectical disputes, they stem from the same source. Their contest can never be settled by a simple victory of one side over the other because they have too much in common. Both begin from a shared recognition of the inter-connectedness of all things. The arrogant branch reasons from that premise toward the view that you cannot fix anything without fixing everything. But in order to fix everything, you have to think pretty big. In order to implement such megalomaniacal fantasies, you may have to become a totalitarian dictator (e.g., Stalin or Castro). No wonder Fidel Castro used to give such long speeches. For those who cannot say anything without saying everything, it's hard to give a short speech.

The humble form of systems theory also starts with the same premise about the inter-connectedness of all things, but reasons quite differently from that premise. The humble form concludes that, precisely because all things are interconnected, you will never be able to isolate the influence of single causes for complex effects. And because *that* is so, you will never be quite certain what the consequences of your actions will be. The perception of inter-connectedness takes the form of a profound skepticism: about the efficacy of predict-and-control planning; about the adequacy of our knowledge of many of the systems we are dealing with in social policy—the healthcare system, the education system, the system for the allocation of resources known as the economy.

Healthcare, education, the economy—these are all *systems* with many intercon- nected moving parts. But do we really know how these systems work? The humble systems theorist says, *No we do not.* The tradition of humble systems theory ex- tends from Socrates's claim to know nothing, through Christian humility—fear of the sin of pride—and from thence to Kierkegaard's resistance against Hegel's Sys- tem, on down through several branches of modern thought: First, an existentialist strain running from Nietzsche through Heidegger, Sartre, and Camus; second, a skeptical empiricism running from Hume through Russell, late Wittgenstein, J. L. Austin, and Gilbert Ryle; third, a Zen skepticism cloaked in the virtues of "empty mind." Among the best examples of humble systems theorists are Peter Checkland, of "soft systems theory" fame (cf. Checkland 1999; Checkland and Scholes 1999) and Don Michael (1997), who became increasingly skeptical about our ability to know anything or do anything without the unintended consequences outweighing the positive rewards of the best laid plans. To the most humble of systems theorists, all aspirations to improving anything amount to sheer vanity.

For very humble systems theorists, there is a danger of wilting in the face of the overwhelming challenge of improving *anything* when you see how interconnected *everything* is. No wonder scientists have to make such an effort to *isolate* any cause or effect. That's what laboratories are for, and they tend to be expensive.

If you construct a spectrum with Stalin on one (arrogant) end and Socrates on the (humble) other, it's interesting to try to map various systems thinkers along that spectrum. Where would you put Jay Forrester, Russ Ackoff, Gregory Bateson, Heinz von Foerster, Theodore Dobzhansky, Erich Jantsch, or Peter Senge?

Facing the choice between arrogant and humble systems theory, one is always oscillating between looking for new ways to categorize, structure, and comprehend the vast complexity of the world around us, and a tendency to recoil from any truly systematic attempts to succeed at just that. Every time we are confronted with some vast architectonic that tries to find a place for everything and put everything in its place, part of us wants to protest and say, *No, life does not work that way. You cannot tie it up quite so neatly.* Just as Kierkegaard's shriek of protest on behalf of the solitary existing individual took the form of an almost visceral rebellion against Hegel's System,[2] so we find ourselves uneasy with the sheer intrusiveness of philosophies like Rudolph Steiner's, which seems to have penetrated every nook and cranny of life right down to micro-managing the kind of toothbrush one should use. Ken Wilber's work can have a similar effect—not that it is not insightful, erudite, even inspiring. But when confronted with the sheer geometry of Ken's model, after granting the importance and profundity of his insight into the dialectic of the seen and the unseen, it's easy to come away, like Kierkegaard from Hegel, itchy about the neatness of the architectonic.

IN FAVOR OF ARROGANCE NONETHELESS

Despite the pejorative tone of the word, "arrogant," I would like to sharpen the dialectic—"heighten the contradiction," as dialecticians like to say—by taking the side of the arrogant systems theorist as opposed to the humble, at least for a moment. I would like to make the case for thinking big by taking a closer look at two vast systems: education and healthcare. Both of these systems are famously resistant to reform. Both yield countless examples of the systems theoretical maxim, "You cannot do just one thing." Why? Because when you are operating in the context of a system, if you try to change just one thing, the rest of the system will suck your attempted alteration back into equilibrium with the rest of the system in no time at all. You cannot change just one thing, because all of the other unchanged things in the system will demand that the changed element realign itself with the rest of the (unchanged) system. This is the meaning of *homeostasis*.

Although there have been piecemeal reforms aplenty in America's public education system—from the new math through the whole language approach to reading, to bilingual education, charter schools, class size reduction, peer review, high school exit exams, and countless other experiments—the overall record of educational reform is disappointing. In *Tinkering Toward Utopia,* David Tyack and Larry Cuban document the dismal record of educational reform over the past century (1995). They show how each and every effort at tinkering with one part of the educational system—whether by down-from-the-top policy or up-from-the-bottom experimentation—eventually gets pulled back into the homeostatic equilibrium of the larger system of public education.

An entire issue of *Daedalus* is devoted to the question of public education's resistance to reform. In the lead essay, Seymour Sarason (1998, 2–3) argues that only a systemic approach that looks at all parts of the very complex system of public education has any hope of making lasting changes. "What are the parts of the system?" asks Sarason. "Teachers, school administrators, boards of education, state departments of education, colleges and universities, state legislatures and executive branches, the federal government, and parents." Unless you get all parties involved, and change all parts of the system more or less together, the system will force any part of itself that is out of step with the rest back into conformity with "the way things work." If the federal government wants to raise standards, then you may need a longer school year. But you cannot change the school calendar without involving the school board, which answers to the state department of education, which answers to the state legislature. And surely the teachers' unions will call for more compensation for more days on the job by teachers.

The situation is similar in healthcare. As we witness the seemingly unstoppable acceleration in healthcare costs, and as we contemplate reforms that seem both inevitable and impossible, it may be useful to reflect on some parallels with the arms race during the Cold War. Certainly there is a similar sense of a system out of control. Are we witnessing a system we could call the medical–industrial complex? Just as Eisenhower's alarm over the military–industrial complex led us to label the triangle joining the armed forces, the defense department, and military contractors as The Iron Triangle, so an analysis of escalating costs in the healthcare industry invites description under the image of a Stainless Steel Star joining (1) patients, (2) providers, (3) insurers, (4) suppliers, and (5) lawyers.

Under a fee-for-service *system*, almost all of the incentives aim toward higher costs. Patients have no incentive to save, because their bills are paid by insurers. Doctors get paid by insurance companies, and with malpractice lawyers breathing down their necks, the physicians are under an incentive to order tests and procedures they might omit in a less litigious environment. The lawyers are hired by patients to protect their interests. Since the lawyers are usually paid a percentage of the final settlement, their incentive is to sue for as much as possible, thereby driving up medical insurance premiums, which are then passed on—eventually—to the consumers and the consumers' insurance companies. With insurance companies, too, operating on a percentage of the cash flow, they have little incentive to reduce that flow. Finally, all the suppliers enjoy the benefits of cost-unconscious consumers, over-cautious doctors, and a third-party payment system that continues to pay rapidly inflating bills for supplies. Like the Iron Triangle of old, the Stainless Steel Star has all its incentives reinforcing each other in one direction: Up.

Comparable to the $800 toilet seat created by the Iron Triangle, consider the plastic inflatable cushion for paraplegics. In the early 1960s, before Medicare and Medicaid, that little cushion cost about four dollars. By the early 1990s it cost between $110 and $140. Hey, it's just one more line-item on a bill that gets checked and rechecked. And who would deny a comfort cushion to a paraplegic? Given the opportunity to spend $4 or $140 of his own money, there's little doubt about what a given patient would choose. But under the current *system* that choice is not available. The cost of the cushion rose "uncontrollably" as it was integrated into a high-overhead *system* where the incentives were all upward rather than downward.

The key to the so-called "managed competition" reforms promoted by the Jackson Hole initiative early in the Clinton administration lay in the incentive toward savings introduced by allowing the consumer to pocket whatever he or she saves by choosing the less expensive rather than the more expensive of two health plans. Under the current system, employers are usually responsible for the choice of an insurance plan. The end-user remains cost-unconscious because the end-user may not have a choice of plans. And even if he did, he may not pocket any savings by taking a less expensive plan (unless he is already paying a variable premium over and above payroll deductions).

Understandably, the Clintons and their chief advisor on healthcare reform, Ira Magaziner, thought that the people they had to convince were patients, their employers, and the doctors, so they under-estimated the importance of one point on the Stainless Steel Star: Chief among the suppliers, the pharmaceutical companies. Perceiving that *their* interests would not be met by the reforms, the pharmaceutical companies developed and aired those famous Harry and Louise ads that scared the American electorate into discouraging their representatives from voting for systemic reform. You cannot even change just four things if you leave a fifth but crucial part of a system unattended. We have seen a similar dynamic play out in the private insurance industry's resistance to a single payer plan, and Big Pharma's resistance to the public option in the debates running up to the Accountable Care Act. Sometimes you really do have to think big enough to change everything at once. That was both the strength and the weakness of the Clinton reforms: Their strength lay in the way the thinking behind the reforms, particularly the work of Alain Enthoeven, touched on all parts of the healthcare system. And their weakness lay in the fact that no one, including the pharmaceutical companies, would remain untouched.

STEERING A COURSE BETWEEN ARROGANCE AND HUMILITY

I would like to reflect on what I take away from the dialectic between the humble and the arrogant. First, I hope the examples of education and healthcare make the point that sometimes a little arrogance is in order. As I sometimes muse when working with very large clients in very large systems, *It's a megalomaniacal job, but someone's got to do it.* Just tinkering around the edges is a waste of everyone's time and energy. As the popular saying goes, *No use rearranging the deck chairs on the Titanic.*

At the same time, the history of cataclysmic failures at revolutionary systemic reforms has to give one pause. Beware final solutions, wars to end all wars, and utopian dreams. Far short of fascist fantasies or communist revolutions, just look at the debacle that followed upon the deregulation of electricity in California. While it seemed like a good idea at the time—in the context of a booming economy and falling energy prices—when the worm turned and Enron got into manipulating the wholesale prices, California's consumers ended up paying much higher rates, but still not high enough to keep Pacific Gas and Electric from going bankrupt. A well-intentioned systemic reform turned out to have unintended consequences in the context of scenarios that no one had anticipated during the boom years of the 1990s.

My colleagues and I at Global Business Network are often called upon to address very large issues for very large clients. We use the tool of scenario planning to address precisely the dilemma posed by the need to think big set against the danger of unintended consequences. A single scenario, because it is cast in narrative form, offers a broad tent under which many different issues can be displayed in their systemic inter-relatedness. A set of alternative scenarios offers an even broader canvas on which a number of possible outcomes can be displayed. The narrative form of scenarios speaks to the need to comprehend a wider context. The story form provides a large container for the many pieces of a complex puzzle to come together in a way that is both intelligible and communicable. But further, *a set of stories* undercuts the arrogance of a single-point prediction or forecast. Precisely in their plurality, alternative scenarios reflect a necessary humility about the future. It is unpredictable. Scenario planning provides a necessary antidote to the kind of predict-and-control pretensions that drove McNamara and his whiz kids at the Pentagon into the Vietnam War. If only we had learned. We now know that, during the latter years of the Clinton administration, a team at the State Department under the leadership of Thomas Warrick put together a set of alternative scenarios under the project title, The Future of Iraq. Some of those scenarios described the prospect of looting and insurgency following a military "conquest." When Bush the lesser took office, however, his military planners dismissed the Future of Iraq scenarios and placed their faith in a single point forecast of grateful Iraqis welcoming U.S. forces into Baghdad as beloved liberators. Like McNamara and his whiz kids, Donald Rumsfeld, Dick Cheney, Paul Wolfowitz, and the lesser Bush exuded arrogance.

In addition to providing a way of accommodating a range of eventualities that may differ *factually* (e.g., will there, or will there not be a surplus of electric energy in California over the coming decade?) a set of alternative scenarios can also serve to articulate futures that differ based on prevailing *values*. And this is important. Part of the pride of the arrogant systems theorist lies in the mistaken belief that values can be reduced to mere subjective preferences. *Facts*, according to this mistaken view, are objective and calculable, whereas values are merely subjective tastes and whims. Facts are supposedly representations of the *real*, while values are just reflections of our wishes. But this view of the relationship between facts and values is wrong. Values have consequences. Values are efficacious. Values make things happen in the world.

Values throw an added wrinkle into challenging systems theory: Precisely because "value systems" are plural, not monolithic, there's really no hope of scaling some highest peak to gain a totalizing view of absolute reality. People try. Fundamentalists think that they have access to the One True Way. Radical

Islam, the Christian Right—such systems reflect the totalizing impulse of arrogant systems theory. They have a place for everything, and can put everything in its place. But that way lies madness ... and bloodshed, as the historical record so often attests.

A popular bumper sticker can be less crudely translated, *feces occur.* Accidents happen. Contingencies are unavoidable. The best laid plans will often run awry. Yet we cannot for that reason sit on our hands and accept paralysis. Some of the things we want to change about the way we live demand systemic, not incremental, reform. So the best we can do is to combine the arrogance of systems thinking with the humility of alternative scenarios.

SYSTEMS THEORY AND ETHICAL PLURALISM

There is another reason for combining both branches of arrogance and humility, and it has to do with a deeper level beneath their common trunk. Not only do both branches share the common trunk of recognizing the interconnectedness of all things. Further, they share a common tap root of moral righteousness that must be tempered by holding both together rather than letting them grow off on their own. The arrogant systems theorists tend to be crusaders, namely the neo-cons crusade to supplant radical Islam with (Christian) democracy in the Middle East. They derive clarity and strength from their righteousness. Howard Dean and his enthusiastic followers likewise derived clarity and strength from the righteousness of non-violent, peace-loving people. As paradoxical as it may sound, pacifists are usually passionate about their pacifism. They care.

What is one to say that could appeal to both hawk and dove? Is there a message that will lessen the arrogance of the hawk even as it emboldens the humility of the dove? I think there is, and it has to do with our understanding of values—what they are and how they work. Values are more than subjective preferences (e.g., for chocolate over butterscotch), even as they are less than universal truths like the laws of physics. The arrogance of the hawk derives from mistakenly confusing the way values transcend whims with the way the universality of physical laws transcend the particularity of, say, social customs. Read that sentence over again: The arrogance of the hawk derives from mistakenly confusing the way values transcend whims with the way the universality of physical laws transcend the particularity of, say, social customs.

Newton's inverse square law really does have broader reach than, say, good manners as defined by Emily Post. But just because values are more universal than local customs, it does not follow that values have the universal reach of physics. To think so is to commit the *phallusy* of misplaced physics—to render unto values the universal reach of mathematics. And this is wrong.

Unfortunately, efforts to show what is wrong with universal ethics are usually misconstrued as defenses for a subjective relativism that says I can like what I like, you can like what you like, whatever. And this way lies nihilism—no values whatever, just whims and tastes. Therefore efforts to chip away at the universal validity of crusader ethics come to look like attempts to push virtue down a slippery slope toward vice: If The Good is not good for everyone everywhere, then it's every man for himself. But this pitting of absolutism versus relativism is puerile and simplistic.

The fact that values are not universal is a feature, not a bug. If values were universal, if, for example, there really *were* a single right answer to the question of whether individualism is superior to collectivism, or vice versa, then the very idea of moral integrity would collapse into naturalistic necessity. I would *have to* aspire to rugged individuality, just as the sunflower *has to* tip toward the sun. I would have no choice, just as the sunflower has no choice. And without choice, where is there room for anything like integrity?

No, values are, as W. B. Gallie once put it, "essentially contestable" in a way that long division is not. Values are also essentially contestable in a way that tastes and whims are not. It is precisely this third way between particular and universal, between subjective and objective, between whim and law, that defines the nature of values and how they work. And it is precisely this more-than-particular-but-less than-universal nature of values that justifies and legitimates pluralism as superior to nihilism on the one hand or absolutism on the other.

Many years ago I wrote about this dialectic under the rubric of "the social philosophy of some" (Ogilvy 1976). My mantra: *not one, not all, but some.* Not subjective relativism, not totalitarian absolutism, but a pluralism in which there are *some* ways for *some* people to get along together. The trouble with such pluralism, though, is precisely its imprecision. "Some" is such a vague and indefinite word. It lacks the elegance and simplicity of "One." It lacks the clarity and grandeur of "All." Rhetorically speaking, "some" is a loser. No wonder my book is seldom cited.

Accepting the challenge that Monty has posed—to place our understanding of systems theory in the context of our autobiographical, intellectual journeys—I now see how my early philosophical if unsuccessful defense of ethical pluralism led quite naturally to my later, more worldly preoccupations. First there was a plunge into consumer segmentation by values rather than demographics—five years of working with Arnold Mitchell, the inventor of the Values and Lifestyles (VALS) program at SRI International (formerly Stanford Research Institute). There we conducted national probability sample surveys to see not what people *ought* to value—philosophers' work—but what they actually *do* value—social scientists' work. For the next thirty years I poured most of my energy into corporate consulting using the tool of scenario planning, an approach to the future that abjures prediction and control for the sake of making decisions in the face of irreducible uncertainty.

I now see how both of these endeavors—VALS and scenario planning—offer empirical support for a pluralism that, in its earlier version, lacked rhetorical force. Both consumer segmentation and scenario planning presuppose a pluralistic openness to *some* ways of valuing, *some* futures, not just one right way. At the same time, both in the work with VALS, and in scenario planning, I have never accepted the slide down a slippery slope from *one* to *any and all* value systems or *any and all* futures. The pluralism implicit in the VALS segments was not a nihilism that said anything goes. Not all lifestyles allow humans to flourish. Likewise, in the discipline of scenario planning, I found it necessary to differentiate my approach from a value free approach that saw only *different* scenarios, not *better and worse* scenarios (Ogilvy 1992, 5–6; Ogilvy 2000).

The linkage between ethical pluralism and systems theory had to be worked out in practice, not just in theory. By finding practical implementations for pluralism in real world systems, I hope I have found a stronger defense of pluralism than was to be found in philosophical theory and the problematic rhetoric of *some*. Systems theory and ethical pluralism turn out to be strong partners. Both of them can join in a dialectical dance linking the arrogance hard problems require with the humility hard problems demand.

NOTES

1. Among the best overviews of the range and history of systems thinking, see Capra (1996, esp. chaps. 2–6).
2. Kierkegaard's resistance to the all-inclusive totality of Hegelian philosophy runs through virtually all of his writing, but it's most explicit in his *Concluding Unscientific Postscript* (1941), 99–113.

REFERENCES

Adorno, T. 1979. *Negative dialectics.* Trans. Ashton, E. B. New York: Seabury Press.
Bateson, G. 1972. Part I: Metalogues, *Steps to an ecology of mind.* New York: Ballantine Books.
Butler, J. 1987. *Subjects of desire.* New York: Columbia University Press.
Capra, F. 1996. *The web of life.* New York: Doubleday Anchor.
Checkland, P. 1999. *Systems thinking, systems practice.* Chichester: John Wiley & Sons.
Checkland, P. and J. Scholes. 1999. *Soft systems methodology in action.* Chichester: John Wiley & Sons.
Emery, F. E., ed. 1969. *Systems thinking.* New York: Penguin.
Joy, W. 2000. Why the future doen't need us. *WIRED* 8 (4). Retrieved from www.wired. com/wired/archive/8.04/joy.html
Kierkegaard, S. 1941. *Concluding unscientific postscript,* Trans. Swenson, D. and Lowrie, W. Princeton, NJ: Princeton University Press.
Laing, R. D. 1969. *The politics of the family.* London: Tavistack.
Michael, D. 1997. *Learning to plan and planning to learn.* Alexandria, VA: Miles River Press.
Ogilvy, J. 1975. Reflections on the absolute. *Review of Metaphysics* 28 (3): 520–546.
———. 1976. *Many dimensional man: Decentralizing self, society, and the sacred.* New York and London: Oxford University Press.
———. 1992. Future studies and the human sciences: The case for normative scenarios. *Futures Research Quarterly* 8 (2): 5–65.
Popper, K. 1945. *The open society and its enemies.* London: Routledge.
———. 2000. *Creating better futures.* New York and London: Oxford University Press.
Sarason, S. 1998. Some features of a flawed educational system. *Daedalus* (Fall): 1–12.
Tyack, D. and Cuban, L. 1995. *Tinkering toward Utopia.* Cambridge, MA: Harvard University Press.
Ways, M. 1967. The road to 1977. *Fortune* Jan. 1967: 93–95.
Wittgenstein, L. 1961. *Tractatus Logico-philosophicus.* Trans. Pears, D. F. and McGuinnes, B. F. London: Routledge & Kegan Paul.

SYSTEMS PATTERNS AND POSSIBILITIES

Linda E. Olds

Professor Emerita, Linfield College, McMinnville, Oregon, USA

Six guiding intuitions and values have informed my life and work: the conviction that truth lies "in the between;" the importance of integrating polarities; the centrality of pattern and multiple facets; epistemological and ontological concerns for wholeness and coherence; the role of metaphor, models, and symbols; and dynamic organicity and congruence in living what we know. These resonances have contributed to my work in systems theory, specifically in teaching, theory-construction, philosophy of science, integrative models of personality, faculty development and higher education, and religion–science dialogue. Possibilities and perplexities for future systems theory are outlined for education; the study of consciousness; the challenge of changing stuck patterns; transpersonal/systems models of self; positive roles for boundaries; the relevance of emotion; and ontological issues.

In systems perspective, intellectual autobiography becomes a story of resonances, tracing a set of predisposing themes through the levels of one's life and work that eventually find emergent voice and congruence in systems models. Benefitted by hindsight's pattern-seeking sweep, I begin by articulating six overarching intuitions I bring to the conversation around systems thinking. I then proceed to summarize how systems models reflect these intuitions and have been expressed in my professional work, and conclude by raising some concerns for the cutting edge of systems theory today, where I see some of the most exciting unresolved dilemmas and questions, and how they connect with my current emphases.

AUTOBIOGRAPHICAL NODES AND PREDISPOSING INTUITIONS

Truth in the Between

The fundamental intuition throughout my life has been that truth, however we define it, lies "in the between." A quintessential liberal arts college student, I aspired to a Renaissance grasp that was already receding in possibility both through temperament of the times and the sheer level of complexity and diversity to be integrated. Exposure to the thinking of Alfred North Whitehead riveted my eventual choice to major in religion at Oberlin College, a major that seemed to open the widest field of interconnections to all dimensions of reality. Not only did Whitehead's (1978) philosophical portrayal of organic process avoid dichotomizing models of Ultimate Reality and an evolving, creative universe, but also affirmed a rudimentary form of consciousness experiencing (which he called prehension) as inherent in all parts of the unfolding universe.

Yet even as I embraced religion as a major, and pursued complementary interests in psychology, biology, art history, and philosophy, I knew none offered a definitive home, a predicament that seemed to leave me facing an immensely lonely, albeit intriguing path. Each field of knowledge extended an invitation to a distinctive intellectual circle, yet my resonance and excitement matched closest the areas where the circles intersected and overlapped. From each discipline's viewpoint, that mandorlic-shaped region of overlap resembled existentially the edges of medieval maps where dangerous beasties lie more than it reflected the passionate domain of interconnections which I longed to explore. Still I could not betray my inner sense of "between places" as the locus for truth and insight, and have sought to cultivate and speak from these places of interconnectedness, solitary as that minority location has felt much of the time in academia.

Professionally I have aspired to embody this intuition of "the between" in my commitments wherever possible to cross-disciplinary and interdisciplinary exchange, research and scholarship, faculty development, and teaching. Typically half of the courses I have taught over thirty-three years of teaching in a liberal arts college setting have had an explicit or implicit interdisciplinary focus, reflecting especially the diverse contributions of cross-cultural perspectives, gender studies, and psychology and spirituality. Within what has been my main discipline and academic base in psychology, I have aimed to introduce non-reductive systems models into courses from introductory psychology to theories of personality. My commitment has been to foster models which respect the important perspectives of each sublevel in this multileveled discipline and explore their interconnections, rather than aspiring to reduce any level of explanation to another, whether to biochemical substrates, instinctual homeostasis, reinforcement contingencies, or sociocultural constructs. In fact, my overwhelming concern about the present state of systems models is whether they too harbor a kind of metaphysical reductionism.

Integrating Polarity

The second reverberating thread of my intellectual/emotional life honors the theme of moving beyond polarities in the interests of orchestrating some third new possibility. For me the search for understanding has always required the language of "and/also" rather than "either/or." This has made me an integrator in most contexts and given me a powerful desire to foster communication between conflicting forces or perspectives, arriving at a larger creative harmony. Yet my recurring role as mediator at numerous levels has also made me relatively comfortable with conflict, chaos, opposition, and ambiguity as a field of possibility that can generate more creative solutions through transforming win/lose alliances to win/win dialogue. I resonate to the quantum principle of complementarity whereby dichotomous constructs like wave and particle are reframed as resonating reciprocities, reminding us of the ever-present role of the observer and the limits of expressing insights through language. System theory's ability to transcend dichotomous concepts like mind/matter and self/other likewise helps reconceptualize our intellectual stuck places.

Early in my professional research in psychology, this resonance for integrating polarity led me to explore the cognitive question of why some people end up as either/or dichotomous thinkers and others manage an operating position that seeks a third, integrating point of view. This question brought me in turn to the study of gender roles as one of the oldest sets of polarity humans have generated and metaphorized throughout world cultures (e.g., Yang/Yin), clustering cultural expectations around these poles with profound consequences for freedom of choice and personality development. In my book *Fully Human* (1981) based on qualitative clinical research, I explored the developmental roots, cognitive facets, and cultural implications of androgyny, that is, the integration of metaphorically "masculine" and "feminine" modes of relating within one person. My deepest ongoing interest has been in alternatives to dichotomous either/or thinking through the capacity to use polarities as springboards for engaging new syntheses. My work, writing, and life reflect also an encounter with the polarities of science and religion, and of West and East, as I have sought to build models congruent with insights from the world's scientific and spiritual traditions, as well as Western and Asian cultures.

Pattern and Facet

The perception and experience of pattern has contributed a third resonant principle throughout my life, particularly patterns reflected at multiple levels of reality. If the previous two predilections had not led me to systems theory, this search for pattern surely would have. For as Gregory Bateson (1979) expressed so beautifully, standing with Whitehead and Ervin Laszlo among my adopted intellectual mentors, the centrally woven fact we encounter at all levels is "the pattern which connects" (8). This taste for pattern, and its contributions to new ways of seeing, expressed itself also in my college efforts to augment my Indo-European language study with Chinese, a language of resonating calligraphy, ideographic image, and syntactical context, which launched an ongoing connection to the organic patterning of Chinese worldviews (Olds 1991).

Crystals likewise have held a lifelong fascination for me as teaching metaphors. Their multifaceted holographic structure and mysterious evolution from the "mother liquid" suggest analogs in other domains not only for Jungian archetypal influence (Jung 1969, par. 155) but for physicist David Bohm's (1980) concepts of an explicate order emerging from a hidden implicate order. Facets allow mutual and multiple reflections in all dimensions and thus provide a nonreductionistic image of reality as interconnected pattern. For me, the search for holistic models of even ultimate reality has focused less on metaphors of oneness and unity, although the Asian language of nonduality is deeply resonant, and more on patterns of interrelatedness. In Buddhist sensitivity, ultimate reality as emptiness means "empty" of separate identity, yet full of connection and embeddedness. Thus the Hua-yen Buddhist image of Indra's Net (Cook 1977) has become for me the quintessential metaphor for systems thinking: the cosmic image of Ultimate Reality as arrayed in a infinite net, every intersection of which contains a crystal node reflecting all other parts of the net. This shimmering patterning needs only a more dynamic reverberating quality to more fully reflect the oscillations and resonance of field models like chaos and dynamic systems theories.

Wholeness and Coherence: Ontology and Epistemology

Fourth, my aspiration has been toward wholeness and coherence in theory construction and the pursuit of inquiry. This passion is resonant with my concern for thinking in-the-between, integrating polarity, and seeking the wider patterns, with wholeness best understood as the most inclusive frame of interconnectedness. Early in my career I discovered R. D. Laing's (1967) caution that our so-called facts or data ought more accurately to be understood as "capta" (62), seized from the fabric of reality according to our viewpoint. Data apart from viewpoint are impossible, and resting with one viewpoint alone can potentially distort and compartmentalize knowledge. I have sought instead integrations that aim at discovering how the best insights from multiple perspectives might fit together in a coherent worldview that can be lived.

The concern for coherence leads quickly into the territory of epistemology and ways of knowing, for academic disciplines frame and anchor their paradigms within competing epistemological modes, such that the search for truth is largely about which models are most trustworthy as sources of knowing. Accompanying my professional work is always the epistemological concern for whether our models of reality are adequate to the complexity of the truth we seek, rather than attempts to reduce complexity solely a la Ockham's razor to a threshold below that which may actually exist.

While postmodern contexts and careful training have led me to be cautious of Truth with a capital T, I nonetheless am unable to surrender the notion of truth as a meaningful concept of approximation, and thus my interest in systems theory has been ontological as well as pragmatic. Like Bateson, my concern and attraction to systems thinking also has been epistemological (Bateson and Bateson 1987) and anchored in a commitment to nonreductionism and nondualism. I am invested in exploring alternative, complementary hermeneutics or modes of knowing that allow a more adequate representation and mapping of domains of experience without distortions from imposed levels of the hierarchy. My systems thinking is thus epistemologically and ontologically inquisitive (1992a), with all the perils and opportunities that entails.

Metaphor, Models, and Symbol

Fifth, my concern for epistemology has led me consistently to an interest in models and metaphors as ways of seeking interconnections between domains and achieving resonance between realms of inquiry. The issue of validating the accuracy of a model within different domains is a challenging one, but despite inherent limitations in establishing the specific parameters of applicability within any one domain, I retain tremendous respect for the importance, centrality, and heuristic fruitfulness of metaphor in the process of truth-seeking and theory construction, whether in science, psychology, or religion (Barbour 1974).

My interest in metaphor is articulated in my book *Metaphors of Interrelatedness* (1992b), an effort to relegitimize metaphorical modes as an important domain of cognitive and psychological functioning, as well as explore systems theory as an interdisciplinary model for bridging dialogue between psychology, science, and religion. Metaphor likewise resonates with Jungian and post-Jungian emphases on symbolic, "imaginal" dimensions (Hillman 1975) of individuation (Jung 1966) and maturity. More recently I have pursued a metaphorical investigation of alchemy as a rich symbol system anchored in the laboratory language of science, yet aspiring to reflect the transformative processes of psychological and spiritual quests, allowing a mirroring of wholeness without and within. Jung's and quantum physicist Pauli's mutual exploration of the archetypal relation of matter and psyche reflect a parallel dialogue in psychology and science (Meier 2001). Metaphors allow resonances between realms, and facilitate the search for correspondences so inherent in systems thinking.

Indeed the primary problems and conflicts of our times are in many ways attributable to an inadequate development of metaphorical, symbolic thinking, with its attendant capacity for humility in the face of partial perspective, yet aspiration for integrated understanding. Without this metalevel metaphorical skill, there is little to prevent a developmental stuckness or collapse into literalism and polarized dichotomous thinking that generates types of fundamentalisms across many domains. Metaphor remains under suspicion in reigning epistemological hierarchies which position experimental models above other empirical ways of collecting data, as well as within traditions which see tension more than complementarity between historicity and symbolic/mythic levels of resonance (Eliade 1963). Our global problems reflect not only the insufficient use of metalevel cognitive skills allowing metaphorical bridges to multi-perspectival thinking, but also the lack of integrative worldviews adequate to framing new syntheses for our times.

Dynamic Organicity and Congruence: Living Our Knowing

Sixth, and finally, I experience life's organicity as fundamentally dynamic, the patterns we embody as oscillating and reverberating. My deepest feelings of connection to the universe have been mediated by nature, and the Chinese heritage of the *Tao Te Ching*, rich in the natural metaphors of ever-changing water, has served as the Asian parallel to Whitehead's dynamic organicism. We are metamorphic beings, our universe is a living whole, and our theoretical and emotional understandings must constantly be open to a new surrender. Change must be fundamental in any languaging of the universe; evolution is a natural mother tongue.

The ever presence of change is not an easy awareness, however, since the quest for truth, understanding, and pattern often echoes the psychological need for security, as Maslow (1966) articulated in exploring the risks of cognitive pathologies in science. Clinical psychology can offer insight into ways early childhood efforts to make sense of reality may freeze into lifelong reverberating loops, much as chaos models for bifurcations between oscillating patterns may allow a way to explore these habit-fields that resist change once sufficiently constellated. The ongoing oscillation between the perceived transiency of life and the intuition of a deeper unfolding pattern, however, has given birth to the insights of both science and religion.

This intuition of organic change has kept me close to the dynamic question of congruence: that is, how do we live the insights we know, and has led to an ongoing concern for elaborating a systems ethics of interrelatedness. I resonate with Bateson's work in that direction expressed in *Steps To an Ecology of Mind* (1972), where he identifies the need to make decisions within the context of the largest, most encompassing system or level of wholeness of which we are a part. My highest aspirations for congruence between physical, emotional, cognitive, relational, and integrative realms supported my choice to pursue a Ph.D. in the scientist-practitioner field of clinical psychology and the integrative strengths of a graduate program which embedded individual and group processes within community psychology contexts and commitments as well. This multilevel concern for congruence, growth, and change has likewise informed my ongoing professional interest in articulating models of personality and self development resonant with systems, cross-cultural, and transpersonal insights of West and East.

The task of living truth in congruence with what we know takes us back to the theme of complexity and the scientific danger of committing the "fallacy of misplaced concreteness" (Whitehead 1925), the tendency to mistake our abstractions from the complex fabric of space/time for actual concrete data. In psychology, our search for knowledge is often mediated by methods that abstract from complexity in the interest of controls enabling cause-effect conclusions, yet the data thus remain largely statistical averages, not predicting to the individual case. Extending Manicas and Secord's (1983) effective analysis of this predicament, we can argue that our methods must aspire to greater complexity or they risk remaining inapplicable to the individual situations we had hoped to aid in clarifying.

Finally, my passion for congruence is also the other side of a passion for transformation: how do we apply what we know to transforming not only our worldviews, but the way we work and live together? It is the question of "So what?" which we must ask of all we learn. Does the model make a difference, allow us to change the way we live? Does it generate William James's (1902/1982) sense of pragmatic truth, truth that transforms who we are, how we act? It is the pressing question of our time: whether we can develop ways of understanding interrelatedness capable of reflecting value and generating transformational perspectives that can foster peace on this planet, sustainable and distributed patterns of cooperative co-existence, respect for diversity and harmony, and multidimensional wisdom. We must ask at least this much of our truths, that they direct our attention to our daily reality and how much more richly we might live (Olds 2001).

CONCERNS, CONTRIBUTIONS, AND CHALLENGES

Systems theory has resonated with all the deep currents and sensitivities of my own life and thinking. It allows for a definition of the basic unit of reality or analysis in terms congruent with intrinsic interconnectedness. A system can be defined as "an ordered whole in relation to its relevant environment" (Laszlo 1972, 38) or as a "holon" (Koestler 1978). Systems theory explores the evolution of holons, of systems embedded within larger systems or holarchies (a term more congruent than hierarchy), and the unfolding of greater complexity (Kauffman 1995) as an intrinsic property of systems as they adapt and evolve, self-stabilize and self-organize (Laszlo 1972). Systems theory allows for the interdisciplinary search for resonance, correspondence, and isomorphism between levels of reality, yet frames this exploration in terms of emergent properties and nonreductionism, thus contrasting with many reigning and often divisive scientific models.

Systems theory is particularly strong in avoiding dualism, especially the kind of mind/matter or mind/body dualism that still plagues much of psychology despite advances in such fields as psychoneuroimmunology. Bateson's (1979, 234) articulation of mentality as "immanent in certain sorts of organization" and complexity and Laszlo's (1972, 154) concept of "biperspectivism" are particularly useful contributions. Bateson claimed that pattern and "information about a difference," rather than number, were the language of evolution (Bateson and Bateson 1987). Further constructs (summarized by Capra 1996) from nonlinear autopoietic systems (Maturana and Varela 1987) and chaos theory have made the classical systems contributions of von Bertalanffy (1968) and Miller (1978) even more dynamic. Systems thinking emphasizes nonlinear causality or multicausality, as in Sperry's (1988) stress on the importance of both traditional bottom-up and top-down directions of influence in evolution, with each emerging whole contributing a new level of influence, constraint, and choice to emerging process. Finally, systems theory is at least in principle open-ended toward the question of ontology, a dimension that lends itself to bridging dialogue between science and religion.

Systems theory is a model that can inspire a life's work. In my own professional life, I have focused its influence in five areas. First, systems models inform my teaching, both within the field of psychology and my extensive interdisciplinary commitments. In contrast to most introductory psychology courses and texts which replicate them, I have taught psychology from the students' beginning contact as a multileveled discipline where biological, behavioral, emotional, cognitive, interpersonal/social, cultural, and integrative/transpersonal dimensions inform and complement each other. None are to be considered primary or privileged in explaining behavior; all contribute to the richness of understanding the human being. Yet these emphases can be framed in terms of levels of emerging or widening complexity, not as separate subdisciplines or specialties studied in virtual isolation. Psychology espouses the importance of integration, but in practice reflects hierarchical judgments regarding both method and content, and risks fragments into data-driven, theory-impoverished exploration. I consider one of the major unfinished tasks of our time the need to widely integrate systems approaches into the very teaching of each academic discipline.

Second, my work with systems theory has addressed the need for more theoretical integration in the field of psychology, which has had a long ambivalent historical relationship to theory itself (Koch 1981). To embody a position as a theorist in such a context has not been without challenge. My scholarly work in psychology has primarily focused on the attempt to reintroduce the importance of broad-based theory-building (Rychlak 1968), the effort to revalidate the importance of metaphor and models as important constituents of theory construction and research, and the exploration of models of wholeness (androgyny, systems thinking) as examples of broadly integrative heuristic frames. In addition systems theory has facilitated my epistemological concerns for a closer examination of assumptions behind psychological paradigms and a more central discussion of contemporary philosophy of science for psychology. Parts of psychology have tended to operate with continued allegiance to positivist models of science, participating less in interdisciplinary debate with postmodern perspectives that challenge those premises, and I have tried to contribute to reengaging this discussion of epistemology.

Third, my ongoing concern and contributions have focused also on evolving models of self that can allow for integrative, systems insights. Much of my scholarly work is currently involved in articulating models of personality which build on all levels of behavior and experience, thus integrating the contributions of research in biological temperament and emotion; behavioral reinforcement and modeling; attachment theory and object relations insights into the early formation of interpersonal pattern; cognitive preferencing and reframing of ego-constructs; phenomenological attention to lived experience; existential dimensions of authenticity and dynamic being-in-the-world; symbolic, imaginal capacities (following Jung and Hillman) which facilitate movement to a more integrated wholeness of self; and transpersonal contributions to post-ego levels of consciousness (Olds 2009).

Wilber's psychological models (1996; 2000) have been especially important here as a complement to systems thinking. It has interested me greatly that his overarching and evolving opus has integrated many systems concepts (1995), although in a way that keeps them anchored less optimally for transcending the very inner/outer dichotomies and domains of experience he so effectively describes. I also find very helpful Bateson's (1972, 318) efforts at expanding the notion of "I" to encompass the entire set of reverberating loops and fields of information exchange in which we participate, and his desire to stretch the meaning of mind or self beyond the bounded person. My own commitment is toward an understanding of multileveled "selfing" and evolving levels of consciousness that resemble Wilber's (1996) distinctions of pre-ego and trans-ego development. I particularly appreciate the contributions of chaos theory (Abraham, Abraham, and Shaw 1990; 1992) in introducing models of personality that stress dynamic change even more than classical systems models.

Fourth, my work has involved a concern for faculty development and contemporary higher education, which is undergoing a paradigm shift from community to corporate models. The problems of systems dynamics in organizations, of how one identifies recurring patterns and orchestrates change in such contexts, are central themes for me. I am an ardent proponent of facilitating cross-disciplinary exchange and challenging the boundary divisions academic departments enact only too easily.

Finally, my ongoing contributions lie also in a concerted commitment to dialogue between the sciences and religious perspectives, a polarity illustrating one of the major bifurcations of our time. Systems perspectives can remind us of the moebius-strip-like character of ultimate truth, each path beginning in what seems like an opposite side, but leading to congruent and intertwined insights. Advocating systems theory as an integrative model, however, is not without its predicaments. Science is wary of the ontological overtones systems theory could carry, and religious perspectives are wary that these overtones are indeed too optional. Probably the central challenge for any integrative thinker is being partially misunderstood by both fields that one aspires to bring into closer dialogue. How does one remain adequate and congruent with the best in both perspectives, without reductionism or forcing models into a closer fit than can be supported?

POSSIBILITIES AND PERPLEXITIES FOR FUTURE SYSTEMS THEORY

One of the most exciting aspects of systems thinking is its profoundly heuristic nature. Systems models stimulate extensive theorizing across interconnected fields, and thus the research possibilities and theoretical questions proliferate rapidly. In this section I wish to raise a number of unfinished possibilities for systems theorizing that particularly capture my attention.

First, we need more focus on education and in most disciplines considerably more congruence between the ways we teach our fields and systems thinking. Without integrating systems habits of thinking and models into the very way we introduce and teach such disciplines as psychology, we replicate the divisive, unintegrated focus on separate fact or method. If we are to influence the worldview of our times in ways that might heal our fragmented approach to global issues, we must encourage habits of interconnected thinking across the curriculum of schools, colleges and universities. We cannot afford the luxury of conventional intellectual habits, and the efforts of correcting them later with goodwill or spiritual initiative. Our scientific worldviews are value-laden and value-replicating, and we must assume more responsibility for how we teach and the myths of separateness unwittingly inculcated through conventional disciplinary habits. Systems models are making their way more fully into graduate training in psychology and research paradigms, accompanied by greater access to complex mathematical modeling and multivariate statistics, but without more undergraduate education in systems models, these graduate programs remain under-accessed. The majority of college students become citizens, not graduate students; systems models are needed throughout our culture and cannot risk being seen as esoteric.

The educational relevance of systems theory is further reflected in the challenge posed by dualistic thinking habits in culture. Systems perspectives involve reframing assumptions and contexts; they require a move to a higher level of perspective, a jump of levels, not an attempt to pit previous hierarchical levels against each other. The intent of systems thinking is and–also, not either–or; systems theory is not an alternative to any one domain. Systems thinkers need to be alert to the possibility that further cognitive developmental levels are needed to fully understand systems thinking. Again, the educational question emerges of how we can better engage these integrative, synthetic levels of thought beyond the Piagetian linear abstract reasoning that typically crowns our educational system. The work of Robert Kegan (1994) on metalevel cognition is especially relevant here.

In psychology, we need far more attention to transcending the mentality/matter, mind/brain duality that still characterizes much of the discussion even in the rapidly emerging, relegitimized field of consciousness studies. Chalmer's identification of the "hard" problem of consciousness, that is, the challenge of relating the interiority of experience and exteriority of brain function, remains open for alternative formulations (Shear 1995–1997), although much contemporary discussion has turned to a monism where matter is primary and consciousness treated as a now interesting epiphenomenon. Systems insights allow an alternative biperspectival framing (Laszlo 1972), with mind and matter as inner and outer reflections of the same phenomenon, a rich heritage that needs attention in an age where systems theory is increasingly associated with outer perspectives alone.

In Wilber's four quadrant model for the investigation of reality (1995, 1998, 2000, 2006), he distinguishes an upper-left domain for the exploration of inner experience and consciousness (phenomenology), a lower-left quadrant focused on shared cultural interpretations of reality (postmodern constructivism and hermeneutics), an upper-right quadrant for exploring outer data like atoms, molecules, and organisms (classic science), and a lower-right exploration of social organizations and interconnections between externally observable realities (where he positions systems theory). Wilber's relegation of systems theory as an "outer" inquiry into group forms and functions may not do justice to more ontologically-rich systems models, but the risk remains that many contemporary systems models are insufficient to challenge materialistic and dichotomous paradigms. More integration into systems theory of quantum models of brain functioning, Laszlo's (2003) explication of multileveled coherence and connectivity, and Bohm's (1980) model of the unfolding of explicate observable order from an ultimate super-implicate dimension would be useful in working on transcending this potential mind/matter dichotomy.

Working from the background of clinical psychology, I have come to be interested in an array of interconnected issues for contemporary systems theory. First, we need far more attention to the topography of personality as pattern and the challenge of changing patterns at all levels of reality. An overwhelming phenomenon in psychological and organizational life is the tendency for humans to develop repetitive interpersonal and intrapsychic patterns. Chaos theory contributions to systems notions of pattern have been particularly fruitful (e.g., Masterpasqua and Perna 1997; Abraham, Abraham, and Shaw 1990; 1992; Barton 1994; Vallacher et al. 2010). Personality can be construed in terms of oscillations of subpersonality tendencies around strange attractors and bifurcation points. The more I work with systems perspectives, the more concerned I am not only with how these patterns form, but how one intervenes in a pattern to allow for change toward a more open, less stuck dynamic. Family therapy has long reflected systems notions of feedback loops and positive and negative spirals of change, but more attention needs to be paid to systems perspectives on recursive patterns of behavior (habit) in working with "individuals" in therapy and groups in conflict. Conforti (1999) has addressed this concern helpfully from the perspective of Jungian archetypal field theory, although we need to integrate this emphasis more explicitly and dynamically with other levels of personality and transpersonal dimensions. Likewise systems theory needs more connection with work on energy systems reflected, for example, in the study of ch'i (Qi), the Chinese concept for matter/energy, or the multileveled model of the Hindu chakra system.

My current work on a transpersonal systems model of personality focuses on developing a model of selfing that can reflect the more active verb languages of field theory, energy patterns, chaos and nonlinear systems dynamics alongside the rich array of perspectives contributed from traditional personality, developmental, and transpersonal theory. In field/systems theory terms, I would construe personality as a developmentally connected set or spiral of evolving identity fields, each characterized by patterns expressive of the skills and emergent properties congruent with that level of identity. In telescoped summary, at least four patterns of identity in this personality holarchy present themselves as noteworthy and significantly different from each other: *pre-ego habiting* (moving from the baby's symbiotic identity to differentiated sensing, rudimentary object relations, and reinforcement repertoires), *ego or ego-ing* (with increasingly abstract cognitive skills and languaged identities), *post-ego selfing* (with holistic integration of polarities and imaginal potentials), and a *trans-identity aming* (with nondual capabilities), to borrow Keen's (1970) existential use of the term "aming" and link it instead to Wilber's notion of "unity consciousness" (1993; 2001). Other intermediate identity patterns or levels can be integrated for greater nuance, comprehensiveness, and link to other theorists and multiple phenomena (e.g., Wade 1996; Washburn 1994; Wilber 1996; 2000; 2006), but these four pattern levels seem most likely to evoke the sense of a "quantum leap" between them. The challenge of translating noun/state language into verb/field language is ongoing.

Each level of resonance or pattern of identity once evolved would constitute a kind of energy field, archetype, or strange attractor that would stabilize that particular constellation of cognitive/emotional skills and emergent properties of consciousness. Once activated, the patterning at each level of development typically takes precedence until certain further evolving conditions of complexity or thresholds are reached that allow growth or "quantum leaps" to a new energy level, providing a matrix for a broader, more integrated identity. Occasionally larger leaps across levels may be facilitated by special circumstances or resonance with more integrative fields (as in meditative experience). My overriding clinical interest lies in the question of how we access the ability to change and evolve these selfing patterns. The brilliance of chaos theory applied to personality lies in its relevance to understanding the regularity of reverberation, repetition, and stuckness in human experience. What factors help precipitate growth to another level; which factors hinder? How do we change personality or interpersonal energy patterns, while integrating and incorporating old levels with new, without precipitating reactive oscillations toward extremes that simply represent a polar opposite and a collapse of genuine alternative possibility? What are the parallel dynamics at organizational and institutional levels?

A closely related clinical interest concerns the need for more articulation of the positive role of boundaries in systems theory. Although certainly not inherent in systems theory, the intuition and positive valuing of interconnectedness can generate a tendency to treat boundaries as ultimately illusory or negative; it is easy to underestimate the relevance of boundaries as positive mediators of connectedness. This differential perception of the value of boundaries in development introduces further gender considerations. With women's developmental pathways more often marked by the relational self of self-in-relation theory (Jordan et al. 1991), and men's development typically partaking of a more firmly bounded ego identity, there may be gender-related differences in resonance to the very notion of an interrelated self or immanental universe (Olds 1999). A strength of systems theory as an operational metaphor lies in its capacity to articulate a model of interrelatedness without resting on gendered assumptions, but systems models may have different implications for women's and men's development toward wholeness and the relationship to boundaries. The challenge remains to articulate the limits to healthy porousness and reciprocity in human interactions, much as the cell needs to govern its own processes despite relying on an ongoing transaction with its environment. Systems thinking offers a congruent model for reflecting on boundaries, but implications for maintaining boundaries as part of healthy interconnection need to be made more explicit.

The role of emotion and feeling as part of mind/sentience is another clinical and potentially gender-related area needing increased attention in systems models. In psychology the role of emotion in human experience was neglected alongside mental activity under behavioral influence, and the field is still moving to recover the study of emotion as a core dimension of cognitive functioning, following the much cited work of Damasio (1994). Systems theory is almost entirely construed in terms of cognitive fields, with emotions constituting epiphenomenal precipitants from pattern. Chaos theory only partially remedies this neglect of the feeling realm. I am concerned to find better ways to reconceptualize the relationship of mentality and feeling such that this dichotomy too may be transcended and integrated.

Finally, my ongoing concern has been to explore the possibilities of systems thinking for integrating scientific and spiritual insights into reality. This ontological interest places me in a small subset of contemporary systems theorists, although this was less so among the writing of such pioneering thinkers as Bateson and Laszlo and the significant work of Joanna Macy on Buddhism and systems theory (1991). As systems thinking has gained wider exposure, I have come to be concerned much more with the extent to which systems thinkers may indeed be fostering a solely materialistic cosmology, deriving mentality as an emergent property alone. Thus though systems thinking actually is open-ended with respect to its ontology, and I believe cannot preclude the possibility of the co-arising of matter/mentality as an expression of a larger more hidden super-implicate order or cosmic consciousness, it certainly often aims to explain within its purview the evolution of matter/consciousness without recourse to any larger questions.

Although I aspire to a worldview that does not privilege the best of either scientific or spiritual intuitions, I have hoped that systems theory might foster and sustain more of this possible integration. Wilber may well turn out to be more accurate than I had earlier hoped in assessing the current limitations of systems models for ontological understandings. Yet Wilber's four quadrant model leaves ultimate reality, despite his highly articulate and inspired intentions, as a kind of transcendent, though informing dimension from and upon which the whole of epistemological reality perches. Though Wilber may be correct in sensing the extent to which much systems theory is uninterested in the possible existence of that transcendent/immanental dimension, I believe he underestimates the significance of systems models in moving our thinking toward more congruence with spiritual intuitions of interconnectedness and ultimate reality. In sum, I am concerned that more and more of the systems discourse, whatever the origin, is being framed in ways that occlude the spiritual resonance that systems theory might carry as we aspire to interdisciplinary dialogue. Although I am pleased to see the ethical dimensions and implications of systems thinking reach more and more articulation through ecological movements in particular, I remain concerned that the ontological grounding and resonance of systems understandings remains less explored than its potential richness deserves. My hope is that these systems theory intuitions be broadly taught and discussed, not only in the sciences but in the humanities, for the heuristic value of these concepts promises major insights for our times.

REFERENCES

Abraham, F. D., R. H. Abraham, and C. D. Shaw. 1990. *A visual introduction to dynamical systems theory for psychology.* Santa Cruz, CA: Aerial.

———. 1992. Basic principles of dynamical systems. In *Analysis of dynamic psychological systems*, Vol. 1, Eds. Levine, R. L. and Fitzgerald, H. E., 35–143. New York: Plenum.

Barbour, I. G. 1974. *Myths, models, and paradigms.* New York: Harper & Row.

Barton, S. 1994. Chaos, self-organization, and psychology. *American Psychologist* 49 (1): 5–14.

Bateson, G. 1972. *Steps to an ecology of mind.* New York: Ballantine Books.

———. 1979. *Mind and nature: A necessary unity.* New York: Bantam Books.

Bateson, G. and M. C. Bateson. 1987. *Angels fear: Towards an epistemology of the sacred.* New York: Macmillan.

Bohm, D. 1980. *Wholeness and the implicate order.* London: Routledge & Kegan Paul/Ark.

Capra, F. 1996. *The web of life.* New York: Anchor/Doubleday.

Conforti, M. 1999. *Field, form, and fate: Patterns in mind, nature, and psyche.* Woodstock, CT: Spring.

Cook, F. 1977. *Hua-Yen Buddhism: The jewel net of Indra.* University Park: Pennsylvania State University Press.

Damasio, A. R. 1994. *Descartes' error.* New York: Grosset/Putnam.

Eliade, M. 1963. *Myth and reality.* New York: Harper & Row.

Hillman, J. 1975. *Re-visioning psychology.* New York: Harper & Row.

James, W. 1982. *The varieties of religious experience.* New York: Penguin.

Jordan, J. V., A. G. Kaplan, J. B. Miller, I. P. Stiver and J. L. Surrey. 1991. *Women's growth in connection.* New York: Guilford.

Jung, C. G. 1966. *Two essays on analytical psychology* (rev. ed.), Vol. 7 of *The collected works of C. G. Jung* (2nd ed.). Princeton, NJ: Princeton University Press.

———. 1969. *Four archetypes*. Princeton: Princeton University Press.

Kauffman, S. 1995. *At home in the universe: The search for the laws of self-organization and complexity*. New York: Oxford University Press.

Keen, E. 1970. *Three faces of being: Toward an existential clinical psychology*. New York: Appleton-Century-Crofts.

Kegan, R. 1994. *In over our heads*. Cambridge: MA: Harvard University Press.

Koch, S. 1981. The nature and limits of psychological knowledge. *American Psychologist* 36 (3): 257–269.

Koestler, A. 1978. *Janus*. New York: Vintage Books/Random House.

Laing, R. D. 1967. *The politics of experience*. New York: Ballantine.

Laszlo, E. 1972. *Introduction to systems philosophy: Toward a new paradigm of contemporary thought*. New York: Harper Torchbooks.

———. 2003. *The connectivity hypothesis*. Albany: State University of New York Press.

Macy, J. 1991. *Mutual causality in Buddhism and general systems theory: The Dharma of natural systems*. Albany: State University of New York Press.

Manicas, P. T. and P. F. Secord. 1983. Implications for psychology of the new philosophy of science. *American Psychologist* 38 (4): 399–413.

Maslow, A. H. 1996. *The psychology of science*. South Bend, IN: Gateway Editions.

Masterpasqua, F. and P. A. Perna. 1997. *The psychological meaning of chaos*. Washington, DC: American Psychological Association.

Maturana, H. R. and F. J. Varela. 1987. *The tree of knowledge: The biological roots of human understanding*. Boston: Shambhala/New Science.

Meier, C. A., Ed. 2001. *Atom and archetype: The Pauli/Jung Letters 1932–1958*. Princeton: Princeton University Press.

Miller, J. G. 1978. *Living systems*. New York: McGraw-Hill.

Olds, L. E. 1981. *Fully human*. Englewood Cliffs, NJ: Prentice-Hall/Spectrum.

———. 1991. Chinese metaphors of interrelatedness. *Contemporary Philosophy* 13 (8): 16–22.

———. 1992a. Integrating ontological metaphors: Hierarchy and interrelatedness. *Soundings: A Journal of Interdisciplinary Studies* 75 (2–3): 403–420.

———. 1992b. *Metaphors of interrelatedness: Toward a systems theory of psychology*. Albany: State University of New York Press.

———. 1999. Immanence and relatedness: Psychological and ontological reflections. In *The annual review of women in world religions*, Vol. 5, Eds. Sharma, A. and Young, K. K., 41–61. Albany: State University of New York Press.

———. 2001. The Columbia basin as a metaphor for an interdisciplinary approach. *Issues in Integrative Studies* 19: 221–225.

———. 2009. Wilber and Jung: One map, two tastes? In *Spheres of awareness*, ed. J. Lough and P. Herron, 155–172. Lanham, MD: University Press of America.

Rychlak, J. F. 1968. *A philosophy of science for personality theory*. Boston: Houghton Mifflin.

Shear, J., ed. 1995–1997. *Explaining consciousness: The hard problem*. Cambridge: MIT Press/Bradford.

Sperry, R. W. 1988. Psychology's mentalist paradigm and the religion/science tension. *American Psychologist* 43 (8): 607–613.

Vallacher, R. R., P. T. Coleman, A. Nowak and L. Bui-Wrzosinska. 2010. Rethinking intractable conflict: The perspective of dynamical systems. *American Psychologist* 65 (4): 262–278.

von Bertalanffy, L. 1969. *General systems theory* (revised edition). New York: George Braziller.

Wade, J. 1996. *Changes of mind: A holonomic theory of the evolution of consciousness.* Albany: State University of New York Press.

Washburn, M. 1994. *Transpersonal psychology in psychoanalytic perspective.* Albany: State University of New York Press.

Whitehead, A. N. 1925. *Science and the modern world.* New York: Mentor.

———. 1978. *Process and reality*, corrected ed., eds. D. R. Griffin and D. W. Sherburne. New York: Free Press.

Wilber, K. 1993. *The spectrum of consciousness,* 20th anniversary ed. Wheaton, IL: Quest.

———. 1995. *Sex, ecology, and spirituality: The spirit of evolution.* Boston: Shambhala.

———. 1996. *The atman project: A transpersonal view of human development,* new ed. Wheaton, IL: Quest.

———. 1998. *The marriage of sense and soul.* New York: Random House.

———. 2000. *Integral psychology.* Boston: Shambhala.

———. 2001. *No boundary: Eastern and western approaches to personal growth.* Boston: Shambhala.

———. 2006. *Integral spirituality.* Boston: Integral Books/Shambhala.

THE STARRY NIGHT SKY

GUY BURNEKO

The Institute for Contemporary Ancient Learning, Seattle, Washington, USA

This is a brief intellectual autobiography telling of how I came to be captivated by evolutionary theories of a self-organizing universe and their meaningful connections with intercultural lore from other settings, notably Daoist and NeoConfucian traditions. This marriage of themes led me to thinking about a universe system of nonlocal connectivity irreducible to subjects and objects. Herein, or hereas, our self-awareness appears as a fractal of the complementarity, mutual coproduction and coinherence of mind and/as cosmic nature the nondualizing (self)experience of which is conducive to extreme long-term ecosocial sustainability. Understanding ourselves in contemplative attentiveness to embody the evolutionary self-organization of cosmogenesis as expressed in the conduct of life and our relations with the natural world we simultaneously experience ourselves as a (co)conscious dimensionality of *creatio continua*. The intrinsic delight of this outshines the extrinsic gains we seek through excessively utilitarian orientations to the world and results in a reduced demand on the natural environment.

This is a story of how I have come to delight in cosmogenesis, the self-organizing evolution of consciousness and the universe experienced as not-two different things, and how this intrinsic system/delight may be a sustainable alternative to excessively manipulative utilitarian demands on nature for extrinsic gain. Interculturally borrowing the language of early Chinese sensibility, I also characterize this delight as a fractal or microcosm of the self-organizing system/awareness of coevolving Heaven, Earth, and Humankind whose co-emergent body and mind we more-than-sustainably express in our nondualizing and nonreductive ecosocial consciousness and conduct (Burneko 2004, 2010a, 2010b). Where everything is interconnected, in the quantum sense Laszlo (2003) emphasizes, is biocosmically coevolutionary, as with Margulis and Sagan (1995), ecosystemically emergent, according to Morin and Deacon, complementary in the Jungian sense and in those of Kafatos and Nadeau (1990, 1992), Jahn and Dunne, reciprocal in the Confucian, and creatively chaotic (or "pumpkinified") in the Daoist senses (Girardot 1983, 265), I cannot say with finality that it all works according to one certain rule or order (cf. Hall and Ames 1995), for example, definitively separable into subjects and objects, nature or consciousness. Conversely, our imagination, intellect and choice seem as much a part of the universe process on Earth as are, for instance, electromagnetism or baryon density.

From relatively early boyhood in Rome, NY, USA a little above the 43rd parallel, I was captivated and enchanted by the starry night sky. Of a crisp autumn evening sometime between homework and sleep, I would find my place in the backyard, crank my head back the requisite number of degrees to get my bearings on Polaris, and travel for a few minutes outside of home and school spacetime into a sidereal order whose magnitudes, as Osarqaq sings, "moved my inward parts with joy" (in Brower 1971, 7). I had some help in this. My Dad colluded in staking me to a subscription of *Sky and Telescope*, taking me to amateur astronomer club meetings, and physically sharing with me the down-in-the-cellar labor of grinding and polishing our own six-inch parabolic mirror for the telescope we never quite finished making.

It was these visits in the night skies that set my course for a lifetime of intellectual, geographical, and emotional exploration, and I can name several of the admirable navigators on this wonderful and sometimes puzzling reconnaissance. They all nourished my young soul, but it was years before I saw how they were all interconnected in my story of life and world. Not even childhood fairy tales or the roisterous outcomes of "The Bremen Town Musicians" (Grimm 1922) were without place and season; and chief among the inspirations and solaces of early youth were *The Wind in the Willows* (Grahame 1908) and *The Secret Garden* (Burnett 1910). I can still feel my way into the skin of brazen Toad the (aspiring) adventurer, dulcet Mole the homesteader, and Badger the thoughtful curmudgeon. Still a canary yellow wagon invites me to new reveries and settings. And for all my life I will be moved with joy and recognition as Mary Lennox addresses herself to the garden robin just as if she were speaking to a person: "Would you make friends with me?" (Burnett 1910, 52). For that is effectively the same silent appeal I also made to unknown celestial others myself, to those stellar, galactic and extragalactic intelligences I was pretty sure were gazing around with as much reflective, delighted curiosity as some of my school friends and I were gazing.

The writings of Fred Hoyle (1950), George Gamow (1952), and their cosmologist colleagues a little later only enriched and secured my sense that the universe (as we had by then come to interpret it) was an integral whole, and evolving as an integrated process-event of potentially numerous dimensions. And since I did not then quibble over the connotations of the word evolution, worry over single-ordered versus many-ordered metaphysics or feel yet any postmodern queasiness about overarching master-narratives of Unity or Origin, the inference I drew was that it was a living universe. But it was not until I read a particular sentence from Sir James Jeans' (1930) book *The Mysterious Universe* that my youthful and subsequent thought-life began to foliate from a particular seed of insight that has remained an ever nurturing and animating one.

About the evolving system, sang Jeans with sweet insouciance into a boy's heart: "The universe begins to look more like a great thought than like a great machine" (1930, 158). And the passion and intrigue this statement fostered in me christened my first cognitive sense that the world of matter and the ecology of life were not separate from the world of consciousness and human feeling. I then first experienced the nondual understanding and the thrill, for want of a better word, that we simultaneously inhabit, embody and voice a universe whose tides and thoughts, mind and nature, are variations and complements of one another in an ever-concoursing-self-organizing-unfolding without, so far as I cared to understand it, any end. Ah, it is not so that youth is wasted on the young. Give us but light, air, food, and love and a tall star to steer by.

The next chapter awakening for me a universe "stranger than we can think," as some scientist has exulted, opened about the time I was finishing high school and getting ready to go off to Fordham, a Jesuit university in New York City (someplace between the Third Avenue El and the mid-late '60s). It was easily marked on the frosty morning my mother tossed me *The Saturday Evening Post* she had opened to an article about the visionary paleontologist Pierre Teilhard de Chardin. My first teenage response to his thinking is best indicated by an image of myself about three paragraphs in beginning a slow, rhythmic slapping of my thigh to a subvocalized, "Holy shit; This stuff all fits together." And it's remained a working lifelong hypothesis since then that the life of consciousness is both a continuation of and a context for the life of the material ecologies of cosmos that accompany it. Mind and nature form, in this lively view, an irreducibly afoundational intersystem, a psychocosmic complementarity and a nondual mutuality. Regardless whether one is stipulated as the source of the other, we never find one apart from the other. And in any case, the meaningfulness of either is a function of both, or so I began to think. I was long later enchanted to find resonant reflections offered in Gregory Bateson's *Mind and Nature* 1979), Edgar Morin's statement that "The world is present inside our minds, which are inside the world" (2008, 62), and in the charmingly evocative ontohermeneutics of Zhuangzi who "did not propose any specific ism. ... [but] merely wanted to *alert* us toward living the polyphonic ambiguities in the polythetic self involved logicality of the universe" (Wu 1990, 256). It was the Asian thinkers who won me to the (inter)existential (auto)hermeneutics of a self-organizing (*ziran*) universe whose optimal mode of ecohumane conduct as enacted by the sage or contemplative is not the utilitarian one of the (supposed) part dominating ongoing wholing for extrinsic gain, but the more intrinsically rewarding coevolutionary self-delight of irreducible "experience-as-such" (undivided into objects by/and subjects) as interpreted, for instance, in Guenther's systems theoretical reading of Tibetan *rDzogs-chen* tradition.

From Teilhard, I learned of noetic, organic, and inorganic systems as interliving and interrooted, and from within their self-organization intimating yet further registers of awareness and eco-(self)-understanding in a groping, perhaps, but ever broadening *itinerarium mentis in Deum/Naturam*. Any contest henceforth between the deeper meanings of science and spirituality seemed beside the point. As another poet is said to have written, "there is another world, but it is in this one." And I was on my way. The universe was growing; I was growing (with) it; and in the heady idiom of the '60s, the ripening of my generation coincided with the maturation of the planet itself. Each of us, as body, mind, and soul was a mode of the always-ongoing.

We are no longer so smug as to believe any generation has cornered the market on either sagacity or great woe. But the ideas in youth that connected Jeans and Teilhard with, say, Shklovskii and Sagan's *Intelligent Life in the Universe* (1966), *The Diamond Cutter Sutra* Buddha 1969), or a two-volume series of essays entitled *Adventures of the Mind* (Thruelsen and Kobler 1961) (the first books I ever bought with my own money)—along with the music of the '60s and continued nighttime correspondence with the northern celestial hemisphere—all combined to evoke a hope-filled sensibility later articulated for me in Erich Jantsch's pregnant systems notion that all life, especially human life, appears as a process of self-realization in which the need for meaning is a powerful autocatalytic theme of the evolution of consciousness and of cosmos (1980, 307–309 passim). And God, undefined, of course, appeared with Jantsch less as an a priori and external Creator of the universe than as the emergently evolving Mind of the universe (1980, 308). To me, this was numinous and functional mystical insight. Nor will I forgo suggesting that by it we achieve glimpses of our responsibility, especially concerning terrorist, racist, profitist, ecocidal, and variously abusive absolutist outlooks, to revision ourselves and our (thinking about the) world. For, as the Buddha in different ways intimates, all that we are is the result of what we have thought (cf. *The Dhammapada*, 1965). Thomas Berry (1988) speaks of this revision as reinventing the human, and Stuart Kauffman (2008) as reinventing the sacred.

I was not a scientist. Math confused, frightened, and angered me; and I was also frustrated that I could not share in its just barely discernible beauties. Algebra seemed an affair of smoke and mirrors, although geometry made sense as did earth science, chemistry, and biology. But in science and learning overall, I respected the process of imaginative reasoning by which small bits of this and that with suitable inference and extrapolation could lead to big picture, even philosophical and mythic sensibilities, like the one William Irwin Thompson somewhere expresses about the self-sacrifice of first-generation supernovae and their subsequent (re)birth as (the organic elements in) Main Sequence you and me, or the cosmological insight of Brian Swimme that "We are all of us arising together at the center of the cosmos" (1996, 112).

Theories may become outdated, but our care in thought—if not always our faith—continues. Nor was it wasted on me, as I continued reading here and there in the myth, religion and literature of the planetary noetic repertoire, that science, art, and spirituality were complements to one another in the musing of the world. Indeed, science, art, philosophy, literature, myth, and religion seemed increasingly narratives in themselves and analogs of one another. Science (as theory and paradigm) seemed like myth with decimal points, and literature like thickly described (qualitative or participatory) science. It was as if the interpenetration of diverse modes of being and genres of understanding expressed in cosmogenesis a family or kinship character whose cousinage included multiply veracious genre-epistemologies—not to say related ontohermeneutics (Cheng 1995; Durkheim 1963). Coming one day in the Smithsonian upon Einstein's words about mystery as the source of all true art and science (and, I think, *re-ligio*) lent the *imprimatur*, if one were needed, to the consciousness that connection and new growth are always in play in the ecohumane and, as David Abram (1996) puts it, as the "more-than-human" imagination. This is even more strikingly presented in terms of the originary cosmogonic complementarity that is infolded into all subsequent events as "the basis for the part-whole complementarity that is evinced at all scales" in the conscious universe (Kafatos and Nadeau 1990, 167).

So I walked intoxicated out of a wonderful undergraduate college education largely in literature, philosophy, and theology unable to read the Latin of my diploma and was soon preoccupied by an Austin Healey which, like Mr. Toad, I drove fast, far, and wide for a year on back country roads before selling it one summer day to raise the money to make the flight to Fairbanks—as far away as I could go without falling off the edge, it then seemed—and graduate school. It is easier to see now than it was as a young man then that going North, not to say several times zones West, was a continuation of childhood exploration fantasies about getting widely oriented in spacetime and meaning. But from boyhood going-to-bed lucubrations about "absolute nothing: no black, no white, no top, no bottom" to fantasies of traveling across intergalactic space alone in a small craft to later hiking in the Brooks Range and on the tundra, and to continuously ongoing reading, nosing around, and thinking, I suspect I was also looking for the parameters and the metrics of new worldmaking and worldmeaning. So much enthusiasm was invested in learning all about everything that I probably also turned into the Nowhere Man off and on. Yet I remembered from the *Daodejing* that nonpurposive thinking and a certain abating of ego success-insistence (*wu wei*) served in opening the doors of perception. Call it homing, call it roaming; call it as Keats did travel in the vale of soul-making (see Jones 1985).

Although few go to Alaska foremost to get a Master's in English, there I found the imagery and language that homes the world in all times and places, friendship in a community of creative recusants, and the great benison of earth, sky, and extreme climate. So by the light of several observatory quality black and white glossies of the nebulae in Orion, The Crab, and such like, and to the low late-night music of The Moody Blues, I passed a couple of subarctic winters studying ancient and modern mythopoeia and a little cybernetics while running along the way into the novelties of: freezeplug heaters, rappelling, moose, fishstrips, Ian McHarg, Paolo Soleri, ice fog, *The Whole Earth Catalog*, Doris Lessing, mukluks, ravens, Norbert Wiener, honeybuckets, snowshoes, breakup, Carlos Castaneda, *aurora borealis*, Buckminster Fuller, John Lilly, Carl Jung, and the first *soupçon* of René Thom's (1975) *Structural Stability and Morphogenesis* (although it was some time before I actually read that). I also read R. A. Durr's (1970) *Poetic Vision and the Psychedelic Experience* in writing my thesis ("Out and In: A Consideration of the Lyrics of Acid Rock") on visionary literature, Asian philosophy, and the musical group mentioned above.

I had known two things about myself as a boy, well before college and grad school. One was learned in family politics: if I did not have enough words I would be suffocated. The other thing, more generously tuned, was that if I knew (at least) a little about a lot of different things, I could talk with almost anybody about something of interest to him or her, and to me. In other words, I understood learning, scholarship if you will, and creative thinking, as ways to enhance and improvisationally enrich interhuman relations. I am not an especially remote person, but I knew my strength was in ideas and knowledge and whatever modicum of understanding might ensue from them. So I let what I knew, thought and read plus intuition, humor and fellow-feeling be the gifts I could offer and share with others, my visas, so to speak, through life. My emotions were also more-or-less evident, and these were especially engaged to the degree my intellectual imagination had room to play, and vice versa. As I much later read, there is no state of cognition that is not also a state of affection. My frequent mistake was to make more of cognition than it warranted or to suppose, on the basis of my early exposure to polemical language, that wording experience was actually being there.

Nevertheless, I wanted to be able to share genuinely with a wide variety of persons. I also had an educational, journalistic, advocacy, or messenger tendency. And I sought consciously to participate in the evolution of consciousness on Earth—through both interpersonal and intellectual, even ontological, conversation: turning-together, moving-with, being-as another, as in Confucian *shu* or self-likening with other beings. These interlinked aspirations I vaguely knew about myself, but never expressly admitted to all in one place. And the book travel in and out of school along with geographical travel were both concomitants and metaphors of that self-organizational myth/experience in which I microcosmically embodied and communicated the self-learning and (auto)hermeneutics of a universe becoming conscious of itself.

Not by or of myself alone, of course—but as a guy response-able, in my own way, for the emerging experience. My mission, message and advocacy were: that the world we know is not all there is to know, could well be different, is the way it is to the degree we are the way we are, and is not separate from ourselves; all it takes is a living vision; trust yourself. We and our world co-evoke one another: there is not (necessarily) an altogether a priori elephant waiting for us to scope out its lineaments or some one fixed, inalterable way the life/mind of universe works. Trust yourself, real-ize your Self seems to be the refrain. This Self is also this all-connected yet interminate cosmogenesis, our co-worlding.

Over time, the languages of cosmology, archetypal psychology, philosophical hermeneutics, world mysticism and of the theory of coevolving and self-organizing systems, for examples, lent themselves well, (nondualistically, interculturally, and transdisciplinarily), to communicating our growthful possibilities, and to articulating what Berry (1988) calls "the dream of the earth." In (often poorly and glibly) learning the various disciplinary, cultural, and attitudinal languages available to me, I also realized as I grew older they were composing an idiom of their own—on their own—that is, a syncretic but authentic language beyond my ego perspectivated intentions (as Gebser might put it). I see, also, that the language and concepts of systems and evolutionary thinking form just one (kind of) language, a dialect. It is one I relish, but it is no more widely beloved among us or apt for various themes and gifts than, say, are the languages of: Kabbalah, Yup'ik, neoplatonism, set theory, birds, or eukaryosis, of *via negativa*, the *dolce stil nuovo*, radical *nirdvandva*, or of postmodernism, images, numbers, silence, quantum indeterminacy, logical-empiricism, *Daxue*, music, love, class warfare, mushroom inspiration, hip-hop or trance and magic in the painted caves. We need to communicate in every tongue and noetic structure we have, for ecosocial sustainability in "the necessity unity" of mind and nature links greatly with cogrowthful diversity (Bateson 1979; Morin and Kern 1999; Morin 2008).

Another way of observing this is to reflect that each language, as Whorf (1956) intimates and George Steiner (2001) confirms, co-constitutes and unfolds a world. A deep reliance on one tongue (discipline, method, culture, state of consciousness, ideology, etc.) alone reveals some and deeply eclipses other realities. By this token, a monocrop overcommitment to the one language of whole systems where not enriched with genuinely transdisciplinary, intercultural, and philosophical reach or coupled with true empathy can lend itself to a kind of pomposity or salon mystification that only closes persons out, defeating the very premise of systemic holism. As Morin (2008, 93, 104) sagely puts it, "There is no omniscient vantage point," "Why forget this?"; "The idea of totality becomes all the more beautiful and rich the more it ceases being totalitarian. ... It is more radiant in the polycentrism of relatively autonomous parts than in the globalism of the whole." We learn to sing sustainingly with every voice: rational, arational, discursive, and concursive.

And Blake's alert, "Go! put off Holiness/And put on Intellect" (in Erdman 1965, 249) reminds us that although holism is sister to holiness and health, yet we are called in real lifetime to perform as our very selves, not merely to advertise, ongoing-wholing as the work of integrated twenty-first-century interbeing. We are called to outgrow ourselves, our consciousness, and our institutions, not just to design models and fundamentalizing heuristics. Indeed, any time we are authentically involved in an art or a science, a polity or a *numen*, we are making an experiment of our life, taking an existential risk, making an offering. This is death/rebirth whether under the signs of bifurcation, fluctuation, chaos, and catastrophe or those of wisdom, compassion, *metanoia*, and *kenosis*. Ours is both a matrix and a practice of worldmaking and meaning-sharing, and the price of sustainability is more attentiveness to the intrinsic value of our relations and experiences with nature and one another than to ulterior ego-gain and manipulation.

Among the languages I encountered, some nevertheless stood out as major resources of interpretation and (co)creation. I also hear, now, that for me the mother tongue, English and English language literature, is beloved not merely for its thematic insights but for its rhythms and patterns, for its connotations as well as its definitions, and, most deliciously, for its etymologies. I also see as languaging other patterns and rhythms of natural and mental phenomena. Language is participative, constitutive and enactive in an irreducibly ontohermeneutic cosmogenesis, not merely re-presentational. And evocative enchantment is as valid an ontomethodology as reductionistic discursion; every cerebral seminar has root, and fruit, in biocosmic ecosemeity.

In language, *langue et parole*, I found anew that mind and nature were alike systems of (co)self-evolving pattern, periodicity, cadence, beat, difference, movement, and growth—what Steiner (and Jeremy Campbell [1982], Bunn [2002], de Santillana and von Dechend [1969]. or *Zohar*) might call grammars of creation. And meaning is not so much of essences as of relations: that is, as much as meaning inheres in individual words and things it is (nonlocally) distributed throughout/as the field/ecology of (their) relations. It's all self-referential music/coherence, in this sense: the musing of and with and *as* (not just *about*) the cosmos that is part created, part perceived—as amusing poets still sing. Rhymes, rhetorics, analogies, algorithms, and wave forms are all kindred forms of reasoning; each is preservation and transformation of the symmetry of the interminate field. We might take this to be the quantum vacuum field, the field or continuum of being, Gaia, or experience-as-such, prior unity. Something like this is succinctly stated in James H. Bunn's "philosophy of rhythmic composition" *Wave Forms,* which he introduces by saying: "One does not refer to nature . . . one refers with nature" (2002, 1).

Under the Alaskan auroras' long-whispering incantations I, while poring over the texts, and theories of literature, poetics, science, and culture, began as a young grad student to see, as Blake had put it and Frye and others following him, that that world is most real and vital that is most clearly, completely and integrally conceived and imagined. It is when we are rapt in attentiveness that we are most ourselves. The mere passive reception of input by the senses after the manner of Locke and Descartes is but part of the self-organization of a more broadly hermeneutic ontology: contemplative attention, interpretation, creative imagination and poetic intellect are wider holarchic modes of continuing creation. We participate in world making not only with one another, but as the voices of the (ever-present) first day in hermeneutic call and response. The intrinsic benefits of participation outlive the extrinsic rewards of domination. Proposed Zhang Zai long ago, that which fills the universe we may consider our body, and what directs the universe our nature (1960).

The ill-shaped and unclear task I visited on myself then, in my late twenties, in partly mythopoeic and religiophilosophical terms and in partly scientific ones, was one that I now identify as one of a functional mysticism, practical wisdom, or *phronesis* linked with the global noetic repertoire of nondual sensibility. It is the attempted knack of nondually languaging worlding in transdisciplinary, intercultural ways, a version of functional cosmology, says Berry (1988). As a clue I have this from Zhuangzi: the ten thousand things and I are born together, all interchanging, swapping our stuff (1981).

So little by little, sometimes only partially wittingly in the self-organization that is life, I blaze my wandering trail: by way of National Endowment for the Humanities and other stipends and fellowships (myth, symbol, and ideology studies at Claremont, Chinese literature and philosophy at Stanford, studies on consciousness and reality formation at Princeton), teaching in unique university programs (Antioch, CIIS), and in independent scholarship and occasional publication (see www.beyondthematrix.com/inst/). Most of my travel has been in North America, Western Europe, and The State of Aloha. I married while in the most delicious doctoral experience anyone can ever have known (at Emory); and on graduating went, with my resourceful wife and our young daughter, to teach in China for two years. All along the way, I engaged ideas as an artist engages colors. There has been divorce and enduring fatherhood, hurts and fears and hopes and love and wonder. I live today partnered with a woman who writes beautiful novels and paints; my luminous daughter and her family now live in Sweden.

I have seen that as our minds change so changes our world. As changes thinking, so alter circumstances. I do not think it's always one-way or causal, for thinking and world(ing) seem polythetically to co-implicate one another. But hijacked jetliners pummeling the World Trade Center illustrate as causes and as effects the connection between our thinking, everybody's thinking, and the modes of our shared worlding. The crises of culture and consciousness (as interpreted by, say, Speth (2012) or by Palmer and Zajonc (2010) are crises also of the Earth and its meanings. Our attitudes and values perhaps even more than gravity and the CO_2 content of the air shape our shared world futures. Likewise, Earth lessons its own sustaining ecosemeity where we heed. Thus I let unformulizable Dao be my polestar, cynosure and hinge of the concelebratory selfgrowing unfolding.

The polestar is supposedly a pretty constant beacon, around which appear to cycle in seasonal inconstancy the other stars of the Northern skies, so its metaphorical association with the wobbly and productive ambiguities of the-Dao-that-cannot-be-told in Chinese lore deserves some interpretation; and offering that I offer a look at the kind of images, ideas and experiences that have claimed my attention in more recent years of thinking about self-organizing eco-noetic evolution. (It's not for me a forgone conclusion that "evolution" is linear in the random-variation-natural-selection version we commonly think of. And just what is consciousness?; Or is it even a "what" at all? I do think process is interpretation and interpretation is process. But this is only to suggest again the genuine systems mysticism that cosmogenesis and meaning/mind/heart (*xin*) are covalent.)

I have always been interested in the theory of myth, and in some specific mythic themes and images. In the myth of Hermes, for instance, there is a great deal going on. And much of it is unpackaged by Karl Kerényi in his book *Hermes: Guide of Souls* (1986), by his astute translator Murray Stein in his own book, *In Midlife* (1983), and in N. O. Brown's *Hermes the Thief* (1969). Any time we hear about Trickster, as well, Hermes is likely in play under some name or trope of feedback/retroaction, disruption, subversion and the kinds of complex eco-self-(re)organization Morin (2008) celebrates.

Of the things that may be learned from myth, and Hermes's myth in particular, a couple are relevant for studies in organized complexity, evolution, chaos, self-organization, and related multidimensionalities. One is that myth, and poetry more extensively, is multivocal (or polysemous); its images say, presence, and "mean," or connect, many things, perhaps seemingly contradictory things, at once, things that would take many pages and contrasting perspectives to spell out in discursive prose. One multileveled mythopoeic picture is worth ten thousand words. Also, the diverse and holonomously varying meanings of myth and poetry are often far from equilibrium with our habituated ego-rational culture and mentality: their *poiesis* perturbs our consciousness to new regimes. Another thing about myths is that they often have intercultural validity: different cultures' myths in different image-clothing (seem to) show archetypal similarities of structure and meaning worldwide. It's as if there were mutually hybridizing biopsychic attractor basins beneath the surfaces of our cultural diversity, or neurognostic aptitudes for holistic perception (Laughlin and Throop 2001).

Again, given their plurisemeity, myth narratives do not always reduce to one, final, conclusive image, storyline or interpretation. They are dynamic disequilibrating, ongoing processes of meaning-ing, not static, finished meanings (i.e., meaning-products or fixed thoughts). Hence, they are often connected with dreams and transformative rituals. And to the degree they emerge as what Berry (1988, 48–49) calls the spontaneities of the earth and Jung the psychoid archetypal dimension where body/nature/cosmos and instinct/psyche/mind concresce, myths and their imagery may be taken as modes of nondual psychocosmic self-organization and display (Yuasa 1987, 1983; Corrington 1994, 1997). In this sense, mythopoeia is a simultaneous process and interpretation of the (co)evolving psyche/cosmos continuum—a performance of psychocosmic *autopoiesis* and/as emergent self-knowing and delight. This illustrates in a metaphorical way the "law" of complexity/consciousness descried by Teilhard for whom, not incidentally (nor alone, say Primack and Abrams 2006) the psychomental dimension of the universe is always already latent, so to speak, in its material ecologies, as these, in their turn, realize themselves through the eyes of (our) evolving coconsciousness. This adumbrates a transdisciplinary and intercultural *scienza nuova* as we integrate contemplative and biocognitive with (Earth) systems and ecoscience.

Be that as it may, the imagery associated with Hermes helps show some of myth's—and poetry's—order-through-fluctuation and "symbiotization of heterogeneity" at work (Jantsch and Waddington, 1976, 7). Hermes is journeyer and guide, herald, musician, god of meetings and (accidental) findings. The god friendliest to man, god of lucky windfalls and quick-seeing opportunism, Hermes is also god of thieves, of commerce, of waymeetings and liminal boundary-crossings; and most familiarly from our childhood exposure to mythology, Hermes is god of (multivocal) language and interpretation, messages and messengers, texts, and con-versation. Hermes (Mercury) is the Quicksilver Messenger Service, the most agile turnarounds and comebacks. His winged feet have brought us everything from flowers on Valentine's Day to the sacred messages and texts of the gods and goddesses above and below, messages whose interpretation has evoked and informed the sacred and scholarly work of hermeneutics. And of all the titles, epithets and characteristics associated with Hermes, the most absorbing for my interests is that of Hermes *Stropheus*: Hermes the socket—the empty gudgeon in which turns smoothly the pivot and the hinge, the axles of (the meanings of) things. This is because s/he is fluent, current, pliant, existentially transparent, conversant with all tongues and manners and seasons of being. Hermes does not ego-appetitively get (stuck) in the way of the self-organizing conduct of life. Hermes is model of the ego/self-emptying or *kenosis* by which in attentive co-resonance with ongoing experience we ecstatically get out of our own way enough to be filled by it, at-oned with (or not-twoed from) it, from ongoing-wholing, and participatingly real-ize the emergent, intrinsic value of self/other compresence with nothing external(ized) left over to grab at. In Morin's complexity variation of the ontohermeneutics of such *philosophia perennis*, "Emergents feed back on the conditions and instruments of their formation, and, in the process, [sus]tain the perenniality of system" (Morin 2008, 113; Burneko 2004).

Writes Kerényi of Hermes *Stropheus,* this hinge is the "primordial mediator and messenger [who con-versationally] moves between the absolute 'no' and the absolute 'yes,' or, more correctly, between two 'no's' that are lined up against each other... " (1986, 77). Hermes *Stropheus,* then, is the ever-pliantly labile hinge, the faculty or eco-function that allows all things/meanings to (co)grow and optimally—or satisficingly, allow Varela, Thompson, and Rosch (1991, 196–197)—(re)turn (*fan*) beyond being stuck. Hermes is not stuck in one subjectivating position, not freighted with an only object-constitutive ego project, not fixed in context, interpretation, mindset or attitude, and thus is the mythological liberation of all things being themselves to the degree they are like hir fluent or deferential, reciprocal, (*shu*), empty (*wu wei*) of self-subsistence and the inclination programmatically to control or manipulate.

Analogously, Hermes may be said to be in myth what Polaris is in the starry night sky. For while Polaris seems to stay parked in one place, even among the ancients it was understood that the Polestar *axis mundi* varies in a many thousand year wobble-and-tilt of its own, even as the seasonal constellations appear to wheel and vary around it (cf. de Santillana and von Dechend 1969, or Jenkins 1998). Hermes, the readiest wobbler towards the light, the liminal player-with-the-limits, is to the fluidity and polysemeity of myth (dream, imagination, communication, discourse/concourse, Earthly exchange and coevolution) what the ever-varying (careen, or precession of the) polestar is to Heaven's: a fluid and fluent value/function of self-organizingly intercomposing order, chaos and variation, stability and instability. Who manifests this self-organizing system dynamic performs the Dao, is *Dao Shu* or the pivot of the Dao, in Chinese lore (Burneko 2004). Jibes Zhuangzi, s/he who wants right without wrong, order without disorder, does not know how things hang together. Self-organizing autonomies are born, as Morin makes the same point, (2008, 11) in interdependencies—openness to universe and/as one another.

The vasty tumbling of the stars in their drift about the galaxy as galactic clusters themselves move to a music of spheres lost to our ears blends chance fluctuations and novelty with the mechanisms of celestial dynamics just as the stochastic marriage of novelty and regularity, of hell and heaven, of syllogism and synchronicity, enacts, and is enacted in, the narrative and interexistential grammars of story, autopoiesis and mythopoeic creation. The *hula* of the freely turning econoetic and humanocosmic hinge, is the genuine, non-fixed, axle/dynamic of *creatio continua.* As suggests the *Daodejing,* it is the empty (unfixed) space in the hub that makes possible the turning wheel. The no-thing/"not-a-what" that "con-courses," dis-courses and "evens out," all thinging is the "ever-present origin," (according, respectively, to Hermes, Deacon 2012; Bett, 1925; Peter D. Hershock 1996; Zhuangzi 1964 and Jean Gebser 1985). Who has no excessively fixed, dominating nature or essence of his/her own is thus polytropically amenable to—strategically liberates, disequilibrates, accords with, releases and real-izes—all things in sustaining coevolution, and does not thing hirself and other sentient beings as objects to hir own subject/object. We and the worlding we (non-ego-attachedly) co-do are the multipolar constellation of ever-self-renewing meaning-and-being ecologies. Our stability amid things and the sustainability of the life of the environment coinhere as fluency, not stasis or isolation—we sustainably endure and grow to the extent we attentively resonate with the ongoing spontaneities of the Earth and do not seek foremost to control and calculate.

In myth and metaphor, the image of Hermes *Stropheus* is the image of dynamic, not static, balance, of spontaneous order through diversity and fluctuation far from equilibrium, the self-organizing complexity of interrelation and the emergence of holistically compresent aptitudes, meanings and possibilities unforeseen from, nor reducible to, their precedents and parts: parts themselves so interinvolved and coevolutionarily interresponsive that they can not finally be said to have been separate parts to begin with. There is no there there where there is fructile emptiness; yet (t)herein is reborn world and/as self. Accordingly, let image and language recreate and sustainingly enact the pinwheeling order-through-fluctuation.

And the archaic images and meanings of myth, sometimes clothed in science, recycle themselves afresh among us who engage them newly today. These are the navigational beacons and peregrinating lightships of an ever-self-varying yet self-optimizing humanocosmic evolutionary journey, then and now (Burneko 2004). The images and the old etymologies, ancient wisdom, and contemporary sciences compresence all at once the differentiable coimplications of: (1) ecological self-renewal and (ecohumane) interdependence; and of (2) the deep feedback cybernetics of sustainable and sustaining cocreative diversity, symbiosis, and mutually involved events, things, persons, polities and heaven and earth; (3) the plurepistemic, nonutilitarian *sagesse* of indual contemplative, non ego-driven, consciousness; and (4) the creative ontohermeneutics of a paradoxically afoundational world that is also a co-selfing, an imperfectly predictable process that is (its own) interpretation. These are among the variants of a cosmogenic unfolding of complex order-with/as-chaos and self-with/as-other whose nuptial performs dynamic balance, changeful music, and terrestrial-celestial navigational *sagesse*.

Only connect: The imagistic rudder of things (from *kybernetes/kybernetikos*), is also the cybernetic cynosure, the beaconing star, retroactive feedback-focus of attention, attraction and admiration (Morin 2008, 114), in the Polestar constellation called both Ursa Minor and the Dog's Tail, or *Cynosura*, an ancient term used exclusively of the ever-precessing Polestar of the Northern skies. It is similarly a role of the sage to accord contemplatively, yet engagedly, in complex ecosocial attunement with/as the constant-yet-inconstant rhythms of Heaven and of Earth and Humankind. S/he thus resonantly incarnates/nurtures the sustaining oncreating, and is automaieutic pivot, hinge, and midwife of the sustaining ecosocial *poiesis* (Burneko 2004).

All is flow and change, *panta rei*, claimed Heraclitus. *Anicca*, there is impermanence; *anatta*, there is not self-subsistent selfhood voiced the Buddha: Nothing worldly is absolute (1965, 1989). All composite things are in coevolving interdependence and disruption. And this, as with mythopoeia, I think, is a premodern way of nondualistically thinking and speaking autopoietic self-organization with skilful means for its postmodern ecosocial, ecopolitical, and ontohermeneutic implications (see Cheng 1995 or Macy 1991, for example).

In cosmology and in mythopoeia, I found a pedigree for my own tendencies connecting hingelike con-versational, or "turning-together" work with that of the great wheeling of the zodiac I so loved contemplating as a boy. I feel our glowing inter-consciousness and the rhythms and patterns of glittering cosmos are not two. And I affirm with Edith Cobb (1977) that the imaginations that most hold us as children set a course for our lifetimes. So I came to rediscover in elder lore images and ideas that now in contemporary (more-or-less) discursive costume are again fruitful and helpful as we sort out our own world wayfaring. We world as we speak. Trying to say too much at once in my amateur concept-matching (*ge yi*), I stutter and complicate this-here-now-ongoing whose apt dia-logic is better the singing of song than the arguing of a thesis.

When Zhuangzi says the ten thousand things and we emerge together, he seems to mean the world and ourselves polyphonically cocreate and coevoke one another—again, to such a degree that they are perhaps not, strictly, one and other. Zhuangzi also notes that having said this, we already are multiplying co(i)mplications—there's the me, there's the world, there's the talking about the world. As arises and objectifies one, so arises and objectifies the other. Zhuangzi to this says pretty quickly, *Basta!* (1981). And he invokes, correspondingly, a nonuse of ego/mind and a demi-use of language, in "goblet words" and "spillover saying" (Wu 1990, 107) whose overall effect, silly as it sometimes sounds, is to pry us out of our conventional (objectifying, dualizing and fixating) ego-perspective-laden ontology and epistemology into a con-versationally strategic freedom not just with, but *as* the (freedom/emptiness of the) interminate worlding process that is (its own) interpretation or, in technispeak, auto-ontohermeneutic *poiesis*. And we can accompany his ancient understanding with contemporary systems and philosophical hermeneutics to speak, now internoetically and interculturally, of a conversational or a hermeneutic ontology: of a world of intrinsic relational meaning and value, not only of reified, externalized objects and stuff. This allows complex experience of a worlding not premised on fixed ideas/things and their program or template-philosophy, but one interpreted less by such other-referent models and designs than (self)experienced and commun-icated in the self-referently improvisational musics of spontaneously con-versing authenticity. This is a world(ing) according, as Morin has it, to "a musical metaphor of construction in movement that transforms in its very movement the constitutive elements that form it. And might we not also consider the knowledge of knowledge as a construction in movement" (2008, vii). External reference, alleges Whorf (1956), is the lesser part of meaning, coherently self-referential or music-like patternment the greater. And as Berry tells it, the universe is the only genuinely self-referential event (1988).

The sage in his/her own skillfully nonutilitarian engagement with/as language accords with the experience that neither on the side of names nor on the side of things, of subject or object, is there any certainty or stasis. In his/her no-mind coconsciousness (*wu zhi, wu nian*, i.e., non be-egoed nonpurposiveness and nonconcern for praise or blame, or payoffs, etc.) con-versing with/as (co)self-organizing cosmos, (nature, the Dao and other beings), the sage in the situational authenticity of hir speech and conduct naturally, spontaneously, concords with and as all mutually interinvolving persons, events, lifesystems and meanings in their always all-together-self-organizing humanocosmic cobecoming. Redacts the gifted scholar Wu Kuang-ming, "to lose oneself [thus] does not mean abolishing the self (for it is 'the I which does the losing'), but the 'abolition of a fixed subjective standpoint.' We can then selflessly 'follow the respective *yeses*' of things, 'tarry in many ordinaries,' and thereby dwell in the pivot of the Tao and respond endlessly. [Outgrowing] fixation in the subject is called Great Awakening" (1990, 219). And I think the freedom and the skilful languaging of this awakening are conditions and outcomes of the ancient springs of evolutionarily fruitful self-organization in sustainable biocosmic and ecohumane realms (Berry 1988, 81, 90, 195).

If the emergence of genuine novelty, of genuinely fresh understanding and states of awareness are possible, it is likely they will be so new as to seem quite crazy, or silly, compared with our conventional tropes and routine habits of world-doing. The contemplative advent of no-mind, or of what Daoists might have called "the position of no position" and similar notions are ways of indicating that fully to understand something you must be that something. And fully to understand and experience the autopoietics of worldmaking is to be (at-oned with/as) worldmaking: to nonmanipulatively (non)do this we may badly need ecstatically to outgrow and forgo (e.g., *kenosis*), the umbra of ego, Blakean "selfhood" and its always insistent payoff- and cunningly purpose-laden "doings."

The price of our Neolithically structured minds, institutions and states may be a sacrifice (or noetic recycling) that is also a liberation of a fresh order of consciousness, culture and interbeing. Intimated Meister Eckhart, we are made perfect (complete) less by what we do than by what we undergo (1974). And while I am not a quietist, I can see that eco-timely un- or non-doing—precautionary *wu wei*, or "deceleration" is the rebeginning of wisdom (Burneko 2004, 2010a, 2010b; Morin and Kern 1999).

The *Daodejing* murmurs to us that one who knows the way does nothing, yet s/he leaves nothing undone. The old narrative poetries come 'round again, audible as the large boombox of ego and empire is for a moment quieted amid the wide-turning starry firmament we together consider (*con* = with, *sidus/sidera* = the stars). Thus anew we become what we attune to, as always we have been, in the wonderful selfcomposing that is the music of life. Ecological sustainability is in this sense attentively, contemplatively self-aware evolutionary systems dynamics. "Each child," writes Swimme, "is situated in that very place and is rooted in that very power that brought forth all the ... universe" (1996, 104).

We are the process and the interpretation of the process; and we are the concealments and the obstructions of the process and the revealing self-illumination of the process. A scholar of both Buddhism and autopoiesis, Guenther goes a little further in saying of *rDzogs-chen* thinking, for example, that it is a way of experiencing the principle of evolution "in the manner of a free play that determines its own rules as the play goes on ... a process of tuning in to the dynamics of the whole, to its movement toward its next structure. What in a static world view is the end, in a dynamic, evolutionary world view is always a new beginning" (1989, 5). Writes systems theorist Erich Jantsch, "we have become the mind of a universe becoming increasingly aware of itself" (1980, 310). And the scholar of Daoist philosophy A. C. Graham notes from "the outskirts of rationality" that. ...

> practical life contracts awareness to the useful aspects of things
> and relates them by the causality which links means to end:

with the intensification of awareness when freed from dependence
on utility we live in a subjectively heightened reality, in which
conjunctions of chance outside us open up to awareness the
"destined" path for spontaneity within. (1992, 232; Burneko 2010b)

Finally, our mutual teacher, Zhuangzi, teases in provisional conclusion: "Do not be
an embodier of fame; do not be a storehouse of schemes; do not be an undertaker
of projects; do not be a proprietor of wisdom. Embody to the fullest what has no
end and wander where there is no trail." (1964, 94).

REFERENCES

Abram, D. 1996. *The spell of the sensuous: Perception and language in a more-than-human world*. New York: Pantheon.

Barrow, J. D., P. C. W. Davies, and C. L. Harper, Jr., Eds. 2004. *Science and ultimate reality: Quantum theory, cosmology and complexity*. Cambridge: Cambridge University Press.

Bateson, G. 1979. *Mind and nature: A necessary unity*. New York: E. P. Dutton.

Berry, T. 1999. *The great work: Our way into the future*. New York: Bell Tower.

———. 1988. *The dream of the earth*. San Francisco: Sierra Club.

Bett, Henry. 1925. *Johannes Scotus Erigena*. London: Cambridge University Press.

Brower, K. 1971. *Earth and the great weather*. New York: Friends of the Earth/Seabury.

Brown, N. O. 1969. *Hermes the Thief: The evolution of a myth*. New York: Vintage.

Buddha. 1965. *The Dhammapada*. Trans. Babbitt, I. New York: New Directions.

———. 1969. *The diamond sutra and the sutra of Hui Neng*. Trans. Price, A. F. and Mou-Lam, W. Boulder, CO: Shambhala.

Burnett, F. H. 1910. *The secret garden*. New York: Grosset & Dunlap.

Bunn, J. H. 2002. *Wave forms: A natural syntax for rhythmic languages*. Stanford, CA: Stanford University Press.

Burneko, G. 1986. Chuang Tzu's existential hermeneutics. *Journal of Chinese Philosophy* 13: 393–409.

———. 1988. Interdisciplinary, transdisciplinary, and intercultural education: Postmodern noetics and guerilla hermeneutics. *IS Journal/International Synergy* 3 (1): 64–99.

———. 2003. *By the torch of chaos and doubt: Consciousness, culture, poiesis and religion in the opening global millennium*. Cresskill, NJ: Hampton Press.

———. 2004. Ecohumanism: The spontaneities of the earth, *Ziran*, and K = 2. *Journal of Chinese Philosophy* 31 (2): 183–194.

———. 2010a. Contemplative ecology: *Guan* for a more-than-sustainable future. *Journal of Chinese Philosophy* 37 (1): 116–130.

———. 2010b. *Yijing for sustainable ecosocial mindfulness*. Unpublished manuscript.

Campbell, J. 1982. *Grammatical man: Information, entropy, language, and life*. New York: Simon & Schuster.

Cheng, C. 1995. Philosophical significances of *Guan* (contemplative observation): On Guan as onto-hermeneutical unity of methodology and ontology. *International Studies of I Ching Theory* 1:156–203.

Cobb, E. 1977. *The ecology of imagination in childhood*. New York: Columbia University Press.

Corrington, R. S. 1994. *Ecstatic Naturalism: Signs of the World*. Bloomington, IN: Indiana University Press.

———. 1997. *Nature's Religion*. Lanham, MD: Rowman & Littlefield.

Da, A. 2009. Not-two is peace: *The ordinary people's way of global cooperative order,* (Third ed.). Middletown, CA: Dawn Horse Press.

de Santillana. G., and H. von Dechend. 1969. *Hamlet's mill: An essay on myth and the frame of time*. Boston: David R. Godine.

Deacon, T. W. 2012. *Incomplete nature: How mind emerged from matter*. New York: W. W. Norton.

Durkheim, E., and Mauss, M. 1963. *Primitive Classification*. Trans. Needham, R. Chicago: University of Chicago Press.

Durr, R. A. 1970. *Poetic vision and the psychedelic experience*. New York: Dell.

Erdman, D. V., ed. 1965. *The poetry and prose of William Blake*. Garden City, NY: Doubleday.

Gamow, G. 1952. *The creation of the universe*. New York: Viking.

Gebser, Jean. 1985. *The Ever-Present Origin*, Trans. Barstad, N. and Mickunas, A. Athens, OH: Ohio University Press.

Girardot, N. J. 1983. *Myth and meaning in early Taoism*. Berkeley: University of California Press.

Graham, A. C. 1992. *Unreason within reason: Essays on the outskirts of rationality*. LaSalle, IL: Open Court.

Grahame, K. 1908. *The wind in the willows*. New York: Heritage.

Grimm, J. 1922. The Bremen town musicians. Accessed June 12, 2013. http://www. brementownmusicians.com/flash/story

Guenther, H. V. 1989. *From reductionism to creativity: rDzogs-chen and the new sciences of mind*. Boston: Shambhala.

Hall, D. L., and R. T. Ames. 1995. *Anticipating China: Thinking through the narratives of Chinese and Western culture*. Albany: SUNY.

Herman, J. R. 1996. *I and Tao: Martin Buber's encounter with Chuang Tzu*. Albany: SUNY.

Hershock, P. D. 1996. *Liberating intimacy: Enlightenment and social virtuosity in Ch'an Buddhism*. Albany: SUNY.

Hoyle, F. 1950. *The nature of the universe*. Oxford: Blackwell.

Jantsch, E. 1980. *The self-organizing universe: Scientific and human implications of the emerging paradigm of evolution*. New York: Pergamon.

Jantsch, E., and C. Waddington, eds. 1976. *Evolution and consciousness: Human systems in transition*. Reading, MA: Addison-Wesley.

Jeans, J. 1930. *The mysterious universe*. New York: Macmillan.

Jenkins, J. M. 1998. *Maya Cosmogenesis 2012: The True Meaning of the Maya Calendar End-Date*. Santa Fe: Bear.

Jones, A. 1985. *Soul Making: The Desert Way of Spirituality*. San Francisco: Harper & Row, p. 130

Jung, C. G. 1959. *The basic writings of C. G. Jung*. Ed. deLaszlo, V. S. New York: RandomHouse.

Kafatos, M., and R. Nadeau. 1990. *The conscious universe: Part and whole in modern physical theory*. New York: Springer-Verlag.

———. 1999. *The non-local Universe: The new physics and matters of the mind*. New York: Oxford University Press.

Kauffman, S. 1995. *At home in the Universe: The search for the laws of self-organization and complexity*. New York: Oxford University Press.

———. 2008. *Reinventing the sacred: A new view of science, reason, and religion*. New York: Basic Books.

Kerényi, K. 1986. *Hermes, guide of souls*, Trans. Stein, M. Dallas: Spring.

Kongzi [Confucius]. 1938. *The analects of Confucius*. Trans. Waley, A. New York: Random House.

Laozi [Lao Tzu]. 2003. *Dao De Jing*. Trans. Ames, R. T. and Hall, D. L. New York: Ballantine.

Laszlo, E. 2003. *The connectivity hypothesis: Foundations of an integral science of quantum, cosmos, life, and consciousness*. Albany, NY: SUNY.

Laughlin, C., and Throop, C. J. 2001. Imagination and reality: On the relations between myth, consciousness, and the quantum sea. *Zygon* 36 (4): 709–736.

Margulis, L., and D. Sagan. 1995. *What is life?* Berkeley: University of California Press.

Macy, J. 1991. *Mutual causality in Buddhism and General Systems Theory*. Albany: SUNY.

Maurer, A. A., Trans. 1974. *Master Eckhart: Parisian Questions and Prologues*. Toronto: Pontifical Institute of Mediaeval Studies.

Morin, E. 2008. *On complexity*, Trans. Postel, R. Cresskill, NJ: Hampton Press.

Morin, E., and A. B. Kern. 1999. *Homeland Earth: A manifesto for the new millennium*. Trans. Kelly, S. M. and LaPointe, R. Cresskill, NJ: Hampton Press.

Palmer, P. J., and A. Zajonc. 2010. *The heart of higher education: A call to renewal*. San Francisco: Jossey-Bass.

Primack, J. R., and N. E. Abrams. 2006. *The view from the center of the universe: Discovering our extraordinary place in the cosmos*. New York: Riverhead.

Shklovskii, I. S., and C. Sagan. 1966. *Intelligent life in the universe*, Trans. Fern, T. New York: Dell.

Smith, M. 1978. *The way of the mystics: The early Christian mystics and the rise of the Sufis*. New York: Oxford.

Speth, J. G. 2012. *America the possible: Manifesto for a new economy*. New Haven, CT: Yale University Press.

Stein, M. 1983. *In midlife: A Jungian perspective*. Dallas: Spring.

Steiner, G. 2001. *Grammars of creation*. New Haven, CT: Yale University Press.

Swimme, B. 1996. *The hidden heart of the cosmos: Humanity and the new story*. Maryknoll, NY: Orbis.

Thom, R. 1975. *Structural stability and morphogenesis*, Trans Fowler, D. H. Reading, MA: W. A. Benjamin.

Thruelsen, R., and J. Kobler, Eds. 1961. *Adventures of the mind. First & second series from The Saturday Evening Post*. New York: Alfred A. Knopf.

Varela, F. J., E. Thompson, and E. Rosch. 1991. *The embodied mind: Cognitive science and human experience*. Cambridge: MIT.

Whorf, B. L. 1956. *Language, thought, and reality*. J. B. Carroll, ed. Cambridge: MIT.

Wu, K. 1990. *The butterfly as companion: Meditations on the first three chapters of the Chuang Tzu*. Albany: SUNY.

Yuasa, Y. 1987. *The Body: Toward an Eastern Mind-Body Theory*, Ed., Kasulis, T. P., Trans. Nagamoto, S. and Kasulis, T. P. Albany: SUNY.

———. 1993. *The Body, Self-Cultivation, and Ki-Energy*. Trans. Nagatomo, S. and Hull, M.S. Albany: SUNY.

Zhang Zai (Chang Tsai). 1960. The Western inscription. In *Sources of Chinese Tradition v.1*, Eds. DeBary, T., Chan, W-T. and Watson, B. 469–470. New York: Columbia University Press.

Zhuangzi [Chuang Tzu]. 1964. *Basic writings*, Trans. Watson, B. New York: Columbia University Press.

———. 1981. *Chuang-tzu: The seven inner chapters*, Trans. Graham, A. C. London: George Allen & Unwin.

A PASSION FOR PUSHING THE LIMITS

Elisabet Sahtouris, Ph.D.

This is the story of an adventurous life of pushing limits to expand our understanding of ourselves in our universe—as an explorer, as a scientist, as a philosopher, as a political animal, as a mother and grandmother, even as an artist—concluding with the realization that *all we have to go on is our stories*. This is what most differentiates us from other species, even from our own cells: that we tell each other stories of What, How, and Why Things Are as They Are. We do not live as they do in the eternally *Now* moment, deeply interconnected within All That Is; rather we live in a mental trajectory from deep past to far future, making up stories about ourselves and everything else, coloring our perceptions with these stories and acting them out. We make them up differently in art, science, politics, economics, religion, and whatever, but however much we insist they are truths, they remain the more or less plausible human stories by which we necessarily live our lives individually and collectively.

... mind and external reality, being differentiated conceptually, are both merely ideas. From the end of the last century scientists have recognized this idealistic impediment in their work. Werner Heisenberg wrote: The common division of the world into subject and object, inner world and outer world, body and soul is no longer adequate and leads us into difficulties. Thus, even in science, the object of research is no longer nature itself but mans investigation of nature.

... The universe has arisen through objectification and the ball is placed in our hands. We have to practise letting it go if we are to play games with it instead of being its dependent. If, as we have assumed, science is practising a way of finding out, the science of creative intelligence is the natural and only thorough way of continuing the process. It does not supersede the objective research but irradiates and enlivens it.

—Max Flisher, in Science and Objectivity
(http://home.debitel.net/user/RMittelstaedt/Media/subj-obj.html)

SEARCHING FOR UNDERSTANDING AND CONSISTENCY

Almost from the time I rose up onto my two legs, I was free to explore my birth ecosystem—the woodlands and fields of the Hudson River's shores—as freely as any Indian in whose invisible footsteps I walked. I climbed trees to see farther, crossed fences that said "no trespassing," came close to copperheads and bears, risked my life on thin ice—always pushing the limits—but was never hurt beyond a wasp sting due to my own carelessness and knew nature to be benign and friendly. Nature and I had not been parted by theories of science or cultural categories, so I could, for example, take my mind up into any tree too high or difficult to climb and be with a woodpecker there in my seamless world even as my toes still squished deeply into the river mud in search of snail friends. It was a delicious time of innocence and profound knowing of what we now call 'Oneness' that shaped my life and brings pleasure in recalling. More than sixty years later, exploring my early childhood turf after attending my 50th high school reunion, I found myself weeping with joy to find so many of my childhood tree friends alive and well after such long absence.

As I grew old enough to think *about* my experiences, rather than simply live them, I investigated the insides of dead animals, pondered their lives and death, grew curious about how Nature worked and who we humans were in this scheme of things, where we had come from and where we were headed. A wonderful seventh grade biology teacher with a Ph.D. in music and encouragement for my curiosity made me realize I was slated to study science. My parents, however, perceived science as a subject for boys and steered me away from math and physics, into French, music and art, explaining that I had talent and needed to study art after high school. Earning a four-year full scholarship to Syracuse University, I could at least experience broader ideas than those of its Art School, but I did not formally study science until I was married with a child and made my way into graduate school at Indiana University without the requisite background by passing an exam and convincing a few professors I was capable of doing the advanced work required.

By the time I got my Ph.D. and a post-doctoral fellowship in evolution biology at the AMNH (American Museum of Natural History), I had really come to believe in the Western materialist scientific worldview, which was compatible with the materialist Marxist economics I had learned during a few intervening years in Berkeley, where my second child was born in the politically dramatic early 1960s. Needless to say, I had also become an activist and lived out the mid-'60s in the safety of Canada, although I continued organizing anti-war demonstrations there while my brother became a marine colonel in that very war.

My noting the compatibility of a scientific worldview with Marxist economics was an indication of my lifelong need for coherence and consistency in my world-view. I have always been an explorer of new mental and physical territories, diving into new fields or areas of inquiry, even whole new cultures and languages, immersing myself in them with enthusiasm to see as quickly as possible how they looked from the inside, then re-emerging to compare and integrate them with my other life experiences—plowing new territory, sowing, feeding, weeding and harvesting the fruits of my ever-evolving worldview.

Sometimes I literally plunged myself from morning sessions with professors in the hallowed ivy halls of MIT to evening sessions in prison with Black inmates, or from dancing Reggae with the natives of a Costa Rican rainforest to having cocktails at the palace in the capitol next day just to see things from the most different perspectives. Always I have sought new perspectives, looking out for inconsistencies and finding ways of eliminating or resolving them. This has made for a very complex life that has often seemed highly inconsistent to my family and friends, and even to me like a cat's proverbial nine lives in one, but I was always true to the unreachable goals of the true explorer's path, to my soul's deep yearning for wholeness and meaning. How could I act with integrity if I did not know How Things Are in the great scheme of things?

I never thought this unusual until I began to notice how often other people thought it so, and until I noticed how many people have inconsistent worldviews. To me it is very strange that a fully committed materialist reductionist scientist can be equally committed to God on Sundays or that a concentration camp guard can torture his victims all day and bring flowers lovingly to his wife after work or that a culture can tell its children not to take things from each other and then aggress on the people of sovereign nations to exploit their resources.

No one was talking about systems theory when I began to evolve my lifestyle, and even after I first learned about it almost half a century ago, I did not see its implications for such matters as worldviews or belief systems for a very long time; I did not know myself as a natural systems theorist and practitioner. Within the sciences alone, I came to explore biology, physiology, psychology, physics, anthropology, sociology, medicine, foundations of logic and mathematics, ancient sciences such as the Vedic, Taoist and Incan, worldwide indigenous sciences and contemporary alternative sciences, not to mention philosophy of science, in order to arrive eventually at the rudiments of a comprehensive new scientific worldview of my own.[1]

In the animal behavior department on the top floor of the AMNH, while doing my post-doc in the late 1960s, I came to see my own and my colleagues' work as "trivia research" in a burning world. Once again, I was looking for consistency. While I was doing comparative brain/behavior research, the museum's smokestacks were belching black soot all over upper Manhattan even as its pioneering exhibit on pollution, housed in an elaborate and expensive maze of elegant Japanese architecture erected within the great hall, was blaming pollution problems on people who littered. The exhibit, full of sanitized plastic garbage heaps and other evidence, actually ended with a picture of Pogo over a mirror, saying "The enemy is us!" while a speaker admonished, "Don't drop that gum wrapper!"

I was livid and made myself unpopular by pointing out this contradiction and growing even more politically active. It was a mystery to me how people could fail to understand the most basic economic relationships between wealth and poverty, cheap imported goods and the exploitation of foreign labor, corporate polluters and laws protecting them, and so on. Understanding the dire situation of humanity in a win/lose world ever deeper in crises of poverty and other social injustice, warfare, nuclear threat, pollution, desertification, and so on, I became convinced that economics and politics were more likely to answer my big questions of who we humans were and where we were headed than science.

While politics gave me some hope for understanding and improving the world, science did not. It had revealed little other than that humans were large mammals with big brains that had come up through the ranks of Earth's creatures by Darwinian struggles for survival and were doomed to continue in endless competition and conflict by virtue of "human nature." This contradicted my childhood view of benign Nature and was no more inspiring than the broader scientific worldview of an accidental and meaningless universe running down to heat death by Entropy. While I could accept, at that time, a universe without "intention" or God, I felt deep down that evolution could not have had such splendid results if all nature were survival struggle amid aggressive nastiness.

Ethology (the study of animal behavior) was all the rage at the time, with one author after another writing popular books to explain our human aggressions as our evolutionary animal heritage. None of them seemed to have noticed that intra-species aggression almost never leads to killing; that, on the other hand, other species were internally prevented from killing their kind by elaborate built-in rituals and limits that humans lacked. This contradiction forced me to think and gave me an important insight: that our big brains, explosively sudden on an evolutionary timeline, apparently traded safe behavioral limits for risky freedom of choice on how to behave. A corollary of this proposition was that humans alone require ethical guidelines and have to devise them culturally along with forms of governance.

BEYOND THE LIMITS OF ESTABLISHED SCIENCE

One of the most difficult limits of the official scientific worldview for me—in addition to its exclusion of all human experience that cannot be measured by man-made instruments—was the ban on values, the proud pronouncement of science as neutrally objective and therefore value-free. I was fond of pointing out that this was hypocrisy and an abandonment of responsibility, since nothing in science except unused lab equipment and unused statistical tools actually *were* value-free. Allowable scientific questions and research were determined by funding, and scientific funding in the Fifties, when I began studying science, came largely from the military and was well on its way to coming from the whole—as Eisenhower named it—military–industrial complex. Obviously, the *values* of this complex determined what scientific efforts were useful enough to fund, yet scientists, isolated in their laboratories, failed to see science as a cultural endeavor in a cultural context the values of which limited its freedom as much as its own worldview did.

My natural bent toward holistic systems thinking got me into trouble again and again. I was living in a culture that had separated and boxed up just about everything—politics, economics, art, science, religion, ethics, work, play, Black people, White people, rich, poor, you name it—even economics and money were separated. Anyone trying to undo these carefully constructed separations was a troublemaker.

Another difficult limit in science for me was the ban on *anthropomorphism*. This was the heresy of projecting human characteristics onto Nature or empathizing with Nature as alive, intelligent and feeling, the way I knew it to be from my childhood experience. Scientifically, Nature was to be perceived as separate and independent of all human thinking and feeling. A dog, for example, had to be demonstrated to be conscious or intelligent by rigorous definitions of the terms and equally rigorous and measurable experimental testing, not because a human perceived it to be. Otherwise objectivity—the fundamental assumption that natural phenomena are independent of us and can therefore be studied without being affected by experimenters—would be undermined.

Philosophers of science, paying attention to the discoveries of physics, were already recognizing the impossibility of objectivity in an interconnected and participatory universe of energy patterns,[2] but objectivity is a lynchpin of the official scientific worldview, so its impossibility is *still* resisted despite actual research results ruling it out (Wiseman and Schlitz 1998). Of course, while anthropomorphism was taboo, perceiving Nature as mechanics, which I came to call *mechanomorphism,* was mandatory. Whenever I pointed out that since humans had invented machinery, *mechano*morphism was merely second-hand anthropomorphism, I got only dirty or pitying looks.

My training in science taught me love and respect for clear definitions and logical reasoning. Unfortunately, I eventually found the very foundations of Western science and many of its conclusions to be based on faulty reasoning, as I will elaborate. The good side of this was that it challenged me to work for years on a better foundation for science. While politics and economics had come to seem better qualified to help me understand humanity and its future prospects than the science I was taught, I still believed in science at some deep level and gradually realized that its theory and practice could be and were being changed.

Meanwhile, the leftist political groups I affiliated with over the years had proven to suffer from in-house rivalries, hostilities, and elitist practices, thus seeming to me ever more incapable of bringing about the better world they preached. Leaving New York City for Boston in the early 1970s, I worked on scientific research at Mass General Hospital, but soon realized a normal scientific career was impossible for me with my growing doubts and the feeling of swimming upstream against an impossible tide when expressing them to colleagues.

A position as Juvenile Justice Planner for the Commonwealth of Massachusetts taught me that mainstream politics were even more corrupt than radical politics, and I came close to getting fired several times for standing on ethical principles. While I taught a couple of courses at MIT and the University of Massachusetts around this time, without the formal appointments that would have locked me into their "publish or perish" tenure tracks, my fiercely independent spirit has kept me away from traditional universities altogether ever since. I seemed to be a social misfit all around!

In 1974, while on the Juvenile Justice Planner job, I had a unique opportunity to travel to China with nine other scientists through a political organization called Science for the People that had been invited to send a delegation as official guests of the National Science Association of the People's Republic. This was a real adventure, as the United States did not have official diplomatic relations with China yet. We had to get visas through Canada and the Chinese authorities did not stamp our passports, to keep us out of trouble with our own authorities.

Along with the ethology of human nature books of that time, other popular authors were bringing racism back into purportedly scientific studies of intelligence just when our political activity seemed to be ending racism. This pushed my thinking as well into questions of just what *was* intelligence. I queried Chinese scientists for their views on intelligence and was told they had determined that motivation was a better indicator of aptitude than standardized intelligence tests, and had therefore abandoned them.

It was only years later, when I adopted Arthur Koestler's concept of holons in holarchy—natural entities embedded within each other, as, for example, the holarchies of cells/organs/organ systems/bodies, or species/ecosystems/planets/star systems/galaxies or individuals/families/communities/nations/world—that I came to my own definition of intelligence as measurable by the number of holarchic layers and the length of time one takes into account for their well-being or sustainability when making decisions. The *Haudenosaunee* (called Iroquois by the White man), for example, took the well-being of families, communities, and ecosystems over seven generations into account in their deliberations, which is something of an intelligence record in my book of cultures. Because of this intelligence, they made peace among warring nations and devised a Great Law of Peace that became the basis for our own U.S. Constitution, largely through the efforts of Benjamin Franklin.[3]

The Chinese had a definition of science that puzzled us Westerners; they called science "the summation of the knowledge of the people" and said it "walked on two legs." These "legs" were the knowledge of ordinary people and the work of professional scientists. We were there at the end of the Cultural Revolution, during which university buildings had been closed as professors, along with students, were sent to the countryside to learn from peasants. From their perspective, universities were still alive and functioning under these new circumstances. The Chinese were very open with us and fulfilled our request to meet with such professors on farms, where they told us of discoveries made by peasants, in crossing plants, for example, that were theoretically impossible. Their job when they went back to their labs would be to show scientifically why they *had* been possible. This began to explain the Chinese definition of science.

Over a decade later, I asked an indigenous friend, Dr. Greg Cajete (see his fine book on indigenous education, 1994) of the Santa Clara Tewa pueblo in New Mexico, what he saw as the difference between *his* science and ours, given that he was trained in both. He replied that the White man isolates pieces of Nature and takes them into the laboratory for study because his goal is to control them, while the Red man goes into Nature to study then in context because his goal is to integrate with them.

The Chinese authorities did not send professors into the countryside as punishment, but because they genuinely believed that poor peasants had rich scientific knowledge through their practical experience within Nature. This proved true and many ecologically sound techniques of natural pest control and soil management, for example, came out of this venture. This was my first experience of recognizing "indigenous" science as valid, more on which later.

China was rebuilding itself from the ground up without foreign capital investments—a policy that paid off handsomely when China became a strong enough and attractive enough economy in its own right to be able to negotiate terms with foreign investors as equals. This financial independence is an important development in our world that has not happened in most other underdeveloped countries since World War II.

A third confirmation of the value of respecting people's practical scientific experiments and knowledge came for me from various articles in *The Ecologist* magazine, World Bank reports and many other sources showing that all over the world ordinary peasants and indigenous peoples had evolved sound scientific practices in agriculture that far outweighed our own modern knowledge. While Green Revolution production figures deliberately distorted results in their favor, the truth was that production was higher and more sustainable in traditional systems. In Bali and India, the World Bank's projects created such agricultural disasters they had to withdraw to let people go back to their old methods.

In the late 1980s I helped found the Worldwide Indigenous Science Network, in the process of which I learned as much science from indigenous people as I had in universities, and in the 1990s I lived in the Peruvian Andes for a year, confirming that the Incas had developed one of the most successful agricultural sciences in all the world, but that is getting ahead of my story.

Back in Boston from China, an encounter with a very impressive psychic turned my quest for understanding quite suddenly down a totally different track. Having left religion along with home at sixteen, when I began university, had made it easier to accept the scientific worldview without conflict, but now I was questioning both science and politics in my search for a larger, more meaningful worldview. This psychic and new friends I met in her classes, plunged me into esoteric study, reading everything from the esoteric classics to modern accounts of out-of-body, after-death, and reincarnation experiences, along with what was then called "paraphysics"—attempts to explain all manner of "psychic phenomena" within the scientific worldview by stretching its limits.

Thus my disappointment with science led me to its explorative fringes, where I continued to seek scientific explanations of the world and humanity within it among those who had broken out of the official taboos. The paraphysicists certainly had some interesting and even exciting theories. One of them, Itzhak Bentov (1977), whom I had the privilege to meet, had a very appealing wave theory of the universe as a giant toroidal black/white hole in continuous creation, the first such theory I encountered, having only a vague memory of hearing about Lord Kelvin's "smoke ring universe." I now see such theories cropping up again and find them the most influential physics theories in my own evolving scientific model of a living universe.

After considerable effort and repeated failure, I succeeded in having my own out-of-body experiences (OOBEs). Biofeedback devices, which I had first encountered in graduate school, were available for some informal research. With their help I explained my OOBEs to myself in terms of alignment between the frequencies of the powerful mechanical aortic heartbeat waves and slow brain waves. But this did not answer the question of whether I was really leaving my body behind through such physiological synchronies or whether they happened "only" in my mind, as a state of consciousness induced by those physiological events, as mainstream science would insist.

I wrestled with this enigma for years before realizing, one day, that *all* my experience is limited to what my consciousness can perceive, and therefore is *within* my consciousness, as *all* experience of *all* humans is! It took this dive into esoteric experience and years of contemplation of it to understand that through it I had made a hugely important observation with major implications for scientific modeling of our universe, as I will describe later.

Over the years, I have had quite a few "anomalous" experiences I would have repressed or ignored had I not expanded my worldview into the esoteric beyond the limits of science. Just as an example, twice in my life I have read a published piece of literature that had not yet been put into print. One was a book by marine biologist and epigrapher Barry Fell,[4] put into my hands by a childhood friend who had become a geologist. He gave it to me on the only visit I ever paid to his home as an adult, while I was pregnant with my son, so the year is not mistakable. Only many years later when I no longer had that particular copy of the book did I have the wonderful opportunity to meet Barry Fell personally and discover that this book had never been published until over a decade after I read it. The same happened with James Lovelock's first journal article on Gaia, which was put into my hands during my post-doc at the AMNH, therefore in early 1971 at the latest, although it later proved—again, on meeting the author—to have been published for the first time only in 1972. Such anomalous personal experiences were instrumental in forcing me to change my worldview to accommodate them, so they could become unusual, yet normal events.

The most fun I had with science during my Boston years was when I was hired by WGBH-TV to write educational materials for the NOVA/HORIZON series. Discovering that I already knew something about the field of expertise behind every program topic, I realized how broad my interests were, how many areas I had explored and how great my need was for a worldview that made sense of *all* human experience.

A separate WGBH assignment was writing a book to go with a proposed film on public education for physically and mentally challenged youth. I set out across the United States to interview the best teachers in this field and had the great privilege of meeting profoundly handicapped people who impressed me as highly evolved souls. I was also amazed to discover that even deeply challenged students tended to achieve whatever their teachers believed they could achieve. It might have been difficult for me to understand this had it not been so consistent with a worldview I was resonating with strongly in the then new and fascinating "Seth books" by Jane Roberts, published in the '70s and into the '80s, still being reprinted today.[5]

Seth, a discarnate entity dictating about a dozen books through Jane, title by title and sentence by sentence as her husband Rob wrote them down over the years, taught a consciousness-based universe, introducing the concept of humans creating reality from beliefs, both individually and as cultures. It was the broadest, most coherent, internally consistent and intellectually satisfying worldview I had encountered, yet classed as esoteric literature because of its unusual origins. Seth spoke eloquently on cosmic physics, chemistry, psychology, biology, medicine, sociology, evolution, human history, religion, philosophy, politics, art, and other subjects. Many later channelers seemed highly influenced by Jane's material, but, for me, none could add anything to it. Jane, who, as a poet and novelist, had little knowledge herself of any of these fields, did not call her own dictations channeling and in Seth's voice consistently urged people to doubt the material and think things through on their own.

In a recent symposium of leading edge Ph.D. scientists, I found the courage to ask how many were familiar with the Seth books and more than half raised their hands. All of Jane Roberts's papers are archived at Yale University and are still much visited there by people from all over the world. As I write this article I am scheduled to speak once more at an annual regional Seth conference (the Rocky Mountain Seth Conference). When the mechanistic worldview has been honored and laid to rest at last, I believe its successor will owe more than ever acknowledged to the mysterious Jane Roberts/Seth alliance.

MIDLIFE RETIREMENT

In retrospect, one of the best decisions I have made in my life was to take a "midlife retirement" in Greece, that turned out to last from the end of the 1970s, when my children had grown up, to the beginning of the 1990s, when I returned with a book published in New York and a new fledgling career in development.

As a dear friend and MIT colleague said on my return, "How dare you take off for a thirteen year holiday in the Greek Islands and come back ahead of those of us who kept our noses to the academic grindstone?!" I had certainly not intended that, but I came to accept that he was right and that it had happened precisely because I did *not* stay in academia, with all its categorizing and separation of "disciplines" and constraints on free thinking. Without those limits I was able eventually to write my own evolving story of a living Cosmos in which the Earth is an evolving living entity and human history a coherent pattern of development within its living context.

There were so many benefits of that retirement period leading up to writing that book that it is difficult to describe them. I went to Greece with the intention of staying only two years or so, though I sold my house to do it, writing novels to explain the human condition to myself. This was partly because I felt science had failed me in my search and partly because I was greatly inspired by having met and spent time with Henry Miller, whose great love of Greece and marvelous philosophy are wonderfully expressed in his book *The Colossus of Maroussi* (1958). It is also the case that it had not crossed my mind that I *could* pursue science on Greek islands, though, in the end, Greece gave me back, in fullest measure, my original motivation for pursuing science along with the leisurely opportunity I needed to evolve my own version of evolution biology and its relevance to humanity at present.

Greece felt very quickly like home and looked very much like all of Earth to me, with its three-fourths sea and one-fourth pinkish-beige pieces of land and island. I called it *MidEarth*, literally the name of the Mediterranean Sea, because it was culturally and geographically a link between East and West as well as between North and South. During my first few weeks there, before I even settled down, two anomalous experiences proved the magical nature of this land.

The first happened in Epidaurus on my first visit by boat and a Greek bus that dropped me some five kilometers from the gate in early morning mists lifting from fields of blood-red poppies beneath olive trees as far as I could see. I cried with joy at their beauty, thrilled to be the first to arrive that day at the great ancient theater with its magnificent acoustics. A few years later, I would be among the twenty thousand people it held to watch Eirini Papa (Irene Papas to Hollywood) perform Greek drama there under a full moon, dressed in black robes, greeted after the play by Melina Mercouri, just appointed minister of culture, stepping off a helicopter in a gold lame pant suit to rush out on stage. But this day I was alone in the vast theater and amazed how the sun-whitened bare bones ruins of temples and hotels could reveal the original splendor of the grand healing spa this was, with its stone friezes of lions and flowers, its fountains, statures and chariot race tracks, the gayety of comedy played alongside tragedy in deep psychological lessons about the actions of gods and mortals in a layered universe where everything affected everything else.

Preparing to continue from there by bus to Nauplion, my next stop on this three-day tour, I went to the government pavilion near the theater intending to cash a travelers check, only to find there was no place to do that, no way at all to get any cash. Banks had not been open before I left my island, and I had only a few coins in my pocket, not nearly enough for the Nauplion bus. I was completely stymied by this unforeseen dilemma, having no way to go on, nowhere to sleep, and, with nothing else to do, spent my last coins on a Greek brandy. As I sipped it, an agitated waiter suddenly ran up to me, grabbed my arm and pulled me from my chair. I had no idea what I had done to offend him and get myself thrown out. He dragged me to the door and pointed into the road, as though to yell "Get lost!" at me, when I saw it—a bank on wheels had pulled up! A vehicle like an old RV with a side door and a clerk inside, who cashed my travelers check. I stepped off dazed by the cash in my hands and watched it pull away again without attracting the attention of anyone else. The waiter still looked shocked himself as I regained the presence to thank Hermes the Trickster, the god of travels, for this magical good fortune. In all my years in Greece, I never saw such a "bank" again! I also thought of Seth, who taught that we manifest our realities . . .

The second anomalous incident happened within a few weeks later on the Greek island of Kos, considered the birthplace of the twins Apollo and Aphrodite. Kos is tiny and there were only a handful of day-trip tourists among the ruins as there were no hotels on the island. Walking across a flat field of sand with a friend, I was picking up various seedpods and small shells in spiral form, marveling at how many versions there could be of this elementary form, which was to become so important in my model of the universe. My reverie took me deep into a cosmos of wheeling galaxies when suddenly the sand some twenty yards from us whirled up into the air forming a perfect funnel that swept a graceful curve in our direction and smacked right into us.

As the day was otherwise completely calm, without so much as a breeze, my friend, getting the connection, asked in amazement "How did you *do* that?" I replied, "I didn't!" and then, on further reflection, added, "But I may have attracted it." He looked at me strangely and asked, "Does the motion in a vortex go inward or outward?" Without having thought about it for a moment, I shot back "Both ways!" I knew this with a certainty—that it *had* to be centripetal and centrifugal at once. Never having taken a single physics course, I could not explain it; I simply knew it as it surfaced in my consciousness then and there on the island of the Twins. I was really sure now that the vortex was the real key to how the universe worked, though it took much longer to figure out how.

I mention these two incidents, as I did the matter of reading things before they were in print, because they were such startling clues that reality was far more malleable than materialist science had taught me it was, and that it was very powerfully linked to my own consciousness. It was one thing to find the Seth books intellectually appealing; it was quite another to have their concepts confirmed so dramatically that they became undeniable.

Mostly, after that, I lived in Greece very simply and less eventfully, in a small old stone house with relatively few possessions. I fixed up the house, gathered fuel wood with a borrowed donkey, washed clothes by hand, went fishing, carried water from wells, cooked more simply, took long walks alone gathering wild greens and mushrooms along the way by day, thrilling to bright moon and stars by night, generally appreciating a very close relationship with my natural setting and enjoying Greek social life with its music and fellowship.

In Greece I learned to undo the nagging Puritan ethic that something useful had to be done every minute of the day. It was difficult for me to learn the fine Greek art of sitting and doing nothing but pass the time. I was often bored, impatient, guilty and amazed at how much time Greeks could "waste." While I had learned to consider time a precious and limited commodity, they saw time as abundant and unlimited. After a few years and lots of practice, I was actually able to spend hours in thought without guilt. I learned that good thinking and writing take time to incubate. Most important, I discovered the real value of letting my mind empty so new thoughts could appear in it.

This came most easily at sea for days and nights on end with fishermen. At first I spent all my time aboard the fishing *kaiki,* which I had bought as an investment, reading whenever I was not helping or preparing food. Gradually I discovered that inspiration comes best when the mind is completely lulled by the rocking waves, at peace with the endless sea and sky. Sometimes at night, when the fishermen slept soundly as cats dropped about the deck, I could find no comfortable position on the hard planks. I would sit up, surrounded by pitch-black sky and sea with no demarcation between them and contemplate my place between the stars and the bioluminescent plankton in the dark waters. Aware of the tremendous difference in their sizes, although they looked so much the same, I knew I was half way between the macrocosm and the microcosm. I will say more about this unique cosmic position when describing the scientific model of a living universe I am presently developing (see last section).

These experiences seemed mystical and led to writing poetry and philosophizing essays in addition to my novels. I did write three novels before I went back to scientific pursuits, committing two of them to flames before returning to the United States. They were a great way to undo the elitist scientific language—some would call it jargon—I had learned in graduate school.

As I lived among simple rural Greek farmers and fishermen, none of whom had more than a few year's schooling or spoke any English, I had lost all my identity as a professional scientist and could not even describe myself as a novelist. My neighbors were clearly puzzled about all the books in my little rented stone house, never having seen any books except in school as children. My linguistic expression, given the difficulties of the Greek language, was that of a toddler first learning to speak, only very gradually being able to share the simplest possible stories of my life and ideas. This also contributed to turning my English writings into simpler story-telling form in good ancient Greek tradition!

Back in the United States in the 1990s, Paul Ray identified and interviewed me as a Cultural Creative (Ray and Anderson 2000), calling my Greek years a shamanic journey into the underworld. At first shocked by this interpretation, I came to see its validity. I had stripped myself first of occupation, house and possessions to make the journey to Greece, then stripped myself of identity through lack of language, all typical of a shamanic rebirth or recreation of self.

One of the greatest lessons I learned in Greece was about cultural assumptions. I was aware of the literature on anthropology that advocated dropping all cultural assumptions and definitions when trying to understand a new culture and was determined to do that as I integrated myself into Greek island life. I had no idea, however, how difficult a task that was, even with the best intentions. Ten years into the process I was still uncovering my most ordinary assumptions. For example, I assumed all people had the same definition of a "problem" as something amiss to be solved, only to discover after many misunderstandings and cultural blunders that something amiss may be a problem but is *not* necessarily perceived as something to be solved. One result of this difference is that Greeks do not run for pain-killers when in pain, nor to therapists if they are not happy. Their entire outlook on and expectation of life is profoundly different from ours by virtue of this one different definition! On the whole, I found Greeks to be a happier people because they were always surprised by life's joys rather than obsessively worrying about what was wrong with them if they had problems and/or were not happy.

From the time I arrived in Greece, I would fling my arms out to the mysterious heavens at night crying "Use Me!" as a kind of non-religious prayer to Whatever might hear it. One day, still effectively a novelist and essayist, I was walking among wild cyclamen in the lovely pine forested hills of my small island when a walking stick insect fell out of a tree and onto my sleeve. Tears welled up in my eyes as I welcomed this utterly unexpected guest reminder of my childhood, when I had gathered up and played with many a walking stick. I had not seen one since. Instantly I knew that I still wanted to understand Nature scientifically and decided to write a book for small children telling the story of Earth's evolution. It was not that I suddenly wanted to become a children's book author, but because I felt that one had to be very true with children and that this would give me the opportunity to tell the story as clearly and simply as possible.

RETURN TO SCIENCE AND HOME

I searched for relevant information in the few books I had brought with me after giving most of my library away and began writing to publishers and universities, begging for articles from scientists whose addresses I was creating from bibliographies. I wanted such up-to-date information that no Athens library would have been worth the boat rides required to get to them, but it turned out that my Greek stamps attracted attention and articles actually began and continued to arrive for me at the local post office. The book went from an edition for five-year-olds to one for ten- to fifteen-year-olds and eventually into what I still see as my "grownup book." The first version was the most difficult, as no one I could find had put the Earth's story into a coherent scientific sequence. Even Jim Lovelock (1982) and Lynn Margulis (1982), who deeply influenced me with their first books on the Gaia Hypothesis—the most holistic analysis of Earth's evolution available—had not done this, as Lynn was focused just on bacterial origins and Jim had been describing how the Gaian planetary system of life and non-life interacted at present.

I sent the young people's version of the book to Lovelock in England and to Margulis in Boston for review. Both answered with very kind praise and while I was working on the adult version—easier, having the basic story done, to fill in details from the scientific work I was receiving—Jim Lovelock actually came to visit me on my island for over a week. Soon after, by now the late 1980s, I was invited to three annual Gaia Conferences organized in England by Edward (Teddy) Goldsmith, founder/editor of *The Ecologist* magazine mentioned earlier. This gave me connections back into a scientific community making real progress toward a more holistic understanding of Earth.

Jim Lovelock became a paragon for me because he was proving that universities, laboratories and grants were not necessary to doing good science. In his countryside kitchen, on a very modest household budget, he had made his own lab equipment, inventing and engineering the Nuclear Capture Device that soon became extremely important to environmental science and medicine, then hitch-hiked all the way to Antarctica on a research vessel to take ocean measurements over a large portion of Earth to back up his planetary scientific hypothesis! Somehow this validated my own pursuit of science on my small remote island.

The first time I visited Jim in Cornwall, he gave me a small paperback book that was inscribed to him with the words "*Closet Gaia, love, Lynn.*" The book was about the work of the Russian geologist Vladimir Vernadsky (Lapo 1982; see also Vernadsky 1926, [1896]), who had seen life as a "transform of rock"—as slow geological activity transforming itself into more rapid metabolic activity. I shouted the proverbial Greek *Eurika!* at reading this, for Vernadsky gave me the seamless world of geobiology.

The Chilean biologists Humberto Maturana and Francisco Varela, working at MIT and the University of Paris, respectively, gave me their new definition of life as *Autopoiesis*—literally Greek for self-creation. If living systems were autopoietic, creating themselves continually, then mechanical systems, I reasoned, should be called *allopoietic*, meaning "other created," because they require external inventors. This distinction contributed a great deal to many essays that developed my thinking and led to my seeing whirlpools, proto-galaxies, galaxies, whirling atoms and particles, all as self-organizing, form-maintaining living entities along with the Earth that ever created itself anew from the same materials in cycles of magma to crust to magma, water vapor to rain to rivers to oceans to water vapor, soil to creatures to soil, and so on. Erich Jantsch's (1980) work on the self-organizing universe fit my developing thought beautifully and many other scientists filled in many other pieces over time.

My own book, now called *EarthDance: Living Systems in Evolution* (2000) begins with words written on the Greek Island of *Angistri* where I wrote its original version:

> This book is a work of philosophy in the original sense of a search for wisdom, for practical guidance in human affairs through understanding the natural order of the cosmos to which we belong. It bears little resemblance to what we have come to call philosophy since that effort was separated from natural science and became more an intellectual exercise in understanding than a practical guide for living.

So steeped was I in Greek culture I did not mention that *philosophia* was actually the ancient Greek word for the later Latin *scientia*. Philosophy *was* natural science, the study of Nature, while *physis*—the Greek word for nature itself—was taken to designate what European scientists so much later came to see as the fundamental science of nature: physics. Though I knew nothing of ancient Greek science in my youth, my big questions of who we were, where we came from and where we were headed drove me to science in search of wisdom to guide humanity on our path into the future. Because I was disappointed in this quest, I determined to answer these questions for myself, within the expanding scientific framework I was now developing.

To develop a new scientific model or worldview as a framework for the human journey, I had to think of the whole universe, Earth within it and humanity within the Earth as a coherent living system with system dynamics. It was not a formal study of system dynamics that inspired me, since this field was still new, but my own mental exercises in thinking holistically and systemically, far away from the academic culture that had separated scientific disciplines into ever smaller fragments and whose professors did not exactly encourage minds questioning the most basic assumptions on which their careers had been built.

Yet as soon as I abandoned novels to weave my scientific story, anonymous but powerful academic authorities started looking over my shoulders again to see just what it was that I was writing and whether I was inserting the proper footnotes. I did not get rid of them until the day my son, who had come to live in Greece himself, said to me, "I hope you'll stand on the courage of your convictions, Mom, and not fill your book with footnotes nobody wants to read. Just tell your story!"

I pondered the story of Western science again and again—of modern physics born of European scientists' love of mechanics, which gave us a lifeless universe modeled on machinery. Was this fundamental assumption of a lifeless, mechanical universe really a "self-evident truth" as scientific assumptions are supposed to be? Descartes, the leading architect of the scientific worldview expounded in graduate schools to this day, came close to a consciousness-based science, rather than one of material mechanism, in the famous meditation leading him to pronounce *Cogito ergo sum*, "I think therefore I am." But in his great love for the practical translations of math into machinery, he chose instead to separate mind from matter, naming God "the Grand Engineer" who put a piece of God-mind into his favorite engineered robot, so that man, too, could think and invent machinery that would eventually be as complex and lifelike as God's! It seemed to me this was God in the image of man, rather than the other way around!

In my own words, Descartes had made nature allopoietic, with only man as autopoietic by the grace of God. (Woman was pure robot like other animals in his scheme of things.) True to Greek myth, if not to Greek science, God the father was overthrown by his obstreperous, if inventive, human sons, who determined that their fine minds were not God-given after all, but had arisen, like their bodies, from a long series of fortuitous local accidents within an accidental universe. It *had* to be accidental to explain it without a purposeful inventor, without purpose of any kind! *This* new version of the universe had miraculously exploded out of nothing and, despite the staggering amount of impressive natural machinery, including man himself, that it gave rise to on its meaningless journey, was headed back into nothingness by the great Law of Entropy.

While Descartes had understood that there can be no machine without a conscious and intelligent inventor, his followers eventually explained away the magic of life emerging from non-life, consciousness from non-consciousness and intelligence from non-intelligence by coupling non-equilibrium thermodynamics with random accident, as, for example, in Ilya Prigogine's work (Prigogine and Stengers 1984). But, it seemed to me, this foundation for science was utterly illogical! Machines, by definition, are purposive devices invented by intelligent beings and assembled from parts to carry out specific tasks. They do *not* "arise" by accidental particle or atomic collisions, and no saying they did can make it so. If nature is mechanism, logically it *must* have an inventor as Descartes proposed; if there is no inventor, it cannot be machinery.

Nevertheless, historically the materialist reductionist science of celestial and biological mechanics had practical applications in engineering, so while it was anathema to the Church, which had been ruling European society through the allegiance of governing royalty and was not happy with scientific rejection of God, science was extremely appealing to a rising European bourgeoisie building an industrial revolution. Thus science gained the power to spread its materialist worldview throughout society and was eventually elevated to a kind of secular priesthood in its own right. Within its ranks, theoretical physicists are an elite that appears to have special dispensation for proposing very far-out theories of How Things Are. Biologists, however, have been second-level scientists, subject to the "established" laws of physics to the point where life's amazing capacities for generating ever new creatures and ecosystems had to be defined as *negentropy*, a temporary swimming upstream that could increase order locally within the drearily deteriorating universe's entropic process toward heat death.

Negentropy is credited with the descent of man, according to Darwin, his predecessors and his followers, as the natural creature of an evolutionary process of accidental events and survival struggles over billions of years. This story of biological evolution has become virtually axiomatic in the scientific worldview, although its recognition of humankind as this kind of evolved creature has had questionable social benefits, justifying the exploitation of fellow humans, often cruelly, along with the rest of the natural world, which is now suffering a degree of devastation that threatens even human survival. The lack of moral accountability of science for social interpretations of Darwinism, along with its failure to see the grave inadequacy of the Darwinian hypothesis, has led to social ills from chaining children to machines for the sake of profits to the Holocaust and, even now, to the current tyranny of the quarterly bottom line competition that pushes large corporations to dishonest accounting and to exploiting the cheapest possible third-world labor under inhuman conditions. The entrenched neo-Darwinian belief that man is doomed to perpetually hostile competition—the scientific belief underlying these social ills—is, as I will attempt to show, a serious misinterpretation of the evolutionary record.

The definition of autopoiesis as life led me quickly to see that the universe could be described more elegantly and logically as self-creating living systems, from tiny living particle and atom vortices to the greatest of galactic vortices and the entire universe itself. To be continually self-creating, vortices had to have a medium to feed on or be self-contained in the form of toroids, as in Lord Kelvin's smoke-ring universe, quite popular with physicists until Einstein stole away their attention. When I got back to the United States, I discussed this with physicist Hal Puthoff (1990), a pioneer in zero-point energy (ZPE) research and he thought it entirely plausible since atoms indeed feed off ZPE to maintain themselves. Another colleague, Foster Gamble, is currently developing a detailed model of atoms as clusters of vortices.

I pondered the question: What if Galileo had looked down through the new lenses of his day arranged into a microscope, so he could see into a drop of pond water teeming with gyrating life forms instead of up through a telescope into the heavens, already conceived in his time as celestial mechanics? Might biology, rather than physics, have become the leading science into whose models all others must fit themselves? Might scientists then have seen life not as a rare temporary and accidental occurrence within the inevitably destructive tide of entropy, but as the fundamental nature of an exuberantly creative universe?

Instead of projecting a universe of mechanism without inventor, assembling blindly through collisions of particles, then atoms and molecules, until a few such aggregates came magically to life and further evolved by accidental mutations, I proposed that there is reason to see the whole universe as alive, self-organizing at multiple fractal levels of living complexity—as reflexive systems learning to play with possibilities in the intelligent co-creation of complex evolving systems.

It seemed more reasonable to project our life onto the entire universe than our non-living machinery, which is a derivative extension of human capability and therefore a truly *emerging* phenomenon, rather than a fundamental one. I found it possible to create a coherent scientific model of a living universe, a model that is not only justified by the findings of science, but can lead to the wisdom required to build a better human life on and for our planet Earth as the ancient Greeks intuited it should.

REENTRY AND CONTINUING ADVENTURE

Before I left Greece, I organized a large Earth Celebration event in Athens that was covered by MTV, my book was published in New York and I got invitations to speak in England, Scotland, The Soviet Union, the United States, and Costa Rica. Jim Lovelock had sent me a used computer to replace my trusty old typewriter and although the Internet had not yet reached the Greek islands, I had moved to Hydra, which had a lawyer's office where I could send and receive faxes.

The conclusion I had reached in the book was that we humans will have to learn very quickly to organize ourselves by the principles of living systems within the larger living system of our planet or do ourselves in as a species. It became obvious to me that indigenous cultures know far more about this than Western industrial culture does, so I set out to learn from them, soon getting involved in forming the Worldwide Indigenous Science Network, with meetings in Mexico; Calgary, Canada; and Taos, New Mexico.

I began to feel South America calling to me. Alan Ereira's BBC film on the Kogi Indians of Columbia, *Message from the Heart of the World: the Elder Brother's Warning* (1992), had a profound effect on me when I saw it in Greece so I looked up Alan in London, and soon had an invitation to visit the Kogi with a friend in New York who knew them as well. Though I did not go, I soon responded to my dearest oldest friend's invitation to come live with her in Tucson, Arizona while I worked on reentry. The year was 1991.

Reentry shock! It was much harder than I had anticipated, much harder than had been the entry into Greek culture. I felt like the proverbial fish out of water—sometimes literally in my hunger for the sea. From Tucson I visited Hopiland to continue work I had begun with Hopi elders, especially Thomas Banyacya, to help him tell the Hopi Prophecy in the UN General Assembly after the 43-year effort to do so made by the Hopi and their many helpers. In 1992, I was unexpectedly asked by the UN in Geneva to participate in an international congress on indigenous peoples in Chile as an advisor, just before the big "Rio '92" UN meeting on the environment, where I had been asked to be a "Wisdom Keeper" in the company of many wonderful religious and indigenous people. Since I had no job or income, these invitations seemed a magical answer to the call of South America I was feeling so strongly. I then moved to Washington, DC on an inner call, where I got involved with hosting an annual Native Prayer Vigil between the Washington Monument and the White House that still happens each October.

In Washington, I woke suddenly one morning in 1994, having heard a voice that said "Go to the June solstice festival in Peru with Mazatl!" No visual images, just that voice. Mazatl is Aztec, a sacred musician and artist. Tracking him, I discovered that six other people had had the same dream call, as had Mazatl himself, who cancelled a concert with Peter Gabriel to take us! Two days later a check big enough for the trip showed up in my mail—a small grant I had applied for and never heard about—and I spent it all to go without a moment's hesitation.

Just before this trip, I went to Ireland to speak at the International Transpersonal Association meetings in Killarney. The preceding year I had met the crew of Roger Payne's whale-watching yacht in Key West, Florida, while visiting a friend there, and had tried to recruit enough paid passengers for a Galapagos cruise in hopes of gaining my own free passage. After failing miserably despite the strong intention I held for that to happen, a man who heard my talk in Ireland came up to me afterward and invited me to teach biology seminars while following whales a year later, aboard the ocean-going, whale-watching sailboat of his California-based marine biology research institute!

Again, intention had produced results, if form an unanticipated direction. Again and again I have been shown that this is the essence of what we call magic: the paradoxical focus of desire or intent while at the same time letting go of the outcome. It is not easy to desire and let go of the desire simultaneously, but when we achieve it, it works!

The colorful crowds of the June solstice festival in Cusco, Peru (winter there, with crisp bright sunny days), awesome Machu Picchu, the splendor of Lake Titicaca, pre-Incan Tihuanaco in Bolivia were all new wonders for me. While walking a street in Cusco one day shortly before we left, the inner voice spoke once again, telling me to come back there in the fall for at least six months. I was very reluctant, as it would be the rainy season and I knew almost no one, did not speak any Spanish and did not want to start over that way in yet another culture, however attractive it was. I fought the relentless inner call for twenty-four hours, then succumbed and announced my plan to return. Needless to say, the money to do so showed up, and permitted me to stay there almost a year on what would have been gone in a few months in Washington.

While there I had a unique opportunity to make a difficult trek with indigenous friends over a 5,000-meter (16,250 ft) high snow-covered pass to visit a traditional Andean community never yet visited by even an anthropologist.[6] I had made almost only indigenous Quechua friends in Cusco, learned Spanish, investigated Inca history and started an indigenous coalition devoted to restoring Inca agriculture—possibly the finest and most extensive agricultural experimentation and development in the history of the world—as well as to reviving traditional medical knowledge, music, weaving, storytelling, and other aspects of Inca culture.

I was also informally adopted by a fourteen-year-old medicine priest in training named Puma, who introduced me to his marvelous grandfather teacher and all his family. By the following year, I had Puma lecturing and teaching workshops in the United States, where he became very active in leadership youth groups devoted to ecology and indigenous wisdom. As I write this he is 23 and just completing his training, which began at age three with dream teachers and continued from age six, when he was struck by lightning—an Andean sign of a medicine man—and his grandfather took over his training.

All of these and other experiences in indigenous worlds contributed enormously to my understanding of humans in nature, of interspecies communications, of the deep spiritual consciousness of all nature, of the awesome scientific knowledge indigenous people gained all over the world. They also gave me my own spirituality in ways I like to think of fondly of as "reverse missionizing," though it was never, ever pushed on me. Rather, it happened naturally, because their spirituality, undivided from the rest of their lives, was so reminiscent of my childhood experiences in nature.

Not long after I returned from Peru and resettled in California, where I had taught the whale-watch biology seminars for one delicious summer, that wonderful Renaissance man, Willis Harman, then president of the Institute of Noetic Sciences founded by moon-walking astronaut Edgar Mitchell, asked me to write a book with him on how biology and society would change if we acknowledged consciousness as the source of material evolution rather than its late emergent product. I was delighted by the opportunity to formalize this worldview, which I had come to but not stated publicly, and the book, *Biology Revisioned* (1998), was written as a dialogue between us, continuing, in a sense, the dialogues we had had by fax during my last years in Greece.

I had also republished the book written in Greece as *EarthDance: Living Systems in Evolution* (2000), which introduced not only the concept of holons in holarchy (mentioned earlier) but a very important and basic cycle of evolution from individuation through tension and conflicts to negotiations and collaborative schemes leading to higher biological unity, exemplified in the evolution of the nucleated cell dominating the second half of Earth's evolution as a collaborative enterprise of previously hostile archebacteria, which dominated the first half. This species maturation cycle links the well-known Type I and Type III ecosystems—the first made of young aggressive species, the latter of mature cooperative species—to show their underlying progression. In a 1997 article called "The Biology of Globalization" I extended this analysis of the evolutionary cycle to describing the human process of globalization. Because Darwin did not see beyond endless hostilities over survival in nature, the emergence of this pattern of maturation to the less visible but profoundly cooperative schemes of mature ecosystems such as coral reefs, prairies and rainforests is very relevant for our own species, now being called to such maturity. It is simply not the case that we are doomed to endless competitive empire building and warfare, whether by dictators, nation states or multinational corporations. Rather, it is our evolutionary heritage and imperative to grow up as a species, to find our way to being a cooperative, healthy global family!

Another book opportunity came when I was asked to write the text of a book illustrated by an exhibit of Earth's evolution created at Hewlett-Packard and called (like the book) *A Walk Through Time: from Stardust to Us* (1998), with an introductory chapter by Brian Swimme. While the publisher—Wiley, in New York—was concerned about scientific reputation and did not permit the use of the word *consciousness* in describing nature, I *was* able to describe nature as intelligent from the get-go and to update neo-Darwinism to show Earth as a living entity in evolution, with an ecological systems perspective, rather than a view of individual species in their habitats.

Because businesses, like other social institutions, are now suffering from having been modeled on mechanisms rather than living systems, and because ecosystems are ever more easily seen as wonderfully efficient and effective economic systems that allocate, transform, consume and recycle resources, living systems are of ever more interest in the business world (see, e.g., Hawkens 1993; Kiuchi and Shireman 2002). Thus my speaking engagements around the globe have included opportunities to speak to management in big businesses such as Siemens, Hewlett-Packard, and Boeing, as well as to Brazilian businesses and MBA programs in the United States and Brazil. But I also speak to many other kinds of organizations suffering the same "mechanical failure," from government agencies and universities to the World Bank, as well as to traditional religious organizations, such as Catholic and Episcopalian, to newer religions, such as Unity and Religious Science, and was invited onto a science panel at the World Parliament of Religions in South Africa.

Some of my most precious experiences have been when priests or nuns have actually asked me to help them update their theology by helping them think through new concepts of God and religion. If those practicing traditional religions based on revelations can be open to scientific thinking, then perhaps science can follow suit and open to the deep inner knowledge to be found in religious belief and practice.

TOWARD A SCIENTIFIC MODEL OF A LIVING UNIVERSE

My very favorite activities are symposia of like-minded scientists and philosophers gathering to share and work out new scientific worldviews or paradigms. Through these wonderful dialogues it is ever more obvious to me that the revolution happening in science is forcing reconsideration of its most fundamental assumptions, that is, of the basic beliefs supporting the current scientific model of our universe or cosmos and ourselves within it.

Western science set itself the task of describing reality—an objective world that could be studied without changing it. But quantum physics and other scientific research has shown objectivity to be an illusion as mentioned earlier, so even our concept of reality must be called into question. My biggest breakthrough on this matter came from meeting one indigenous culture after another, such as, for example, Lakota, Australian aboriginal, and Peruvian Andean Runakuna (Quechua), that saw reality as the totality of human experience while recognizing there were other realities for the other living beings of the universe and wide differences even in human experience of the world. Thus their world or universe models were omnicentric, with each sensing being at the center and the social/scientific task to find a shareable public description of reality for humans that respected individual deviations from it as equally real.

This made a great deal of sense to me because of the recognition reported earlier that no one, not even any scientist, has ever had any experience of the world outside of his or her consciousness, and some important ones, such as Gregory Bateson (1979) and Harvard's Nobel Laureate biologist George Wald (1984) had seen consciousness or mind in all of biological evolution. Thus, our scientific models of the universe must begin with consciousness and can only be formulated as models of human experience of the universe. As Western science was developed, the scientists (almost exclusively men) were so enamored of the increase in human power that came from the inventions of math and its translation into physical mechanism, that they projected these inventions onto the whole universe, with God as temporary inventor before dropping Him.

As I worked on the requirements for an Integral Science from my own perspective, I felt a strong need to end the sharp distinction between physics and biology, to avoid having either one forced into the mold of the other. Rather, I seek out new models of cosmic physics that are naturally compatible with seeing the universe as embedded living systems. Since familiar biological life forms—from nucleic acids to bodies—take on fundamentally toroidal (vorticular) structure, which is the simplest structure meeting the definition of autopoiesis and is evident in proto-galactic clouds, galaxies and planetary energy configurations such as Earth's electromagnetic field and surface weather patterns, I gravitate toward cosmic physics models that begin with this elementary living geometry.

The beauty and usefulness of autopoiesis as a definition of life lies precisely in helping us see beyond our narrow focus on familiar life forms to their relationship with both smaller and larger entities from subatomic to galactic. The simplest entities I could find that fit the definition were a whirlpool in a river, a tornado, a proto-galactic cloud. I reasoned that any differential gradient, whether in water, our atmosphere, the supernova dust cloud that gave rise to Earth or the earliest universe itself, would cause things literally to curl in on themselves—to form vortices that held their form as matter/energy was pulled into and spat out again by them.

Having come to a vortex theory of an autopoietic living universe—a universe of self-creating living geometry—I gravitated toward physicists working with vorticular, toroidal models of macrocosm and/or microcosm, especially looking for models with two-way (centripetal/centrifugal) motion. It is apparent that more and more physicists *are* coming to see inwardly and outwardly spiraling waves as the very essence of cosmic creation.

Exciting maverick physicists such as Walter Russell (1978 [1926]; 1994 [1947]), Itzhak Bentov (1977) and Nassim Haramein (2001; 2013), see the universal processes of creation and destruction as closely coupled and mutually necessary. In their unified field physics, these processes are radiation and gravity or entropy and centropy; their biological version is anabolism and catabolism. In Haramein's model of black/white wholes as the fundamental nature of all entities in the universe at all scalar levels (what I would call holarchic levels)—that is, particles, atoms, cells, bodies, planets, stars, galaxies, and the entire universe—fluctuations in the density differentials of the vacuum or ZPE (zero point energy field) at the event horizons of particles change their geometries and thus those of their atoms in turn, giving rise to the different elements of the chemical table. If the dynamic entropy/centropy balance shifts too far toward centropy, particles disappear back into the vacuum; if the balance shifts too far in the other direction (away from the centropy holding them together) the particles composing atoms become increasingly radioactive. The table of elements ends just before the dynamic balance is lost altogether, dissipating particles as unfettered radiation.

Cosmic objects never exist in isolation, so their internal dynamic balance must be held within the complex sea of wave interactions among all objects at all scalar levels. These interactions must surely affect the internal dynamics of any entity, either disrupting or enhancing them. The work of Wolff (2002) and of Schwarz and Russek (1999), as well as that of Haramein, has made this clear.

Bacteria, protists (single nucleated cell creatures), multi-celled creatures, ecosystems and the Earth itself can be seen as five fractal or holarchic levels of biological systems. The scalar location of all Earth's creatures—from bacteria to baleen whales—at a size level halfway between the microcosm and the macrocosm cannot be accidental. Rather, it can be seen that they evolved precisely in the most complex possible region of entropy/centropy dynamics in the universe. Earth's surface (or event horizon) must also be subject to standing waves produced by the interference patterns of colliding Earth and solar radiation, Earth and galactic radiation, Earth and supercluster radiation. If the vacuum energy gradients prove to be particularly steep at Earth's surface, where temperature, water, carbon and materials mobility provide other favorable conditions, toroids within toroids within toroids can curl up into complex life forms as nowhere else in the universe, except other planetary surfaces with similar conditions.

This model thus holds out the possibility of a completely new approach to explaining the origin of the biological creatures of Earth—to which science has, until now, restricted the category *life* (opposed to *non-life*). From a physical perspective, we may be able to see planetary creatures as a special case of autopoietic complexity arising through the unique interaction of energy gradients in patterns of wave interference at the surfaces (event horizons) of planets with particular compositions and conditions determined by their energetic relationships with their star and universal bodies at other scalar levels.

Cosmic autopoiesis—the self-creation of a living universe—thus promises to become an elegant view of the whole, with essentially the same production *and* recycling process at all scalar or fractal levels, and uniquely complex life forms generated at planetary surfaces. Thus my explorations, unfettered by the limits I was taught as a scientist, brought me back to my passionate belief in science and enabled me to begin work on a coherent and self-consistent model of a living Universe[7] that will undoubtedly keep evolving for the rest of my life in this particular world.

NOTES

1. This worldview is somewhat elaborated in the last section of this article and may be found as "A Tentative Model of a Living Universe, Parts I and II," at http://via-visioninaction.org in the *Articles* section under my name.
2. Objectivity—the presupposition that there is some kind of reality independent of individual perceptions—asserts that there are facts that transcend subjective reality. This concept was championed by theorists such as John Stuart Mill, David Hume, Emile Durkheim, and Max Weber, and later challenged by Polanyi, Kuhn, Feyerabend, and others.
3. This was scarcely acknowledged before the late 1970s and is detailed in Lyons et al. (1992).
4. Barry Fell was a Harvard marine biologist who deciphered rock and tablet inscriptions, including the Minoan Phaistos Disk, and became an internationally acknowledged, though somewhat controversial, epigrapher. The book was *America B.C.* (New York: Wallaby Books, Simon & Schuster). It had been given to me in late 1961 or early 1962 although it was not published until 1976, a year after his textbook on marine biology. Fell's other books on epigraphy are *Saga America* (Times Books, 1983), and *Bronze Age America* (Little, Brown & Company, 1982).
5. Among my favorite books by Jane Roberts are: *The Nature of Personal Reality*, 1974 and *The Individual and the Nature of Mass Events*, 1981, both republished in 1994 and 1995, respectively, by Amber-Allen, San Rafael, CA.
6. An account of this trek may be found under the name "Journey to Hapu" by scrolling down my website: http://www.ratical.org.lifeweb
7. See note 1.

REFERENCES

Bateson, G. 1979. *Mind and nature: A necessary unity*. New York: Dutton.

Bentov, I. 1977. *Stalking the wild pendulum*. New York: E.P. Dutton.

Cajete, G. 1994. *Look to the mountain: An ecology of indigenous education*. Durango, CO: Kivaki Press.

Ereira, A., Director. 1992. *From the heart of the world: The Elder Brother's Warning* [VHS]. USA: Mystic Fire Video.

Haramein, N. 2013. Quantum gravity and the holographic mass. *Physical Review & Research International*, 3 (4): 270 292.

———. 2001. The scaling equation from micro to macro cosmos in terms of frequency vs. radius ω (R). Paper presented at the American Physics Society Meetings, Texas.

Harman, W. and E. Sahtouris. 1998. *Biology revisioned*. Berkeley: North Atlantic Books.

Hawkens, P. 1993. *The ecology of commerce*. New York: Harper.

Jantsch, E. 1980. *The self-organizing Universe: Scientific and human implications of the emerging paradigm of evolution*. Oxford: Pergamon Press.

Kiuchi, T., and B. Shireman. 2002. *What we learned in the rainforest*. San Francisco: Berrett-Koehler

Lapo, A. V. 1982. *Traces of bygone biospheres*. Moscow: Mir Publishers.

Lovelock, J. E. 1972. Gaia as seen through the atmosphere. *Atmospheric Environment* 6 (8): 579–580.

———. 1982. *Gaia: A new look at life on Earth*. Oxford: Oxford University Press.

Lyons, O. and J. Mohawk, Eds. 1992. *Exiled in the land of the free: Democracy, Indian nations and the United States Constitution*. Santa Fe: Clear Light.

Margulis, L. 1982. *Early life*. Boston: Science Books International.

Miller, H. 1958. *The colossus of Maroussi*. New York: New Directions.

Prigogine, I. and I. Stengers. 1984. *Order out of chaos: Man's new dialogue with nature*. New York: Bantam.

Puthoff, H. 1990, July 28. Everything for nothing. *New Scientist*.

Ray, P. and S. Anderson. 2000. *The cultural creatives: How fifty million people are changing the world*. New York: Harmony Books.

Russell, W. 1978 [1926]. *The universal one*. Waynesboro, VA: The University of Science and Philosophy.

———. 1994 [1947]. *The secret of light*. Waynesboro, VA: The University of Science and Philosophy.

Sahtouris, E. 2000a. *EarthDance: Living Systems in Evolution*. iUniverse.com.

———. 2000b. The biology of globalization. *World Futures: Journal of General Evolution* 55 (2): 105–127.

———, with S. Liebes and B. Swimme. 1998. *A walk through time: From stardust to us*. New York: Wiley.

Schwartz, G. and L. Russek. 1999. *The living energy Universe*. Charlottesville, VA: Hampton Roads.

Vernadsky, V. 1926 [1896]. *The biosphere*. Oracle, AZ: Synergistic Press.

Wald, G. 1984. Life and mind in the Universe. *International Journal of Quantum Chemistry*, Quantum Biology Symposium No. 11, 1–15.

Wiseman, R., and M. Schlitz. 1998. Experimenter effects and the remote detection of staring. *Journal of Parapsychology* 61:197–208.

Wolff, M. 2002. *Origin of the natural laws in a binary universe*. Manhattan Beach, CA: Technotran Press.

MY LIFE IN CHAOS

ALLAN LESLIE COMBS

Center for Consciousness Studies, California Center of Integral Studies, San Francisco, California, USA

This article presents an informal story of Allan Combs' professional career in terms of his personal life, and the paths that have led him to become a creative and productive scholar. It emphasizes the roles played by colleagues in the fields of chaos theory, systems theory, and general evolution.

> If a system's attractor is strange,
> You will see its trajectory range
> Through every spot
> You can possibly plot
> In the space of temporal change.
> —Ted Melnechuk (1990)

MY PERSONAL STORY

This is a story of the evolution of my ideas about systems theory, chaos, and consciousness, and how these have intertwined in my life. But first let me tell you something about myself.

My initial conditions were fashioned in Ohio during the Second World War. As a kid I was thoroughly attention deficit hyperactivity disorder (ADHD), if such a category had existed at the time. I would have been given loads of Ritalin, were it available, but fortunately I lived on a farm and every day ran everywhere I went until I wore myself out and went to sleep. When I got to school it was apparent that I also was dyslexic, if such a category had existed. Indeed, I was lucky to spell my own name. Teachers regularly pointed out my "laziness," as evidenced by the fact that despite spelling a word correctly now and then, I typically misspelled it several times on the same page. My parents took me to Ohio State University, where a nice professor diagnosed me with "mixed-dominance" and sent me to a lady downtown who made a living by "training your eyes to cooperate with each other."[1] I was also given tutoring in hopes that I might learn to read and write like a normal child. My mother told me she would buy me anything I would read, so I tried her out on a series of horror comic books.[2] After she endured this quietly for a while I threw them away and graduated to books on flying saucers.

In middle school, then known as "junior high," I nearly flunked 7th grade math. Against my teacher's best advice I took 8th grade math the next year. Against my 8th grade teacher's recommendation I took ninth grade math after that. And so it went on to the 11th grade, where I received a grade of "B" and an approval to continue. I passed senior math with the highest score in our school, but still could not spell. None of the teachers encouraged me to go to college, and I was required to take shop instead of advanced literature; a ruling I have always been thankful for, since I learned many practical skills and read the literature anyway. I was also barred form the secret meetings of the National Honors Society, although my friends all seemed to belong. The school principal got wind of the fact that I was planning to continue my education at the university and gave me a pep talk: "Don't be discouraged, now, Allan. It will be hard but you can do it if you really try."

Actually, I did fine in college except for my awful spelling. Typically instructors would give me a "B" and apologize. This was in the days of slide-rules, before mechanical calculators and long before spelling checkers. I labored on, and after two years of physics and two more of psychology, I got myself accepted by a couple of passable graduate programs in clinical psychology. I was interested in theories of personality. I choose the University of Florida, where I hoped to study with Sidney Jourard, one of the founders of Humanistic Psychology, at that time was a new light on the intellectual horizon. I got to Gainesville in time to discover that he had just left for a year in England.[3] I later got to know him, but only after I was booted out of the clinical program for poor spelling and a bad attitude about behaviorism. I busied myself picking up a degree in counseling in lieu of traveling to Southeast Asia as a foot soldier.

Two years later I was accepted into the psychology program at the University of Georgia, rife with money to develop a new science complex, and I was there for nearly a year before I was booted out again, this time by the machinations of a faculty member recently arrived from my old nemesis, the psychology department of the University of Florida. I found this depressing, and I went to one of my instructors, an assistant professor named Ed Mulligan, to ask for a recommendation I could use to help me get in yet another clinical psychology program. He looked at me like I was addled, and asked how I could possibly want to spend my life listening to people moan about their problems. He then offered me a research grant to study the evolution of hearing. I thought about this and decided my luck had changed. It was 1968.

MY PROFESSIONAL STORY

In 1968 the world of science was highly charged. At the time I was a graduate student at the University of Georgia large amounts of federal money had recently created a city of buildings dedicated to virtually all branches of scientific investigation, and outfitted with cutting-edge instrumentation. We were in the midst of the Cold War, and Sputnik had given the gift of government funding to all U.S.

graduate students. Thomas Kuhn (1962) had recently published *The Structure of Scientific Revolutions*, and we all knew that paradigm changes were in the air. I worked in the acoustics laboratory under the auspices of an Air Force grant exploring how the ear detects small signals in loud noises; a project distantly related to the development of sonar and radar technologies. At the same time I was taking courses on invertebrate sensory systems with Robert Taylor over in the department of biology. With him I was learning to record the activity of single nerve cells in crayfish, and warming up for a dissertation that would utilize this skill to study nerve action using mathematical modeling. Despite the fact that I was a psychology graduate student, Taylor was the only professor on campus doing single cell work and I wanted to learn his skills.

I had begun my undergraduate studies in the early '60s as a physics major at the Ohio State University, then shifted in my junior year to psychology and continued in this field, going on to graduate school to find out what makes people tick. At the time I read a number of books by Carl Jung and became fascinated by concepts such as *archetypes* and the *collective unconscious*, and I had developed interests in European phenomenology and Eastern philosophy. Somewhere in the second year of graduate school, however, I swerved back in the direction of the hard sciences, and now I was in a zoology laboratory doing mathematical modeling on crayfish nerve cells. Perhaps this reverse step was due to the enthusiasm for pure science that was in the air those days, which in my case had been encouraged by a young instructor of sensory psychology named Edward Mulligan, who in time became both friend and mentor as well as my major professor. In any event I had found my community, one comprised of faculty and students with passion for their intellectual work. Nevertheless, on weekends and during vacations I enthusiastically read into the new field of Humanistic Psychology. There I became charged by Abraham Maslow's exhilarating book, *Towards a Psychology of Being*, and Carl Rogers' tender but powerful work, *On Becoming a Person*. I also read everything written by the scientist-mystic John Lilly, whose work with dolphin communication was a fascinating application of the technology I was learning in the acoustics laboratory, and whose remarkable experiences with LSD while drifting in a flotation tank of his own invention were an inspiration to a whole generation of spiritually motivated scientists. His most exciting book was *The Center of the Cyclone* (1972), in which he also described his experiences in a strange Latin-American school of esoteric studies operated by Oscar Ichazo, who in turn had been deeply influenced by the Gurdjieff work. I occasionally participated in Gestalt therapy groups and human potentials workshops, and I hoped one day to find a way to bring all these threads together.

The two principal sources of enthusiasm in late 1960s neuroscience were the opening volleys of the investigation of the brain as a chemical organ, and mathematical modeling of nerve cell activity with the aid of the relatively new device called a computer. It had been just over a decade since Hodgkin and Huxley (1952) in England had successfully mapped the chemical mechanisms underlying nerve impulse transmission, and it was already beginning to look like the brain would turn out to be as much an enchanted chemical forest as, to use Sir Charles Sherrington's famous phrase, an "enchanted loom" of electrical activity. But truth be known, I did not have a mind for chemistry, let alone biochemistry. It all seemed like magic to me. And anyway I had dropped Chem. 102 as a freshman after discovering I had been assigned to an 8:00 a.m. lab section on Saturday mornings, and I never looked back. I liked the clean abstract ideas coming from mathematics and computer modeling, as seen in the early neuronal modeling work of Michael Arbib (1964) and Warren McCulloch (1965). I decided that if I were ever to make a contribution of my own it would be through modeling or theory building, and not by carrying out chemical assays on the brains of rats or schizophrenics.

It was about this time, quite by chance, that I made my first acquaintance with systems theory. While browsing through books in the new graduate research library my attention was captured by a volume loaded with interesting diagrams of boxes and arrows. As I now recall, these dealt with how factories work. There were arrows for where raw materials entered and for how synthesized products moved about in the factory to get where they were needed, finally lining up to be loaded on trucks or trains. I was not interested in factories *per se*, having acquired a distasted for working in them during summers as an undergraduate, but these diagrams held my attention. There was wisdom in them that reached beyond written descriptions: they summarized the entire factory operation in a fashion that disclosed its many facets and their relationships to each other in an immediate and explicit fashion like nothing I had seen before. It seemed to me that there was something in this representation of multiple coordinated events captured in pictures that could have interesting applications for understanding the nervous system.

Like so many young scientists, however, I did not pursue the career of research immediately after completing my doctorate. While in graduate school I had discovered that I liked to teach, and during my last few years of study I had paid my way by teaching a variety of psychology courses. In the meantime, during the early '70s the easy research money was rapidly drying up and I saw my own professors burning the midnight oil to maintain productive research careers while dealing with increasing demands on their time and decreasing financial support. It was not an encouraging picture.

I took a one-year teaching position at Earlham College, a small Quaker liberal arts school in Indiana, where I spent half my time in psychology and the other half in biology. Recalling the advice of my major professor, that anyone who liked to "bull shit" as much as I should be a teacher, I found the job rewarding. I have continued to make my living as a teacher to the time of this writing. During the 1970s I worked at a small midwestern college in southern Missouri, where I thrived at first but later found the cultural and intellectual mediocrity of the region stifling. I read Nikos Kazantzakis in desperation, and inspired by Zorba the Greek prepared myself to abandon elitism and join the common people! I became active in a civics club as well as becoming the board chair of a multiple-county community mental health center. These activities were not wholeheartedly Zorba-esque, but sometimes one takes what fortune offers, and in the meantime I read everything I could get my hands on about consciousness and the burgeoning human potentials movement unfolding in the exotic state of California. By the early 1980s I gave up the Midwest, or it gave up on me, and I moved to a job at a small liberal arts college in the mountains of Western North Carolina. There I was blessed with a friendly and stimulating environment, and the time to read widely while teaching a variety of courses. I came to appreciate the value of a broad background of knowledge in the pursuit of my growing intellectual passion, the study of the nature of consciousness.

One book on consciousness that I read while still idling in the Midwest deeply influenced my later thinking about the nature of consciousness and about systems theory as well. Because of its importance to what follows below, let us take some time to review its important ideas. The book was by psychologist Charles Tart (1975) and was titled *States of Consciousness*. In it he explicitly applied a systems theory approach to understanding states of consciousness. Here are the boxes and arrows again! But this time they are used to represent how one state of consciousness differs from another, and how each state is structured. William James had also been interested in states of consciousness a century ago, as indicated in the now-famous lines from *The Varieties of Religious Experience*:

> Our normal waking consciousness, rational consciousness as we call it, is but one special type of consciousness, whilst all about it, parted from it by the filmiest of screens, there lie potential forms of consciousness entirely different. We may go through life without suspecting their existence; but apply the requisite stimulus, and at a touch they are there in all their completeness, definite types of mentality which probably somewhere have their field of application and adaptation. No account of the universe in its totality can be final which leaves these other forms of consciousness quite disregarded. (1902/1987, 349)

Tart was following in James's footsteps. In this 1975 book he presented a landscape diagram in which parts, represented by variously shaped puzzle pieces, could be moved about on a tabletop to form an endless variety of distinct patterns. These parts depicted psychological functions such as memory, emotion, body sense, sense of self, style of reasoning, sense of humor, and so on. For some states of consciousness they form a coherent pattern, or *gestalt*. Such a pattern represents a stable and coherent state of consciousness such as ordinary wakefulness, the hypnotic trance state, or a drugged state such as being "stoned" on marijuana. Configurations that do not form coherent patterns do not yield viable states of consciousness, or in some instances represent only transitory states such as experienced while waking up or falling asleep, or shifting from ordinary consciousness into a meditative or trance state.

Continuing with this systems theory approach Tart proposed several kinds of patterning influences that stabilize a state of consciousness, keeping a person from slipping out of it into some other state. These included *loading stabilization*, *negative feedback stabilization*, *positive feedback stabilization*, and *limiting stabilization*. Tart used the example of ordinary wakefulness to illustrate these ideas. Engaging in work, for instance, is a good example of loading stabilization, which puts some kind of weight or drag on the system. As long as a person is busy washing dishes, cleaning gutters, or writing a dissertation, they are not likely to fall into states of ecstasy, or even fall asleep. Instances of the operation of loading stabilization for other states of consciousness include the repetition of a mantram as a patterning force in absorptive meditation, or chanting as a patterning force for certain states of religious ecstasy.

Negative feedback stabilization refers to the undesirable consequences of slipping out of a state of consciousness. Falling asleep at the wheel endangers one's life, and drifting into fantasies does little to facilitate the completion of a dissertation. Positive feedback, on the other hand, indicates the positive effects of staying awake and on task. We get the job done, or if we are driving we get where we are going. Lastly, limiting stabilization refers to constraints that limit a person's access to "undesirable" states of consciousness. For instance, in the United States the government does its best to limit personal access to mind-altering drugs, and society, in the form of parents, the church, and other rule-enforcement agents, often discourages participation in activities such as chanting, meditation, or trance dancing, which might seriously alter one's state of consciousness. In the same vein, books on magic may be kept in locked rooms on the top floors of university libraries. It was not too long ago that books with erotic content sometimes suffered the same fate. All this is to limit access to materials that might alter consciousness. Through much of the '70s and '80s, often without knowing it, I was working my way toward my own re-conceptualization this important early work by Tart on states of consciousness.

To continue my story, however, in the mid-'80s I happened across an article in a popular magazine on the mind and brain, written by a freelance writer and psychologist by the name of David Loye. I struck up a correspondence with him, and eventually made some of my undergraduate students available to him for preliminary tests on a protocol he was developing to measure cognitive styles. This protocol was based on his earlier theoretical work on differences in information processing strategies between the left and right brain hemispheres and the frontal lobe. As it turns out, his identification of the frontal lobe as the executive pole of the brain, explained in his highly readable book *The Sphinx and the Rainbow*, was a decade ahead of its time. David and I became friends, and he invited me to join him in writing book reviews for the journal *World Futures: The Journal of General Evolution*, operated by a group of systems theorists and evolutionary scholars known as The General Evolution Research Group (GERG). This group, which at the time of this writing includes about 30 members from all about the world, was originally formed by a few social science scholars around the theoretical work of Ervin Laszlo, one of the leading systems thinkers of our age and the originator of *the theory of general evolution* (Laszlo 1987).

Laszlo's theory paints a broad picture of how systems of many kinds grow and change over time. It applies with equal validity to single-celled organisms, complex organisms, and ecologies. And it can be applied to economic and social systems as well. It presents a basic approach to the understanding of many kinds of complex systems, understanding them to be comprised of more or less independent and loosely interconnected subsystems. Each of these subsystems is itself a complex and often chaotic system. The interactions of these subsystems stabilize the larger system over time, and they also recombine to create new and emergent levels of complexity. For instance, individual cells in the human body rely on dozens of complex metabolic processes, each a complex process itself, which interact and catalyze each other. The result at the next level of organization is the stable structure we know as the cell itself. But cells, in their turn, combine to form organs, and organs combine to form whole organisms. At each level—the metabolic cycles, the cell, and the organs—the processes combine to form the structure at the next level up. This larger structure can be more or less complex than the smaller systems that form it, but often it has a certain degree of independence from them. Thus the activity of a living cell is dictated only in part by the individual chemical systems that comprise it. The brain, an organ associated with the mind and comprised of individual nerve and glial cells, is relatively independent in its activity from the dictates and desires, as it were, of the individual cells of which it is formed. In the words of Nobel laureate Roger Sperry (1993), the individual cells are "hulled about" by the overall activity of the brain. Brains in turn form social networks, or societies, but the actions of a society as a whole do not necessarily reflect the actions of each individual brain that forms it.

Viewing the evolution of complex systems as they evolve over time can give useful insights into how they come into existence in the first place. Most systems of interest to us are said to be of the *third type* (Prigogine and Stengers 1984). These are systems that absorb energy from the environment, using it to sustain and build themselves into new and more complex structures, often through *bifurcations* into new forms that involve the creation of new and higher levels of organization. Harvard astrophysicist Eric Chaisson and GERG member (2001) has shown that this general model of the evolution toward increasing complexity characterizes cosmic evolution from the diffuse radiation that filled space just after the big bang through the creation of subatomic and atomic particles, on through the emergence of atoms, molecules, and macromolecules, and on to the origins of life, single and multicellular organisms, and to the human brain and human societies, from hunting and gathering through industrialization and post-industrial civilization. It is a grand picture of increasingly complex organization with the emergence of hierarchical systems and increasingly efficient utilization of energy.

This majestic overview of evolution, which I discovered in Ervin Laszlo's writings, took root in my imagination and I begin to see its potential for understanding a wide range of important ecological, social, and psychological issues. One of the most obvious of these concerns the sustainability of the human species on our planet. For instance, the systems perspective offered by Laszlo's general theory of evolution made it clear that a wide variety of seemingly separate global crises are in fact intimately interrelated. These include the growing shortage of drinking water and tillable soil, the loss of rain forests and with them decreasing biodiversity, rising pollution in the air and water, global warming, and in human society the rapidly mounting disparity between the haves and have nots as well as the markedly uneven distribution of resources between different countries.

The good news from the general evolutionary perspective is that since everything is connected to everything else, it may be possible to make wide-spread improvements by acting on a relatively few "high leverage" points in the enormously complex global system. For instance, it has been shown that to provide access to education for women in third world countries leads to lower rates of population growth, greater available food, an elevation of cultural values such as education and the arts, and a reduction of social and domestic aggression (Eisler, Loye, and Norgaard 1995). All this is related to the fact that educated women are more capable of taking care of themselves and their families, less interested in having large numbers of children to care for them in their old age—a situation common to poverty environments all over the world—and more active in promoting cooperative community values. Thus, relatively small investments of resources spent for the education of women in countries such as India have large payoffs in many ways.

With these ideas in mind, I began to give talks on global sustainability in my university classes, and soon started to lecture to community groups as well. About this time David Loye introduced me to Ervin Laszlo himself, and both invited me to join the GERG community. There I found myself involved in a global network of like-minded systems and evolutionary scholars. During the years since that time I traveled with Ervin and other GERG members to many countries in Europe as well as many locations within the United States to participate in meetings and give lectures on issues of sustainability. In the meantime my interests in systems thinking expanded to include the study of the consciousness and the brain, thus bringing me back full circle to my original studies in psychology and brain science. I owe both David Loye and Ervin Laszlo a great debt of thinks for extending their generosity and hospitality to me, which lifted me into an entirely new world of possibilities for action and scholarship.

One of the most brilliant and eccentric members of GERG was mathematician Ralph Abraham. Ralph was a pioneer of the emerging field of chaos mathematics. He had co-authored a set of short and highly illustrated books on the foundations of chaos theory in what is known as the *dynamical systems* approach. A dynamical system is one that is in a state of motion or change. Thus, it can be said to be following an evolutionary trajectory, meaning that it progresses along a transitional pathway that can, at least in principle, be represented by some mathematical expression. The path of a dynamical system can often be represented with surprising clarity by drawing it as a line on the surface of a topological "phase space." For example, the swinging of a pendulum can be seen as a circle in phase space. The absence of activity in a stone resting on a tabletop can be shown as a point. And the intricate rhythms of the human heart can be seen as a convoluted elliptic form. Patterns such as the latter are said to be *chaotic*. Ralph's books demonstrated many types of dynamical activity with clear and accessible diagrams that had the charm of hand-drawn art from the '60s. For this reason the books were known in the trade as Ralph's "chaos comics" (Abraham 1982–1988). I discovered these in the late '80s and spent three weeks reading them day and night.

Chaos theory actually dates back to the 1890s when Henri Poincaré articulated the 3-body problem, but it really caught hold in the late 1980s when René Thom's catastrophe theory, actually developed in the 1960s, combined with the new concepts of attractors and bifurcations to create an entire nonlinear view of the physical world. It was a view that was both exciting and threatening, depending on how you liked to view the world. Some scientists, who relied on the absolute predictability of nature to ply their trade, met chaos theory and nonlinear dynamics with angst because it indicated that nature was no longer subject to precise prediction; no longer reliable. A surprising number of philosophers found themselves in the same camp. For them the comfortable reliability of the clockwork universe was giving way to the prospect of a world without order. For folks like myself, however, the idea of a cosmos in which one could not know the outcome of every single event in advance was a welcome relief from the vice grip of the traditional mechanistic worldview. Though physical events were still technically "deterministic," the whole thing seemed now much less like a machine and much more like a living organism. Free will remained a distant hope for philosophers and mathematicians, but the old mechanistic theories of the brain, mind, and behavior were dead on their feet, and for a scientific humanist like myself the situation could hardly have looked better.

In the fall of 1989 a colleague at my liberal arts college returned from an American Psychological Association (APA) meeting in Boston to tell me about an interesting session he attended there on the topic of chaos theory and psychology. He knew that I had been reading about chaos theory and systems science, and he supposed that I would be interested in attending a similar meeting the organizer, Larry Vandervert, was planning to hold at the next APA conference in San Francisco during the summer of 1990. I was indeed interested, although I had long since developed a distaste for big meetings, and I replied that I would probably not be attending this one. A few months later, however, I changed my mind, thinking that this would at least be a good excuse to visit old friends in the Bay Area. I called Larry Vandervert at his home in Spokane to see what he was planning. Initially he told me that he had decided not to organize another chaos theory session, but a few weeks later he called back to say that he had changed his mind and was thinking of organizing a meeting. This one would not be a discussion group at the APA convention, but rather an inaugural meeting of a new organization, which we tentatively named The Society for Chaos Theory in Psychology. He hoped that the Saybrook Institute, in San Francisco, might host our gathering during the week prior to the APA convention, and I agreed to call Stanley Krippner, a faculty member there, to see what could be worked out. Over the years to come I was to discover that Larry was an excellent organizer but a very private person. I never learned how he knew that Stanley Krippner would be interested in our gathering, but I did my part and gave him a call. To my delight he was quite friendly, but he told me that he just returned from a trip to South America where he was working with a shaman and he needed a day or two to get his feet on ground. Sure enough, one or two days later he called back to say that the president of Saybrook had approved our meeting and we could use their facilities. We were off and running!

As I said, Larry was a private person, and it was years later that I discovered he had also conscripted Fred Abraham, a neural psychologist, electroencephalogram (EEG) expert, and brother of GERG member Ralph Abraham, above, to help get the meeting organized. Fred had written the first book on chaos theory and psychology, which David Loye reviewed for *World Futures*. Larry, Fred, and I worked together to invite colleagues by phone and by e-mail to participate in the meeting. It seemed, however, that this meeting was already just waiting to happen, because e-mail inquiries about it came in from all around the United

States as well as from Europe and Asia. The hundred or so folks who actually showed up ranged from California artists to European robotics engineers, but most were psychologists and other social scientists interested in applying ideas from chaos theory to their own fields. Stanley Krippner, fast becoming one of the world's leading scholars on the psychology of consciousness, gave a plenary talk on the importance of nonlinear dynamics in understanding the mind and behavior. Another plenary speaker, Karl Pribram, already established as one of the leading brain scientists of the twentieth century for his work on the holographic brain and other topics, emphasized the importance of pursuing a balance between traditional linear dynamics and the new nonlinear or chaotic dynamics. David Loye spoke about the future of the organization we were founding, and stressed the importance of gender equality in its activities and administration. During the conference I did the public introductions and Larry did most of the behind the scenes organizing. Fred sped about coordinating and gathering people into groups based on interest, generally facilitating the whole process. It was quite an exciting event, and in the end we created an enduring organization that, to include everyone present, would come to be call itself The Society for Chaos Theory in Psychology and the Life Sciences, which acquired its own professional journal a few years later titled *Nonlinear Dynamics: The Journal of The Society for Chaos Theory in Psychology and the Life Sciences*. Personally I would have preferred titles that were less long and awkward, but at least it was evident that everyone got in their two cents worth. During the official banquet I met Sally Goerner, a graduate student at Saybrook who would become a longtime friend. Sally (1994; 1999) has since established herself as a leading complexity theorist working in areas as diverse as city planning, green economics, and the design of creative and sophisticated educational programs for primary school children.

During the '80s and early '90s I became involved in several writing projects with colleagues from The Society for Chaos Theory and GERG. I co-edited two volumes of proceedings for The Society for Chaos Theory, one with Robin Robertson and the other with William Sulis. Robin is a mathematician turned Jungian psychologist and a professional magician, and Bill is a Canadian psychiatrist with a strong interest in mathematics and chaos theory. Meanwhile, with Ervin Laszlo's encouragement I edited a special issue of *World Futures* on the topic of *cooperation*, seen through several theoretical and applied perspectives. This issue was later printed as a book in GERG's *General Evolution Series* published by Gordon and Breach. This was my first book, and my first lesson in obscurity. Despite the fact that it included the work of respected authors such as Ervin Laszlo, Ralph Abraham, David Loye, and Riane Eisler—David's partner and author of her own series of influential books beginning with *The Chalice and the Blade*—it was read only by a handful of people. About this time I also helped edit a book titled *Changing Visions: Human Cognitive Maps, Past, Present And Future* (1996) with Ervin Laszlo and other GERG colleagues from around the world which anticipated Richard Dawkins' idea of social *memes* by several years. This project was satisfying and confidence-building to the writer and theorist in me. And academically speaking it was more successful than the previous book, meaning that it was favorably received by professional colleagues and even read by a few regular people.

So by the beginning of the '90s I found myself in the company of fascinating and creative colleagues with whom I shared a wide range of interests. I owe a great deal to my friends in GERG and The Society for Chaos Theory for simply being themselves and fostering an atmosphere in which significant and interesting work is encouraged and supported. Moreover, after that first meeting of The Society for Chaos Theory at the Saybrook Institute I developed a friendship with Stanley Krippner, who became both a colleague and mentor to me. Stanley is one of those great human beings whose intelligence and kindness has touched the lives of many people. It has been a gift to know and work with him. He helped me became an adjunct faculty member for Saybrook, which put me in regular contact with a community of teachers and scholars who shared my interests in spirituality and consciousness. In time I also met faculty members at the California Institute of Integral Studies and other alternative institutions of higher learning. I later came to now Ken Wilber as well, joining his circle of friends.

I cannot overemphasize the importance of the encouragement and stimulation a scholar receives from participating in a community of like-minded people, ones with whom she or he can share ideas and celebrate accomplishments. Universities are supposed to serve this function, and to some extent they do, but working at a university is not a substitute for a community of colleagues with shared interests. Indeed, successful researchers in just about every field find some way to schmoose with each other. I was now experiencing the encouragement, support, and confidence needed to follow my own interests. I began to apply ideas from general evolutionary theory and chaos dynamics to understanding the mind, brain, and consciousness.

Two ideas grew to take a central place in my thinking. The first dealt with chaotic dynamical systems and the second with self-organizing algorithms. My first idea was that mental processes that give form to our conscious experience, such as thought, memory, and emotion, are dynamical events subject to the kinds of processes best characterized by chaotic (also termed "strange") attractors. My second idea was that these processes engage in self-organizing interactions that can be represented by algorithms. Let me unpack these notions by beginning with the processes themselves. The idea is that mental processes such as the flow of emotions, thoughts, memories, and fantasies form a kind of inner weather in which each ebbs and flows in a chaotic-like fashion over time. This inner weather is analogous to the weather outside where temperature, barometric pressure, wind velocity, and humidity rise and fall in a semi-random fashion that in each case can be represented by something like a mathematical chaotic, or strange, attractor. Considering the whole weather system together for a particular geographical region we find a complex interactive process best understood as a multidimensional strange attractor.

Now, all strange attractors have certain features in common, whether they represent the outer or the inner weather. For instance, they change continuously, and they cannot be predicted in detail. The latter fact becomes obvious when we try to predict the outer weather. But strange attractors nevertheless exhibit recognizable patterns. For example, any geographic region exhibits weather patterns that remain recognizable over time. Typically the wind may come up in the late morning during the early months of spring, and in mid-summer it may rain most afternoons, while it may be dry during the winters. This is a recognizable pattern, but it is one that is impossible to capture in linear mathematical equations that would allow detailed predictions to be made over significant periods of time. No matter how much you know about the weather today you can only make an educated guess about tomorrow, and predictions about each succeeding day become even less definite. Beyond a few days into the future the weather becomes virtually unknowable, except that it will continue to look typical. Bringing these ideas together, we say that the form or a strange attractor is globally recognizable but unpredictable in detail. Another feature of interest is that such attractors never exactly repeat themselves. For instance, the weather is never precisely the same on any two days, and in this sense every day is unique.

In the early '90s I created a "chaos laboratory" at the University of North Carolina–Asheville to investigate consciousness and behavior in terms of chaos theory. In one study a group of students and I recorded our moods every ten minutes for a period of two weeks. The results demonstrated that emotions do indeed change from moment to moment, hour to hour, and day to day, in a way that can be represented as strange attractors (Combs, Winkler, and Daley 1994). Our findings were consistent with the data on moods obtained from other laboratories (Hannah 1991), and several investigations of the brain that disclose an essentially chaotic architecture of the electrical activities found there (e.g., Freeman 2001).

The second idea that held central place in my thoughts was that mental processes, undergirded by events in the brain, interact in such a fashion as to recreate themselves over time. In other words, consciousness is a self-creating or *autopoietic* process analogous in its own way to a living cell (Varela, Maturana, and Uribe 1974) where the contents are the product of many underlying metabolic cycles and hyper-cycles. This view emphasizes the mental life as a *process* rather than a structure. It is reminiscent of William James's (1890/1981) descriptions of conscious experience. James characterized consciousness as a *stream* that never actually repeats itself, just as is the case with strange attractors. He further observed that the overall character of this stream is unique for each individual, and thereby defines a person's personality. Here we see a strong similarity with my idea that the mental processes which undergird consciousness can be understood through chaotic dynamics.

When I first began to explore these ideas I was very unsure of myself. On the one hand, I wondered if I was just stating the obvious. On the other, perhaps I was getting into chaos theory and systems thinking over my head. As a trial run I presented my ideas to members of The Society for Chaos Theory at our second meeting, held in Canada during the summer of 1991. These were a kind group of people and I hoped they would be gentle and thoughtful in their response. I only got about halfway through my presentation, however, when a young man near the back stood up and stated that he was coming to very similar conclusions as a mathematical computationalist. He soon joined me on the stage and verified that he was working along the similar lines in developing a computational theory of the mind. He introduced himself as Ben Goertzel, and indicated that he had already written one book on the topic and was working on some others (1993a; 1993b; 1994; 1997). This meeting with Ben, so unexpected and so validating to my own thinking, was one of the most rewarding events of my intellectual life. Ben and I became friends and have shared ideas and collaborated on projects ever since. Among the latter is the creation of an online journal, *Dynamical Psychology*, where we encourage the publication of creative applications of dynamical ideas to psychology.

Under Ben's influence I began to think in terms of computation as well as dynamics. For instance, one can entertain the idea of modeling psychological process with a sufficiently complex computer program. In support of this notion, European systems theorist George Kampis (1991), a student of evolutionary biologist and GERG member Vilmos Csányi, showed that any dynamical process can be represented, at least in theory, by an algorithmic one, and vice versa. Goertzel and Kampis have some differences in view over whether *all* algorithmic processes can be made into computational ones, but these are not important here. The point is that we can alternatively imagine an autopoietic ecology of psychological processes represented as interactive algorithmic or computational processes. In support of this notion, it is possible to construct sets of complex computational codes that interact with each other in such a way as to recreate those very codes (McCaskill and Wagler 2000). This is a kind of autopoietic computational soup in which the interactions of the original codes create an ongoing reproductive ecology. Both Goertzel and Kampis point out that with sufficiently complex interactions of this sort new codes can come into existence that are entirely original, thus transforming the future of the system in novel ways. This is a confirmation, in principle at least, of the above idea that the dynamical interactions of the ongoing events which comprise our conscious experience can create entirely original events; novel thoughts, feelings, perceptions, imaginings, and the like. Thus, consciousness is a constantly evolving system.

Thinking in this way, it was not difficult to imagine that consciousness might progress, or evolve, through successive levels of complexity, like other complex systems such as forest ecologies or the matrices of metabolic interactions within living cells. For years I was fascinated by the idea that conscious experience might have undergone several transformations during the long course of human history. I read Ken Wilber's fascinating book, *Up From Eden*, when first published in the 1981, in which he argued that during the long course of history human consciousness has come through a series of transformations from one structure to another, and still other structures are possible in the future. Much of this book was based on earlier scholarship by the mid-twentieth-century European cultural philosopher Jean Gebser (1949/1986). Gebser was a cultural historian who discovered evidence of an emerging structure of "integral consciousness" in the work of modern poets, artists, scientists, and others. This new consciousness seemed to be multidimensional, carrying with it the ability to see objects in multiple perspectives, such as the models in Picasso's paintings, and through a more fluid experience of time, as in Duchamp's *Nude Descending a Staircase*. This freedom from what one might call Newtonian space–time also appeared in Einstein's theory of relativity and in the new quantum physics, and was experienced as well in certain poets such as Rilke and Lorca. Gebser believed it contained a spiritually luminous quality that he termed *diaphony*.

Having identified this new structure which was coming onto the horizon of human consciousness, Gebser began to search the past for evidence of earlier structures. He found several. These included an *archaic* structure, transitional between hominids and early human beings; a *magical* structure, through which the world is understood in terms of magical thinking and magical causality; a *mythic* structure in which the great enigmas about life and death as well as much else are explained by grand mythic narratives such as the tales of Zeus and Horus; and finally the currently dominant *mental* or rational structure that dictates realities through linear reasoning (e.g., in science and mathematics). A central feature of the newly emerging *integral* structure consciousness was that it incorporates all the previous structures so that, for Gebser, *to live the integral life meant to live all the structures of consciousness at once.*

Interestingly, Wilber did not agree with Gebser's notion of integral consciousness, and in its place saw the whole panorama of the evolving structures of consciousness in a developmental framework. Gebser may well have agreed with the developmental orientation were he still alive, but he had not systematically explored such an approach as Wilber would do in several subsequent books (e.g., Wilber 1998a, 1998b, 2000a, 2000b, 2007). It does not take too much imagination, however, to think of the consciousness of an infant as similar in its pre-linguistic simplicity to the archaic mind of an ancient hominid. And in early childhood we all seem to have been magical thinkers. Perhaps it is not so obvious that older children go through a mythic period before entering rational adulthood, for those who make it that far, but Wilber was among the first to point out that the mythical mind is also a literal mind, associated with a kind of blind following of rules while completely identifying with a particular role in society, such as being a midwife, soldier, scribe, or priest. To emphasize these features he named this form of consciousness the *mythic-membership* structure. With this in mind, it is reasonable to think that this structure corresponds to late childhood or early adolescence.

In fact, Wilber was building a case for the parallel development of consciousness across history and within the individual, a notion similar to the old idea that *ontogeny recapitulates phylogeny*. My own first response to this idea, like that of most psychologists, was to disagree with it as archaic and simplistic. In time, however, the evidence from many sides became overwhelming and I began to see that Wilber could well be right. It was a matter of coming to understand both the individual and historical growth of consciousness in the terms outlined by developmental psychologists such as Jean Piaget (1954), Laurence Kohlberg (1981), Robert Kegan (1982), and other current developmentalists.

The idea that structures of consciousness are developmental, coupled with the notion that they can be modeled in terms of underlying algorithmic processes, eventually suggested the idea that transitions between such structures might be "constructive," that is, they might grow out of the interactions between psychological process which, though in reality dynamical, can be approached as self-constructing algorithmic events of increasing complexity. To put this plainly, Piaget conceptualized the development of intelligence in children as passing through several stages, each defined by particular kinds of thought processes. Piaget called these *schemata* emphasizing that they are basic patterns of thought. When sufficiently complex they combine to form increasingly sophisticated and fluid systems of thought, eventually leading toward transitions to higher or more complex structures of intellectual development. Kohlberg understood moral growth in a similar fashion, each stage representing a particular kind of moral reasoning, while successive stages exhibit increasingly complex levels of moral thinking. Considering all this in terms of computer programs, my idea was that these *schemata* operate like to a soup of programming codes that interact in increasing complexity, and eventually will undergo dramatic bifurcations leading to new and higher orders of processing. In this way, each structure of consciousness can be thought of as a set of self-creating algorithms that grow through increasing levels of complexity toward entire system transitions that amount to increasingly complex and supple structures of consciousness. In the big picture, consciousness shifts gears several times during development, both individually or historically, from the archaic to the magic, then to the mythic, and finally to the mental structure of experience. According to Wilber, and I tend to agree with him, there are several more gears beyond the fourth gear of adult mental development.

Now, keep in mind that each of these structures represents a complete way of experiencing the world. Thus, we have before us the outline of a basic theory of the evolution of consciousness in history and in the person. Evidently, individuals living in each historical period grow from infancy up through the various structures of consciousness to whichever level their own culture and environment supports. Some grow to the highest level common to their own moment in history, while others seem to grind to a stop at less advanced levels. At any time there are people at all these levels interacting with each other and trying to get along together. If this is the case, it is no wonder that we humans often find it so difficult to get along with each other (e.g., see Beck and Cowan 1996; Wilber 2000b).

In each historical era a few people seem to push the envelope and create original ways to experience the world through new forms of intelligence. Wilber's forthcoming book, tentatively titled *Kosmic Karma and Creativity*, argues that the most advanced structures are still in formation and have not yet solidified. In the terms of American philosopher Charles Sanders Peirce the universe has not yet made a habit of them. Or, in terms of Neoplatonism they are still forming at the level of *nous*, or *logos*, just beneath the One, and are only now descending down into the level of *soul* and the world of everyday experience. If this is the case, it is interesting to ask who the evolutionary groundbreakers might be. The answer would seem to be the great artists, moral leaders, scientists, mathematicians, and spiritual guides of each generation. What they accomplish in their own lives helps set patterns for the future.

I first developed many of the above ideas in rough form in the book *The Radiance of Being: Complexity, Chaos, and the Evolution of Consciousness* (1995). Finding a publisher for the book was almost as difficult writing it. My agent was John White, a respected writer who had been Ken Wilber's first agent as well.

Wilber's first book, *The Spectrum of Consciousness*, had endured over thirty rejections before it was finally accepted and published by the Theosophical Press to become a bestseller. My book seemed to be following a similar trajectory, at least in terms of the rejections. Trade book publishers said it was too demanding for the average reader, and academic publishers did not like its "mix of science and spirituality." In fact, it was Ervin Laszlo who actually found it a Scottish publisher in the form of a forward-looking editor by the name of Christopher Moore, who was seeking manuscripts that represented what he felt were original ways of thinking about science and spirituality for the twenty-first century. Most of today's editors only guide a writer though the details of supplying a manuscript in proper form for the typesetter, but Christopher became seriously involved with the manuscript, helping me re-write whole sections of it to make a well-rounded book. As a result, the book was published first in the United Kingdom in 1995 and a couple years later in the United States. In 2002 it underwent a major revision, with new chapters and a Foreword by Ken Wilber, and at the time of this writing is available from Paragon House.

Shortly after the original 1995 publication of the book, Stanley Krippner and I began to work together on the ideas that were in it. With his help and encouragement they were refined in a series of papers that we developed together (Combs and Krippner 1998, 1999a, 1999b, 2003). In the meantime, the basic notion of psychological development as a series of increasingly complex interactive processes has gained support in the work of several significant developmental researchers (e.g., Kegan 1982; Cook-Greuter 1999; Fischer and Bidell 1998), and the idea that the course of the developmental pathway through human history mirrors the developmental path of the child is also finding wide support (e.g., Barnes 2000; Combs 2002; Feuerstein 1987; Wilber 1981, 2000a; as well as histories of consciousness and art such as Gablik 1976, and Richter 1937/1982).

For me, one of the most exciting aspects of all this has been the possibility of pushing the model at the top end of development to see where it takes us in terms of human potentials. With this in mind, Stanley and I published a paper that examines the whole issue of higher states of consciousness (Combs and Krippner 2003). Our conclusions are generally in agreement with Wilber's work on the same topic, namely that the highest structures tend to correlate with the subtle realms mapped long ago by the scholars of Vedanta. But our approach differs in its stress on the inner structural dynamics of experience. In agreement with Wilber, it emphasizes the transformation of one's sense of self, which softens and becomes more transparent at high levels of personal evolution, a notion that has received empirical supported in the work by Susanne Cook-Greuter (1999). It also points to an enlarging sense of wholeness and self-awareness, in large part due to the integration of previously disparate attractors in a person's mental atmosphere, an idea that is also explored from a dynamical systems perspective by psychoanalyst S. R. Palombo (1999).

The richness of dynamical systems approach for the understanding of consciousness has been rewarding in other ways as well. For instance, when applied to the brain and the sleeping mind it leads to a theory of dreams, which Stanley and I have developed over several publications (Combs and Krippner 1998; Kahn,

Krippner, and Combs 2000, 2002; Krippner and Combs 2002). The basic idea is that during dream sleep neuronal processes in the brain form strange attractor patterns. These patterns are also formed in wakefulness (e.g., Freemen 1991, 2001), but while dreaming the brain is suspended in a kind of virtual reality state in which it is shut off from sensory input from the outside world. At the same time the neurochemistry of the brain changes to allow a freer flow of spontaneous activity than during wakefulness. Combine these changes with the fact that certain areas of the brain, such as the limbic system, are more active during dreaming, while others, such as the prefrontal lobe, are less active, and the resulting attractor patterns become highly responsive to the slightest nudge by residual emotions, faint memories from the day, and so on. Perhaps even the whisper of subtle PSI influences can be felt in the brain during dreaming. Evidence from research carried over several years by Krippner (1993) in the Maimonides dream laboratory suggests this to be the case.

This theory of the dreaming brain recognizes the importance of dreaming as a neurological process without overlooking the importance of understanding dreams from a psychological viewpoint as well. It is our guess that once the initial conditions are set and a dream is put into motion, it then tends to follow the natural course of the imagination, which has something to do with the creative interactions of the various processes of the mind, discussed above, and the tendency of the human mind, and the human brain, to create narratives and to understand the world in terms of them. In a sense, dreams are total immersions in mythic and magical experiential realities.

Other applications of the general model of the mind and consciousness discussed in these pages include its use for understanding creativity in the individual. To this end I recently joined forces with Monty Montuori, the editor of this book, Ruth Richards, a creativity researcher at the Saybrook Institute, and David Loye (Montuori, Combs, and Richards 2004), to work on an understanding of creativity modeled after creative processes that universally characterize highly complex systems. This work is based in the pioneering research of Frank Baron (1995), who spent years studying the characteristics of highly creative people, to discover how they differ from ordinary people. His thinking on this topic represents one of the first and finest uses of systems thinking in psychology. Building on his ground-breaking research, we added ideas about how the interacting elements of the self-creating system of the mind combine and recombine to form new and creative outcomes which are then built back into the evolving mind.

Currently I am working again with Stanley Krippner as well as Jamesian scholar Eugene Taylor to explore the enormously rich thinking of William James on the nature of mind and consciousness in the context of our model of consciousness as a self-creating event. Many of James' observations and reflections are nothing short of striking in their accord with this notion. Perhaps this is not surprising, since my own earliest work was inspired by James' writings, and especially his emphasis on consciousness as a process. Moreover, the direct introspective observation of conscious experience, and in particular the mind itself, on which James based so much his psychology, seems to me exactly the right place to start as well. One gets the feeling that the chaotic systems approach to consciousness can become at least one direct continuation of James's own brilliant work, left incomplete after the First World War and the rise of Behaviorism in psychology. Topics in the works include an extension of James's thinking on disassociation, after a century again now finding a central place in psychology, and a further refining of the developmental model of the structures of consciousness placing more stress on James's approach to conscious experience itself.

Now, this brings the story of my ideas about systems theory, chaos, and consciousness, up to date at the time of this writing. Many of my current thoughts are developed in my most recent book, *Consciousness Explained Better* (2009), which emphasizes a process understanding of consciousness as seen though many perspectives. Wilber recently endorsed it as, "the finest book on consciousness written in modern times." Needless to say, this endorsement was rewarding to me after so many years of pursuing an understanding of consciousness.

Recently I was offered a senor faculty position at California Institute of Integral Studies, teaching in an online transdisciplinary doctoral program created by Alfonso Mountori, a friend and also a colleague form GERG. My wife and I have moved to the Bay Area, where we enjoy the rich cultural and spiritual atmosphere of this part of the world.

Now, on reflection it seems to me that life itself is a species of strange attractor. We all communicate ideas and sentiments to others and they to us in a rich ecology of community. The extent of my influence on others, for better or for worse, I can only reckon. Likewise, my own life has been molded by their ideas and sentiments. It seems to me that we are all a bit like social spiders, each darting to and fro on a scintillating web of ever-widening arcs of communication, transmitted across the web by vibrations and felt through our whole bodies. We all inhabit dimensionless networks of thoughts, feelings, and ideas which, no matter how private, or how strongly we feel them to be our very own, take form though a community autopoiesis in which all who play the game of creative thought can make their own contribution to the larger event of the evolution of wisdom.

NOTES

1. Much later, when I was in college myself, a prominent perceptual psychologist said about all this, "I wouldn't take it too seriously!"
2. During this period in the '50s it was widely held that comic books were the downfall of the younger generation. Later it was discovered that the real curse was rock and roll.
3. He died a few years later when his sports car fell on him while he was tuning it. His best advice to me about authorship was, "Write in singing English!" This did not help get me published, but when I did finally make it into print I began to see the truth of it.

REFERENCES

Abraham, R. 1982–1988. *Dynamics, the geometry of behavior*. Santa Cruz: Aerial Press.
Arbib, M. A. 1964. *Brains, machines and mathematics*. New York: McGraw-Hill.
Barnes, H. B. 2000. *Stages of thought: The co-evolution of religious thought and science*. New York: Oxford University Press.
Baron, F. 1995. *No rootless flower: An ecology of creativity*. Cresskill, NJ: Hampton Press.

Beck, D., and C. Cowan. 1996. *Spiral dynamics: Mastering values, leadership, and change (developmental management)*. Cambridge, MA: Blackwell.

Chaisson, E. 2001. *Cosmic evolution: The rise of complexity in nature*. Cambridge, MA: Harvard University Press.

Combs, A. 1995. *The Radiance of being: Complexity, chaos, and the evolution of consciousness*. Edinburgh: Floris Books.

———. 2002. *The Radiance of being: Understanding the grand integral vision; Living the integral life*. St. Paul, MN: Paragon House.

———. 2009. *Consciousness explained better: Towards an integral understanding of the multifaceted nature of consciousness*. St. Paul, MN: Paragon House.

Combs, A., and S. Krippner. 1998. Dream sleep and waking reality: A dynamical view of two states of consciousness. In *Toward a science of consciousness: The second Tucson discussions and debates*, Eds. Hameroff, S., Kaszniak, A. W. and Scott, A. C., 487–493. Cambridge, MA: MIT Press.

———. 1999a. Consciousness, evolution, and spiritual growth: A critique and model. *World Futures* 53 (3): 193–212.

———. 1999b. Spiritual growth and the evolution of consciousness: Complexity, evolution, and the farther reaches of human nature. *The International Journal of Transpersonal Studies* 18 (1): 9–19.

Combs, A., M. Winkler, and C. Daley. 1994. A chaotic systems analysis of circadian rhythms in feeling states. *The Psychological Record* 44:359–368.

Combs, A., E. Laszlo, R. Artigiani, and V. Csányi, Eds. 1996. *Changing visions: Human cognitive maps, past, present and future*. London: Adamantine Press; Westport, CT: Praeger.

Cook-Greuter, S. 1999. *Postautonomous ego development: A study of its nature and measurement*. Unpublished doctoral dissertation. Cambridge, MA: Harvard University. *Dissertation Abstracts International-B*, 60-06.

Eisler, R., D. Loye, and Norgaard, K. 1995. Women, men, and the global quality of life. www.partnershipway.org (Accessed December 15, 1998).

Feuerstein, G. 1987. *Structures of consciousness: The genius of Jean Gebser*. Lower Lake, CA: Integral Publishing.

Fischer, K. W., and T. R. Bidell. 1998. Dynamic development of psychological structures in action and thought. In *Handbook of child psychology: Vol. 1: Theoretical models of human development* (5th ed.), Ed. Learner, R. M., pp. 1–141. New York: John Wiley & Sons.

Freeman, W. 2001. *How brains make up their minds*. New York: Columbia University Press.

Freeman, W. J. 1991. The physiology of perception. *Scientific American* (February): 78–85.

Gablik, S. 1976. *Progress in art*. New York: Rizzoli.

Gebser, J. 1949/1986. *The ever–present origin*, Trans. Barstad, N. and Mickunas, A. Athens: Ohio University Press.

Goerner, S. 1999. *After the clockwork universe: The emerging science and culture of integral society*. Edinburgh, Scotland: Floris Books.

Goerner, S. J. 1994. *Chaos and the evolving ecological universe*. New York: Gordon & Breach.

Goertzel, B. 1993a. *The structure of intelligence*. New York: Springer-Verlag.

———. 1993b. *The evolving mind*. New York: Gordon & Breach.

———. 1994. *Chaotic logic: Language, mind and reality, from the perspective of complex systems science*. New York: Plenum.

———. 1997. *From complexity to creativity: Explorations in evolutionary, autopoietic, and cognitive dynamics*. New York: Plenum.

Hannah, T. 1991. *Mood fluctuations and daily stress: The contribution of a dynamical systems approach.* Paper presented at the Inaugural meeting of The Society for Chaos Theory in Psychology and the Life Sciences, San Francisco, CA.

Hodgkin, A. L., and A. F. Huxley. 1952. A quantitative description of membrane current and its application to conduction and excitation in the nerve. *Journal of Physiology* 117: 500–544.

James, W. 1890/1981. *The principles of psychology.* Cambridge, MA: Harvard University Press.

———. 1987. The varieties of religious experience. In *William James: Writings, 1902–1910,* ed. B. Kuklick. (pp. 1–478). New York: The Library of America.

Kahn, D., S. Krippner, and A. Combs. 2000. Dreaming and the self-organizing brain. *Journal of Consciousness Studies: Controversies in Science and the Humanities* 7 (7): 4–11.

———. 2002. Dreaming as a function of chaos-like stochastic processes in the self-organizing brain. *Nonlinear Dynamics, Psychology, and Life Sciences* 6 (4): 311–322.

Kampis, G. 1991. *Self-modifying systems in biology and cognitive science.* New York: Pergamon.

Kegan, R. 1982. *The evolving self.* Cambridge, MA: Harvard University Press.

Kohlberg, L. 1981. *Essays on moral development* (Vol. 1). San Francisco: Harper & Row.

Krippner, S. 1993. Telepathy and dreaming. In *Encyclopedia of sleep and dreaming,* Eds. Carskadon, M. A., 612–613. New York: Macmillan.

Krippner, S., and A. Combs. 2000. Self-organization in the dreaming brain. *The Journal of Mind and Behavior* 21:399–412.

Kuhn, T. 1962. *The structure of scientific revolutions.* Chicago: University of Chicago Press.

Laszlo, E. 1987. *Evolution: The grand synthesis.* Boston: Shambhala.

Lilly, J. 1972. *The center of the cyclone: An autobiography of inner space.* New York: Bantam Books.

Loye, D. 1984. *The sphinx and the rainbow.* New York: Bantam Books.

Maslow, C. 1968. *Towards a psychology of being.* Princeton: Van Nostrand.

McCaskill, J., and P. Wagler. 2000. From reconfigurability to evolution in construction systems: Spanning the electronic, microfluidic and biomolecular domains. *International Conference on Field Programmable Logic and its Applications,* 286–299.

McCulloch, W. S. 1965. *Embodiments of mind.* Cambridge, MA: MIT Press.

Melnechuk, T. 1990, October 15. Personal Communication with author (e-mail).

Montuori, A., A. Combs, and R. Richards. 2004. Creativity, consciousness, and the direction of human development. In *The great adventure: Toward a human theory,* Ed. Loye, D., 197–398. Albany, New York: SUNY Press.

Palombo, S. R. 1999. *The emergent ego: Complexity and coevolution in the psychoanalytic process.* Madison, CT: International Universities Press.

Piaget, J. 1954. *The construction of reality in children.* New York: Basic Books.

Prigogine, I., and I. Stengers. 1984. *Order out of chaos: Man's new dialogue with nature.* New York: Bantam.

Richter, G. 1937/1982. *Art and human consciousness.* New York: Anthroposophic Press.

Rogers, C. 1961. *On becoming a person: A therapist's view of psychotherapy.* Boston: Houghton Miffflin.

Sperry, R. W. 1993. The impact and promise of the cognitive revolution. *American Psychologist* 48:878–885.

Tart, C. T. 1975. *States of consciousness.* New York: Dutton.

Varela, F., H. R. Maturana, and R. Uribe. 1974. Autopoiesis: The organization of living systems, its characterization and a model. *Biosystems* 5:187–196.

Wilber, K. 1977. *The spectrum of conciousness*. Wheaton, IL: Theosophical Publishing House.

———. 1981. *Up from Eden: A transpersonal view of human evolution*. Garden City, NY: Doubleday.

———. 1998a. *Integral psychology*. Boston: Shambhala.

———. 1998b. *The eye of the spirit: An integral vision for a world gone slightly wrong*. Boston: Shambhala.

———. 2000a. *Sex, ecology, spirituality: The spirit of evolution;* 2nd edition. Boston: Shambhala.

———. 2000b. *A theory of everything: An integral vision for business, politics, science and spirituality*. Boston: Shambhala.

———. 2007. *Integral spirituality: A startling new role for religion in the modern and postmodern world*. Boston: Shambhala.

HUMAN POSSIBILITIES: AN INTEGRATED SYSTEMS APPROACH

RIANE EISLER

Center for Partnership Studies, Pacific Grove, California, USA

A basic principle of systems theory is that if we do not look at the whole of a system, we cannot see the connections between its various components. This article describes the author's personal and research journey developing a new method of inquiry and a new theory of cultural evolution that takes into account the whole of our history (including prehistory), the whole of our species (both its male and female halves), and the whole of social relations (from politics and economics to family and other intimate relations). It reveals connections and patterns not visible using smaller data bases and casts a new, more hopeful, light on our past, present, and the possibilities for our future.

My interest in social systems is not only intellectual. It is rooted in my early life experiences. On November 10, 1938—later known as Crystal Night because so much glass was shattered in Jewish stores, homes, and synagogues—a gang of Nazis came for my father, shoved him down the stairs, and dragged him off. Miraculously, my mother obtained his release, and my parents and I fled my native Vienna to Paris, and from there to Cuba. Had we remained in Europe, we would almost certainly have been killed, as were most of our relatives.

These childhood experiences led to burning questions. Why is there so much cruelty, destructiveness, and hate in the world? Is this our inevitable lot? Or can we create a more peaceful, just, and caring world?

As I grew up, I looked for answers to these questions in books and universities, but I never found satisfactory ones. Then I took a job as a social scientist at the Systems Development Corporation, an offshoot of the RAND Corporation. I did not like the work because my employers were only interested in military systems. But I learned a basic principle of systems thinking: that looking at how different parts of a system interact makes it possible to see more than just the sum of the system's parts.

I was not aware at that time that studying social systems would become my life's work. That was in the 1950s, and many things happened before I returned to the fundamental questions I had never answered. By the time I did, it was the 1970s. Like many of us, I saw that the growing global crises futurists then called the *world problematique* cannot be solved by the system that created them. At our level of technological development, violence to settle international disputes is not sustainable. Neither is the once hallowed "conquest of nature" sustainable at a time when advanced technologies are causing environmental damage of unprecedented magnitude. I saw that a grim future awaits my children—and all of us—unless there are transformative social changes.

But transformation to what? Can we really construct a social system that supports more just, balanced, and peaceful relationships? If so, what does such a system look like? And how can we accelerate the shift to this type of social system worldwide?

As I embarked on my systematic analysis of human societies, I developed the *study of relational dynamics.* This is a method of inquiry that differs markedly from traditional studies of society. To begin with, it draws from a much wider data base. Conventional studies, including most systems studies, focus on politics and economics. The study or relational dynamics looks at the *whole* of our lives—including our family and other intimate relations. Unlike the majority of studies (often aptly called "the study of man"), this method takes into account the *whole* of humanity—both its female and male halves. And rather than examining one period at a time, it looks at the *whole* span of history—including the long period before written records called prehistory.

A basic principle of systems theory is that if we do not look at the whole of a system, we cannot see the connections between its various components—just as if we look at only part of a picture, we cannot see the relationship between its different parts. Using the more complete data base of the study of relational dynamics makes it possible to see connections between different parts of social systems that are not visible otherwise.

Some connections I recognized from earlier studies, such as the work of psychologists documenting the connection between the family backgrounds of "authoritarian" versus "democratic" personalities and religious and racial prejudice, as well as the writings of feminist scholars on the link between social violence and a male socialization for conquest and domination. But I also saw larger patterns that had not been identified within the scope of modern science—patterns that began to answer my questions about viable alternatives to chronic violence, insensitivity, and suffering.

With these patterns in mind, I gradually developed the theoretical strands of *human possibilities theory.* The first strand, drawing from a re-examination of human cultural evolution, is the *cultural transformation theory* introduced in my book *The Chalice and the Blade* and other works (Eisler 1987, 1995, 2000, 2002, 2007). The most recent strand, drawing from a re-examination of human biological evolution and new findings from neuroscience, is what I call *bioculturalism.*[1] Together, these strands provide an integrative conceptual framework for understanding the interactive relationship between biology, culture, and human agency.

FROM CONVENTIONAL CATEGORIES
TO HOLISTIC FRAMEWORKS

Like systems, chaos, evolution, and complexity theory, human possibilities theory recognizes that, like other living systems, a cultural system is not a static entity. It is a human-made, self-organizing, self-maintaining, and self constructing network of component-producing processes.[2] That is, a cultural system maintains itself through the interaction of key components that together maintain and regenerate the culture's basic character.[3]

My first challenge therefore was to identify the key components of cultural systems. It soon became clear that conventional social categories, such as ancient/modern, Eastern/Western, religious/secular, rightist/leftist, technologically developed/undeveloped, and capitalist/communist are not useful in this regard.

Religious/secular, Eastern/Western, and ancient/modern are shorthand for ideological, geographic, and time differences. Right/left and liberal/conservative describe political orientations. Industrial, pre-industrial, and post-industrial describe levels of technological development. Capitalism and communism are labels for different economic systems. Democratic/authoritarian describe political systems in which there are, or are not, elections.[4]

In short, none of these categories take into account the totality of the institutions, assumptions, beliefs, relationships, and activities that constitute a culture. Indeed, these conventional social categories do not even take into account the cultural construction of the primary human relations: the formative childhood relations and the relations between the male and female halves of humanity—even though these relations are basic to our species' survival and to what children learn to view as normal or abnormal, possible or impossible, moral or immoral.[5]

Because the quality of the relations a child experiences and observes plays a critical role in the development of nothing less than the human brain, we need categories that take into account the cultural construction of parent–child relations. Because we are a dimorphic species, we need classifications that take into account the cultural construction of the roles and relations of the female and male halves of humanity. Because people spend most of their lives in the day-to-day relations of family, school, and local community, we need categories that include what happens in the private sphere as well as the larger public political and economic sphere. And because our problems—personal, political, economic, and ecological—revolve around how we relate to ourselves, others, and the Earth, we need social classifications that show what kinds of relations a culture supports or inhibits, be it in families or in the family of nations.

With these matters in mind, my second challenge was to search for patterns, cross-culturally and historically. Using the large data base described above, what gradually became apparent were social configurations that repeat themselves cross-culturally and historically—configurations that are not visible through the fragmenting lenses of old social categories.

There were no names for these social configurations. So I called one the *domination model* and the other the *partnership model.*

The partnership model and the domination model are self-organizing and non-linear. They describe mutually supporting interactions of key systems components that maintain a particular systems configuration.

These interactions establish and maintain two very different types of relations—from intimate to international. One type is based on rigid rankings of domination ultimately backed up by fear and force. The other type is based on mutual respect, mutual accountability, and mutual benefit.

No society orients completely to either the domination model or the partnership model. This is why I called this new integrated conceptual framework for the analysis of cultures the *partnership/domination continuum.* And what I found is that the degree to which a society or time period orients to either end of this continuum profoundly affects which of our large repertoire of human traits and behaviors is culturally reinforced or inhibited.

THE PARTNERSHIP/DOMINATION CONTINUUM

The interaction of the core elements of the domination model and the partnership model can best be understood in terms of systems self-organization theory. This is not a matter of linear causes and effects, but of continual interactions between the core elements of the system.

We see this if we look at some of the most brutally violent, repressive societies of the twentieth century: Hitler's Germany (a technologically advanced, Western, rightist society), Stalin's USSR (a secular leftist society), Khomeini's Iran (an Eastern religious society), and Idi Amin's Uganda (a tribalist society). There are obvious differences between these cultures. But they all share the core configuration of the domination model.

The first component of the core domination configuration is a structure of rigid top-down rankings: hierarchies of domination maintained through physical, psychological, and economic control. This structure is found in both the family and the state or tribe, and is the template or mold for all social institutions.

The second core component is the rigid ranking of one half of humanity over the other half. Theoretically, this could be the female half over the male half. But historically, it has been the ranking of the male half over the female half. Along with this ranking of male over female, we see the higher valuing of "hard" qualities and behaviors, such as "heroic" violence and "manly" conquest and control. I want to emphasize that these are *not* qualities inherent in men but rather qualities stereotypically associated with "real masculinity" in domination ideology.

The third core component of the domination model is culturally accepted abuse and violence, from child and wife beating to chronic warfare. Every society has some abuse and violence. But in cultures orienting to the domination model, we find the institutionalization and even idealization of abuse and violence to maintain hierarchies of domination—man over woman, man over man, race over race, religion over religions, tribe over tribe, nation over nation.

The fourth core component consists of beliefs that relations of domination and submission (beginning with the domination of male over female) are inevitable, normal, and even moral. Hence, in cultures and subcultures that orient closely to the domination model, we find teachings and stories that it is honorable and moral to kill and enslave neighboring nations or tribes, stone women to death, stand by while "inferior" races are put in ovens and gassed, or beat children to impose one's will. In this belief system, there are only two options. You either dominate or you are dominated. Therefore, both war and the "war of the sexes" are inevitable. The guiding belief is that there is no other alternative.

The partnership model has a very different core configuration. The basic template of this model also consists of four interactive, mutually supporting components.

The first core component is a democratic and egalitarian structure. This structure is found in both the family and the state or tribe, and is the template for other institutions. That is not to say that there are no rankings. But they are what I call *hierarchies of actualization* rather than *hierarchies of domination*. These are more flexible hierarchies in which power is viewed not as power *over* but as power *to* and power *with*: the kind of power described in the progressive management literature today as empowering rather than disempowering, as inspiring and supporting rather than controlling.

The second core component is equal partnership between women and men. With this comes a high valuing, in *both* women and men, of qualities and behaviors such as nonviolence, nurturance, and caregiving—qualities denigrated as "soft," feminine," and "unmanly" in the domination model.

The third core component of the partnership model is that abuse and violence is not culturally accepted. This doesn't mean that there is no abuse or violence. But they do not have to be institutionalized or idealized because they are not needed to maintain rigid rankings of domination.

The fourth core component consists of beliefs about human nature that support empathic and mutually respectful relations. Although cruelty and violence are recognized as human possibilities, they are not considered inevitable and normal, much less moral.

Cultures that orient to the partnership end of the partnership/domination continuum also transcend conventional categories such as religious or secular, Eastern or Western, industrial, pre-industrial, or post-industrial, and so on. Contemporary examples include tribal societies as well as pre-industrial and technologically advanced nations.

For example, the forest Teduray, as anthropologist Stuart Schlegel writes, can best be described as a partnership society. He writes: "I used to call them 'radically egalitarian.' But... they have the core configuration characteristic of the partnership model: they are generally egalitarian, women and men have equal status, and they are peaceful." In describing his fieldwork among the Teduray, Schlegel (1998, 244) further writes: "Family and social structure were egalitarian and social relations unranked and peaceful. Decision-making was typically participatory; softer, stereotypically 'feminine' virtues were valued; and community well-being was the principal motivation for work and other activities. Nature and the human body were given great respect. The emphasis on technology was on enhancing and sustaining life" (244).

The agrarian Minagkabau also orient to the partnership model. The Minagkabau are the fourth largest ethnic group in the Sumatran archipelago, numbering about four million people. As among the Teduray, here women play major social roles, violence is not part of Minagkabau childraising, and stereotypically feminine values such as caring and nurturing are valued—not only in women but also in men. In contrast to more domination-oriented ideologies, in the Minagkabau belief system nurture is a basic principle of nature.

As the anthropologist Peggy Sanday reports,

> The Minagkabau weave order out of their version of wild nature by appeal to maternal archetypes. Unlike Darwin in the 19th century, the Minagkabau subordinate male dominion and competition, which we consider basic to human social ordering and evolution, to the work of maternal nurture, which they hold to be necessary for the common good and the healthy society. ... Social well-being is found in natural growth and fertility according to the dictum that the unfurling, blooming, and growth in nature is our teacher. (2002, 22–24)

As among the Teduray, among the Minagkabau mediation for violence prevention and non-escalation have been developed to encourage a peaceable way of life. Sanday writes: "Childcare is not authoritarian or punitive. I have never seen any child hit or even slapped. ... The socialization techniques fit what one would expect from the peacefulness of Minagkabau interpersonal relations."[6]

Over that last several centuries, especially in technologically developed, industrialized Western countries, there has been movement toward the partnership end of the continuum. And this orientation to the partnership configuration is today most clearly visible in Nordic societies such as Sweden, Finland, Iceland, and Norway.

THE NORDIC EXPERIENCE

These Nordic nations are not ideal societies. But they are democratic cultures where there are not huge gaps between haves and have-nots, where women have higher status, and where nurturance and nonviolence are considered appropriate behavior for men as well as women and are supported by fiscal policy.

These countries have a successful mix of free enterprise and central planning. They were the first nations to move toward more industrial democracy, pioneering teamwork by self-directed groups to replace assembly lines where workers are mere cogs in the industrial machine. They have low poverty rates, low crime rates, and have succeeded in creating a generally good living standard for all.

This success has sometimes been attributed to the fact that these nations are relatively small and homogeneous. But smaller and even more homogeneous societies, such as some of the oil-rich nations of the Middle East where there are large gaps between haves and have-nots, orient closely to the domination model. So to understand why the Nordic nations developed a more caring and equitable economics we have to look at other factors.

Table 1
The Domination System and the Partnership System

Component	Domination System	Partnership System
1. Structure	Authoritarian structure of ranking and *hierarchies of domination* in *both* family and state or tribe.	Democratic structure of linking and *hierarchies of actualization* in *both* family and state or tribe.
2. Gender	Ranking of the male half of humanity over the female half, as well as rigid gender stereotypes, with traits and activities viewed as masculine, such as "toughness" and conquest, ranked over those seen as feminine, such as "softness" and caregiving.	Equal valuing of the male and female halves of humanity, as well as fluid gender roles with a high valuing of empathy, caring, caregiving, and nonviolence in both women and men, as well as in social and economic policy.
3. Relations	High degree of fear, abuse, and violence ranging from child and wife beating to other forms of abuse by "superiors" in families, workplaces, and society. Children grow up in punitive, authoritarian, male-dominated families where they observe and experience inequality and inequity as the accepted norm.	Mutual respect and trust with a low degree of fear, abuse, and violence, since they are not required to maintain rigid rankings of domination. Children grow up in families where parenting is authoritative rather than authoritarian and adult relations are egalitarian and equitable.
4. Beliefs	Beliefs and stories that justify and idealize domination and violence, which are presented as inevitable, moral, and desirable.	Beliefs and stories that give high value to empathic, mutually beneficial, nonviolent relations, which are considered moral and desirable.

Adapted from Riane Eisler, *The Power of Partnership,* New World Library, 2002.

One important factor is that in countries such as Sweden, Norway, Finland, and Iceland there is much greater partnership between women and men in both the family and the state. Women have in the Nordic world held the highest political offices, and a larger proportion of legislators (approximately 40 percent) are female than anywhere else in the world.

As among the Teduray and Minagkabau, the higher status of women in the Nordic world has important consequences for how men define masculinity. As the status of women rises, so also does the status of traits and activities that are in domination-oriented cultures unacceptable in men because they are stereotypically associated with "inferior" femininity. These traits become more highly valued in, and by, both men and women. So along with the higher status of women in the Nordic world, came fiscal priorities that support more stereotypically "feminine" values and activities. These more partnership-oriented nations pioneered caring policies such as government-supported childcare, universal healthcare, and paid parental leave.

As a result of these more stereotypically "feminine" caring policies, countries such as Finland, Sweden, and Norway, which earlier suffered from extreme poverty—including severe famines that led to waves of immigration to the United

States—became prosperous. This contradicts still another reason sometimes given for more humane Nordic social policies: that these policies were due to greater prosperity. As Hilkka Pietila documents, in reality, these policies were the cause, not effect, of greater prosperity (2001; Eisler 2007).

Nordic nations also pioneered laws prohibiting violence against children in families. They have a strong men's movement against male violence toward women. They pioneered nonviolent conflict resolution, establishing the first peace studies programs when the rest of the world only had war academies. In other words, in conformity with the partnership configuration, they have worked hard to leave behind entrenched traditions of violence in both intimate and international relations.

In addition, Nordic nations pioneered environmentally sound manufacturing approaches. For example, the "Natural Step," where materials are recycled even after they reach the consumer to avoid pollution and waste, came out of Sweden. These nations also contribute a larger percentage of their annual gross domestic product to international programs working for economic development, environmental protection, and human rights than other developed nations—a fact that frontally contradicts the notion that these nations are more caring because of their homogeneity, since their large investment in the developing world is to benefit people who are very different from them.

These are *not* coincidental developments. They are all outcomes of the fact that the core configuration of the Nordic world orients more to the partnership model rather than domination model.

But without the analytical lens of the partnership–domination continuum, the patterns I just described seem random and disconnected. Indeed, looked at through the lenses of conventional social categories, we cannot even see these patterns, as we lack the conceptual framework to analyze the dynamics of the core components that interact to form the domination model and the partnership model as two underlying possibilities for structuring societies.

BUILDING A NEW THEORY

Human possibilities theory examines a large field of complex interactions, but simplifies these by focusing on core systems dynamics. It examines the complex interactions between four key interactive relationships:

1. The interactive relationship between biology and culture;
2. The interactive relationship of the core elements of a culture;
3. The interactive relationship between cultural beliefs and institutions and different kinds of human experiences, behaviors, and relationships;
4. The interactive relationship of all the above.

Human possibilities theory proposes that the conflict between the partnership model and the domination model as two basic ways of structuring institutions, beliefs, and behaviors underlies human cultural evolution. It further proposes that by examining this conflict we can more effectively predict the outcome of different personal and cultural choices. Most importantly, we can more effectively intervene in our personal and collective futures.

In constructing human possibilities theory, I was influenced by the whole family of new theories variously known as systems, cybernetic, chaos, evolutionary, and complexity theories. Some of my theory-building draws from these theories, some of it parallels them, and some of it expands them by focusing on matters that are not included in them.

My work also draws from other new scholarly strands, including gender and women's studies. And it draws from both new and early research in both biological and social science in its focus on the interaction between biology and culture and between genes, cultures, and individual beliefs and behaviors.

But human possibilities theory provides a new connectivity to some of the insights advanced by earlier scholars by offering the new, more inclusive conceptual framework of the partnership/domination continuum as well as cultural transformation theory and bio-culturalism. It also takes findings from neuroscience, which have largely focused on individuals, and applies them to cultures.

The premise of human possibilities theory that biology has to be considered in studying humanity is certainly not new; it goes back to Charles Darwin, and earlier evolutionary studies. The premise that culture plays a major role in how humans view the world and live in it is also not new. It is the basis of sociology, of classic works such as those of Emile Durkheim, Wilfredo Pareto, Max Weber, Pitirim Sorokin, Karl Marx, and other notable figures in the field. Anthropological studies such as those of Franz Boas, Ruth Benedict, Margaret Mead, and Geoffrey Gorer have also contributed to our understanding that cultural variations are reflected in people's beliefs and actions.

Also not new is the idea key to human possibilities theory that early childhood experiences profoundly affect how we see the world and live in. This is an insight widely discussed and documented in psychological literature, and was foundational to the works of Sigmund Freud, Alfred Adler, Karen Horney, and other pioneers in the field. The more recent work of neuroscientists such as Bruce Perry, Debra Niehoff, Steven Quartz, and Terrence Sejnowski verify this on a biological level.

The tenet that the social construction of the roles and relations of women and men is a key component of culture is also not new. This has been discussed and documented by many feminist scholars, from Charlotte Perkins Gilman and Elizabeth Cady Stanton to belle hooks, Kate Millett, and Susan Moller Okin. Anthropologist such as Peggy Sanday and Stuart Schlegel and cultural historians such as Renate Bridenthal and Claudia Koonz have focused on the connection between culture and the status of women, and social psychologists such as Wilhelm Reich and cultural geographers such as James DeMeo have examined the connection between the cultural construction of sexuality and the totality of a culture's worldview and institutions.

Evolutionary systems thinkers such as Sally Goerner, David Loye, and John O'Manique have in recent years also advanced theories connecting biological evolution and cultural evolution, with insights that in key ways parallel those advanced by the bio-culturalism proposed by human possibilities theory. Other evolutionary systems theorists such as Ervin Laszlo, Allan Combs, Bruce Weber, David Depew, and Ken Wilber have also made important contributions to a more systemic approach to evolution.

The intent of human possibilities theory is not to compete with any of these theories. It is to complement them. I emphasize this because one of the characteristics of contemporary science is its intense competitiveness, which along with the compartmentalization and fragmentation of the modern academy, has made it difficult to bring together diverse insights into a more inclusive and integrated explanatory whole.

TOWARD A UNIFIED THEORY OF EVOLUTION

In searching for an inclusive explanatory whole, I not only reexamined cultural evolution but also biological evolution. Here too I was influenced by new theoretical approaches. In the 1980s a number of international scholars came together in a new group that called itself the General Evolution Research Group (GERG). We spanned many disciplines, from astrophysics, chemistry, and biology to sociology, social psychology, and history. My husband, social psychologist and evolutionary theorist, David Loye, and I were two of the co-founders of this group, which was largely inspired by the systems philosopher Ervin Laszlo. It later expanded to include Ilya Prigogine and other leaders in what is sometimes called the new science.

One of our aims was to re-examine evolution from the perspective of general systems theory. We were not proposing any ultimate causality but rather that evolution is a self-organizing process that can be better understood by transcending the conventional fragmented approach to the study of evolution focusing on the history of particular species.

Today, the principle of self-organization is increasingly recognized in the natural sciences. Examples are the theories about how chemical systems maintain themselves or are transformed at critical bifurcations points advanced by Ilya Prigogine and Isable Stengers (chaos theory) and the biological and evolutionary theories of Humberto Maturana (autopoiesis) and Vilmos Csanyi (autogenesis).

This principle also operates in the living systems we call societies. However, principles from the natural sciences cannot be exported wholesale into the social sciences. There are some isomorphisms between different levels of evolution. But at each new level of evolution, new governing dynamics emerge.[7]

This does not mean that older processes are no longer operant. When life appeared on our planet, physical processes still operated. But now they interacted with newer biological processes. With the emergence of our species, another level of evolutionary dynamics emerged. Consequently, what happens at the human level cannot, as has been proposed by many earlier evolutionary scientists, just be reduced to the principles of natural selection and sexual selection. Although human cultures are living systems in which chemical and biological processes are operant, a whole host of additional processes come into play at the human level.

Charles Darwin, as well as Theodosius Dobzhansky, Julian Huxley, and Ernst Mayr, three of the prime architects of the neo-Darwinian synthesis, all emphasized that human evolution transcends prior evolutionary dynamics. Dobzhansky specifically emphasized the importance of culture in human affairs. He wrote, "The most significant product, and the paramount determining factor, of human evolution is culture" and "culture is not transmitted biologically through some special genes; it is acquired anew in every generation by learning and instruction, in large part through the medium of the symbolic language" (1968, 236).

These are also basic premises of the bio-culturalism I propose. Bio-culturalism posits that in studying human behaviors, we have to take into account the interaction between genes and experiences as influenced by our environments—and that the most important environments for humans at this point in our evolution are our cultural environments. In other words, our human experiences are largely molded by our cultures.

Certainly all human behaviors, including our great capacity for learning, have a biological base. But we humans have a very large behavioral repertoire. Insensitivity, cruelty, violence, and destructiveness are human possibilities. And so also are consciousness, empathy, caring, and creativity. If they were not, we would not be capable of them. And both of these different sets of capacities are part of our biological repertoire, which developed in the course of evolution.

In this sense, sociobiologists and evolutionary psychologists are right in arguing that we need to take biology into account to understand human behavior and human society. But they are not right in claiming that our behaviors today are the result of millennia-old evolutionary imperatives that inexorably drive us to violence and domination.

As Loye writes, to understand and advance the evolution of our species we need a fully human theory of evolution (2003; 2010). Rather than being puppets of highly specialized preprogrammed brain circuits, we are driven by a complex combination of motivations, ranging from survival and reproduction to our needs for self-expression, love, meaning, and self-actualization.

My new book in progress with the working title of *Human Possibilities* analyzes the expression of these motivations in the context of cultural environments orienting primarily to the domination model or to the partnership model. It proposes that our brain neurochemistry is to a large extent the product not of ancient evolutionary imperatives but of adaptations to different environments—and that the environments of cultures orienting to the domination model or the partnership model support the development and maintenance of different neurochemical patterns.

In other words, I am proposing that the issue is what *conditions* lead to the expression, or inhibition, of different aspects of our large and varied human biological repertoire. Even more specifically, the issue is what conditions lead to the expression or inhibition of our great human capacity for caring and creativity or, alternately, for cruelty and destructiveness. And addressing this issue requires studying both biological and cultural evolution from a new systemic perspective.

EXPANDING THE SCOPE OF SYSTEMS ANALYSES

As I mentioned earlier, a distinguishing feature of the study of relational dynamics is that it takes into account the most formative human relations: the primary relations between the female and male halves of humanity and between them and their daughters and sons. It is on this substrate of primary relations that all social organization rests. Not only are these relations key to survival and reproduction; these are also the relations through which people acquire their mental and emotional maps for what is normal, moral, possible. It is where they first learn, and continually practice, either respect for the human rights of others or acceptance of chronic human rights violations as "just the way things are."

Given these seemingly obvious dynamics, one must ask why intimate relations have not been considered important—much less central—in most studies of human society. The reason lies precisely in the kinds of mental and emotional maps most of us have inherited from earlier times that oriented much more closely to the domination model: maps in which anything pertaining to women or children is not considered of real importance.

How limiting this view has been is shown by a statistical study conducted under the auspices of the Center for Partnership Studies comparing measures of the status of women with quality of life indicators.[8] Based on statistics collected by international agencies from 89 nations, this study, *Women, Men, and the Global Quality of Life*, shows that in significant respects the status of women can be a better predictor of general quality of life than even gross domestic product (GDP). While economic development tends to go along with movement toward gender equality, societies with the same GDP can have great variations in gender relations—which in turn correlate strongly with a higher or lower general quality of life (Eisler, Loye, and Norgaard 1995).

This was a pioneering study released in 1995 in time for the United Nations Women's Conference in Beijing. Since then, the systemic importance of the status of women has been shown by other studies. For example, the annual Gender Gap Reports of the World Economic Forum show that nations with the lowest gender gaps are also regularly in the highest tiers of the annual World Economic Forum's Global Competitiveness Reports (Hausmann, Tyson, and Zahidi 2011).

These gender-holistic studies show that economics cannot be understood, or effectively changed, without attention to other core cultural components—and that a key component is the construction of the roles and relations of the female and male halves of humanity. More recently, my book *The Real Wealth of Nations: Creating a Caring Economics* documents the connection between a society's economic policies and practices and what is considered normal in gender roles and relations (Eisler 2007).

Nonetheless, many people still dismiss the ranking of the male over the female half of humanity as "just a women's issue." They avoid dealing with such matters as women's and children's rights, at best inserting a few sentences about them in their books. Even works about systems theory fail to give importance to these relations, and in most cases do not include them.

Indeed, until relatively recently, the construction of the primary human relations between women and men and between parents and children as rigid rankings of domination was not even part of the cultural discourse. It was simply assumed to be natural, even moral.

All this is our heritage from more authoritarian and male dominated times. So also is the fact that worldwide traditions of violence against the majority of humanity—women and children—receive only passing attention, and are in many world regions not even prosecuted as crimes (Eisler 2013). Cultural traditions that blight and take the lives of millions every year are still split off as "just women's issues and children's issues" from the "important" issues that are the proper subject of scientific study—so deeply engrained is the fragmentation of consciousness that makes it possible to marginalize issues affecting the majority of humanity.

This takes us to one of the ways domination-oriented cultures maintain and reconstruct themselves: the fragmentation of perception into rigid compartments that make it difficult to see connections between various aspects of reality. Modern physics demolished this mechanistic way of describing reality in its repeated observation of the fluidity between energy and matter and in the insight that the observer affects what is observed. But these insights, too, are kept in a hermetically sealed compartment, as if physics had nothing to do with anything else that happens on our planet.

This fragmentation of perception constricts and distorts consciousness. It has even suppressed consciousness of a seemingly obvious fact. This is that, if we are serious about cultural transformation in a more peaceful, equitable, and sustainable direction, we have to take into account the cultural construction of the most foundational human relations: the relations between women and men and between parents and children that provide our first mental (and as neuroscience now shows, neural) templates for human relations (National Research Council 2000; Niehoff 1999; Perry n.d.).

CULTURAL TRANSFORMATION THEORY

Looking at cultural evolution through the analytical lens of the partnership–domination continuum offers grounded hope for a more equitable and peaceful future. It makes it possible to see that all around us there is movement toward family and social structures that are closer to the partnership template—albeit against enormous resistance. This is why I want to close with a description of the strand of human possibilities theory I call cultural transformation theory and its implications for research and action.

Most theories of cultural evolution have described a linear progression from "primitive" to "civilized." Cultural transformation theory offers a conceptual framework that is not unilinear but rather multilinear. Specifically, it proposes that the partnership model and the domination model are two basic attractors for social systems; that movement from one to the other does *not* follow a linear progression; and that times of disequilibrium—such as ours—offer the opportunity for fundamental cultural transformation.

Cultural transformation theory proposes that while social systems, like all living systems, seek to maintain themselves, transformative change is possible during periods of systems disequilibrium. It suggests that there are bifurcation points where a system can either move to a different level or return to the old level. Specifically, it shows that cultural evolution has been characterized by the tension between the partnership and domination models—and that we are at a time when this tension is coming to a head.

I want to again emphasize that cultural transformation theory has commonalities with both new theories, such as nonlinear dynamics and chaos theory, as well as earlier theories, because some of what is today presented as new is actually an expansion of earlier insights. For example, the theories of social psychologist Kurt Lewin about how systems unfreeze and refreeze prefigures insights of what can happen in states of social disequilibrium. Feminist theory also prefigures some of the tenets of cultural transformation theory. And many evolutionary studies, starting with Darwin, have shown the unique capacities of our species (for details on what Darwin had to say about our species, see Loye 2010).

However, cultural transformation theory adds important new dimensions to these insights. Many popular evolution theories minimize the importance of human agency; for example, most evolutionary psychologists and sociobiologists maintain that human behavior is controlled by ancestral evolutionary imperatives that developed millennia ago. They basically ignore the interaction between biology and culture, and minimize the fact that we human are capable of conscious choice. By contrast, both bio-culturalism and cultural transformation theory recognize the interactive relationship between biology and culture. Moreover, they propose that, while we are profoundly affected by our cultural environment, we also affect it in an interactive process guided by our conscious goals and plans. In other words, we *can* change our cultures.

Change is of course a constant in the living world. But there is a big difference between change within the parameters of a particular social system and transformative change. The first kind of change does not alter a social system's basic identity or configuration. The second kind of change shifts the system from one basic identity or configuration to another. It is this *transformative* change that is the focus of cultural transformation theory.

I have elsewhere presented data based on findings from archeology and mythology suggesting that the original direction of civilization was more toward the partnership model (see, e.g., Eisler 1987; 1995; 2000; see also Eisler 1993; 1997; 2003). In the earliest cradles of civilization, going back 10,000 years to the beginning of the Neolithic or first Agrarian Age, there are few indications of destruction through warfare or fortifications. We also do not find in their extensive art images that idealize warfare or rape, as we do in the art of later chronically warlike and violent times. While there were some differences in status and in wealth, as the British archeologist James Mellaart (1967) writes, these were not extreme. As the Lithuanian archeologist Marija Gimbutas (1982), the Greek archeologists Nicolas Platon (1966) and Nino Marinatos (1993), and the British archeologist Ian Hodder (2004) write, the evidence supports the conclusion that women were not subordinate to men.

However, these were *not* matriarchies, or societies governed only by women, as nineteenth-century scholars claimed. They were cultures where there was a more balanced relationship between women and men. As reflected in their art focusing on nature and the life-giving powers inherent in woman's body, the belief systems of these societies focused more on the power to give and nurture life than on the power to take and control life.

I have also elsewhere described the prehistoric shift to the domination model during a period of massive disequilibrium. While my focus was primarily on early Western civilization—Europe and the Middle East—the same pattern has been found by scholars in other areas. For instance, a multidisciplinary team of scholars at the Chinese Academy of Social Sciences in Beijing tested the applicability of cultural transformation theory to China and found the same pattern of an early partnership direction followed by a shift to the domination model (Min 1995).

But even after this shift, the partnership model continued to act as an attractor. All through recorded history, there have been periodic partnership resurgences. In Western history, such periods include the early Christian movement and the eleventh- and twelfth-century resurgence of a more stereo-typically feminine ethos expressed by the veneration of Mary and the Troubadour poetry.

Most importantly, modern history has been a time of cumulating challenges to entrenched traditions of domination. The seventeenth and eighteenth centuries brought challenges to the so-called divinely ordained right of kings to rule over their "subjects" and monarchies were, at least in some world regions, replaced by republics. In the same centuries, men's so-called divinely right to rule over the women and children in the "castles" of their homes began to be challenged. The nineteenth century brought movements against economic oppression and domination, the anti-slavery and abolitionist movements challenging the "divinely ordained right" of one race to dominate and even enslave another, and an organized feminist movement challenging traditions of male-dominance. Then came the twentieth-century civil rights and anti-colonial movements, the indigenous liberation movements, and the women's liberation and women's rights movements. Even the environmental movement is a challenge to traditions of domination: to man's once celebrated "conquest of nature."

All these progressive movements are part of a larger movement toward another fundamental cultural transformation—this time from domination to partnership. But for this shift to be completed requires informed and conscious human agency.

TRANSFORMATIVE CHANGE

Until now, the primary focus of modern progressive movements has been the top of the domination pyramid: the so-called public sphere of economic and political relations from which women and children are excluded in the domination model. A great deal of attention has been given to what was once aptly called the "men's world." But the foundational relations—parent–child and woman–man relations in the so-called private sphere—have received far less attention from those working for a more equitable and peaceful world.

By contrast, those pushing us back to more rigid rankings of domination recognize that gender relations and parent–child relations are fundamental to what is considered normal in *all* relations. This connection is why the most repressive modern regimes—from Hitler's Germany and Stalin's Soviet Union to Khomeini's Iran to the Taliban of Afghanistan—have sprung up where family and gender relations based on domination and submission were firmly in place. The systemic importance of these relations is also why, once in power, these regimes have pushed policies that have as their goal the reinstatement of a punitive father in complete control of his family.

This is why so-called religious fundamentalists—be they Muslim, Hindu, Jewish, or Christian—focus so much on the return to a "traditional family" in which men dominate women and children learn never to question orders, no matter how painful or unjust. It is also why fundamentalist leaders fiercely oppose reproductive freedom for women. It also helps explain why they are virulently hostile to gays, as in their eyes gay men violate the God-given order of a man never taking the subservient role of a woman. It is why the so-called Christian Right has in the United States even opposed federal legislation to protect women from violence as well as government funding for shelters for abused women (as in former Senator Laxalt's so-called Family Protection Act). It is also why organizations such as the Promise Keepers offered men the false choice between neglecting or abandoning their families and "regaining control."

Studies of society must take these key dynamics into account. At the same time, we also have to change the political conversation.

Rhetoric about "strengthening the family" and "family values" needs to be challenged by asking what kind of family we want to strengthen and value. Is it a family based on rankings of domination in which a male head of household "calls the shots" and human rights violations are viewed as "just the way things are"? Or is it a partnership-oriented family in which both halves of humanity are given equal value and children learn early on to view relations based on respect for everyone's human rights as normal? Does strengthening the family mean supporting policies that promote families in which a "strong" father is in complete control? Or does it mean supporting nurturing parenting by both men and women? (For a progressive family agenda, see Eisler 2002, 2013).

We also have to show policy-makers and the public at large the connection between these very different family models and two very different types of social policies. If we continue to let the "strong" punitive father, rather than the nurturing parent, be the ideal norm, we cannot effectively counter the cultural drift back to "strong" leaders who, like the punitive male head of household, likewise rely on fear and violence to impose control.

Nor can we realistically expect fiscal policies that support caring and nurturance, such as universal healthcare, childcare, and help for the poor—policies that reflect the ideal of a nurturing and caring parent rather than a punitive father. Indeed, the problem is not, as we often hear, the historic move to capitalism (that is, to a market economy); it is that we have through so-called neo-liberalism and "trickle down economics" seen a return to an economics of domination, where those on bottom (as in the kingdoms and caliphates of old) are to content themselves with the scraps dropping from the opulent tables of those on top, and where freedom is used to justify exploitation by those in control, whether it is the exploitation of people or of nature.

This is one of the lessons from the last several decades in the United States, which have been marked by a massive regression to the domination model through the rightist–fundamentalist–corporatist alliance. And it is not coincidental that, starting with the defeat of the Equal Rights Amendment, which first brought this alliance together, it has invested enormous money and energy in trying to push us back to one of the fundamentals of domination systems: a family where children learn early on to equate difference, beginning with the most fundamental difference in our species between male and female, with superiority or inferiority, dominating or being dominated, being served or serving.

This regression is most virulent in the resurgence of so-called religious fundamentalism in the Muslim world, where despotic control by the male head of household is the model for despotic control in the tribe or state, so much so that even when there are democratic elections a majority of people have voted for repressive fundamentalist regimes such as Hamas in Gaza and the Muslim Brotherhood in Egypt.

From this perspective, we can see that the struggle for our future is not between religious and secular values. The real issue is what kind of religious or secular values are being advanced: partnership values or dominator values.

At the core of many religious teachings are stereotypically "feminine" values such as caring, sharing, and nonviolence. For example, Jesus taught partnership values: stereotypically feminine values such as caring, empathy, compassion, forgiveness, and love. By contrast, the leaders of the Christian right focus on hate-mongering, scapegoating, sexual control over women, and violent discipline of children—all designed for dominator systems maintenance.

The political agenda of fundamentalists—whether Muslim, Hindu, Jewish, or Christian—is a domination agenda. It is re-imposing a system of rigid top-down control: strong-man rule in both the family and the state, the ranking of the male half of humanity over the female half, and fear and institutionalized violence to maintain a system of top-down rankings—be they man over woman, man over man, race over race, or religion over religion.

Today's religious fundamentalism, however, is not an isolated phenomenon. It is part of a larger worldwide regression to the domination model. It has gone along with the again widening gap between haves and have-nots, a mass media that idealizes "heroic" male violence and marginalizes women and anything stereotypically considered feminine, elections where politicians are for sale to the highest bidder, and escalating violence and environmental destruction worldwide.

That is the domination side of the picture. Yet there is also the partnership side: the continuing worldwide movement toward real political democracy, environmental sustainability, and economic, social, racial, gender, and family equity.

Many so-called "private" issues are becoming political issues—issues that people did not even talk about not so long ago, such as the global pandemic of violence in the name of tradition against women and children. We are beginning to have a children's rights movement. The international women's movement is growing. And both national and international agencies are beginning to recognize some of the dynamics I have described—that raising the status of women is key to economic development and that violence against women and children is a training ground for using force to impose one's will on others—and hence a training for national and international violence.

In these and other ways, we are moving toward the truly systemic partnership movement that can bring about transformative change. But unless we build the solid foundations on which more partnership-oriented societies can be built worldwide—and shift from domination to partnership in our primary gender and parent–child relations—we will continue to see regressions to the domination side. And at our level of technological development, these regressions may threaten nothing less than our species' survival.

CONCLUSION

Human possibilities theory is grounded in a holistic/systems perspective that has been gradually emerging. The new conceptual framework of the partnership/domination continuum offers a dynamic/nonlinear rather than mechanistic/linear model for living systems, focused on self-organization rather than predetermined directions.

Human possibilities theory—which includes the methodological approach of studying relational dynamics, cultural transformation theory, and bio-culturalism, helps advance this holistic/systems perspective in a number of ways. The theory:

1. Examines the interactive field of human biological and cultural evolution through the new analytical lens of the partnership/domination continuum;
2. Proposes a multilinear rather than unilinear model for human cultural evolution;
3. Proposes that human behaviors—and even brain neurochemistry—are to a large extent products of adaptations to cultural environments orienting to the domination model or the partnership model, rather than being the automatic result of ancient evolutionary imperatives;
4. Highlights the importance of the cultural construction of the relations between the male and female halves of humanity and between them and their children, recognizing that it is through these primary relations that people acquire their basic mental, emotional, and neural maps for *all* relations;
5. Shows that we humans do more than just adapt to our cultural environments in a mechanistic manner, but are also creators of our cultural environments;
6. Shows that cultural transformation is possible in periods of systems disequilibrium;
7. Shows the possibility of transformative change through a systemic approach that takes into account the totality of a social system, including the primary human relations as the substrate on which all social organization rests.

These principles are of immediate utility. The disequilibrium of the rapid technological changes of modern times—now accelerating as we move from the industrial to the postindustrial knowledge/service technological age—has caused great social and economic dislocation. But it has also made possible great changes in both consciousness and social organization through progressive social actions.

However, this movement has not been linear. It can best be imaged as an upward spiral toward the partnership model countered by enormous resistance and periodic regressions to the domination model.

Our future will not be decided by impersonal evolutionary or systems dynamics. It will be decided by conscious, self-directed human agency. We are not prisoners of "selfish genes." We have it in our power to consciously and creatively move to a more equitable and fulfilling partnership way of life.

The problem is not, as we are often told, "human nature." The human yearning for caring connection, for love, for creating rather than destroying, for living in peace rather than war, for mutually respectful and beneficial rather than tense and violent relations in all spheres of life, is integral to human nature. This yearning lies behind all the progressive modern social movements that have over the last centuries challenged traditions of domination.

Now is the time to broaden and deepen this movement by changing traditions of domination and violence in the most formative human relations: the gender and parent–child relations where traditions of domination have been the most resistant to change. Systems science can make a big contribution to this urgently needed change through an integrated approach that fully takes these relations into account.

We owe it to our children and to future generations to show that a partnership future is not a *utopia* or no place, but a *pragmatopia* or possible place. We can make this possibility a reality by using our creativity to build partnership cultures worldwide.

NOTES

1. Eisler, R. *Human possibilities* (work in progress).
2. These interactions have been described by Maturana and Varela as autopoiesis, by Prigogine and Stengers as auto- and cross-catalysis, and by Csanyi and Kampis's concept of autogenesis.
3. There are in cultural systems feedback and feedforward loops, continual auto-catalytic and cross-catalytic processes that maintain the system's basic character. I use the term "feedforward" in the sense of "top-down feedforward" proposed by Karl Pribram, rather than in the sense of the older "bottom-up feedforward," such as the passage of a visual image from the retina to the cortex.
4. The categories democratic/authoritarian come closest to partnership and domination, but they are generally used only to describe political arrangements (the presence or absence of "free elections"), and are only occasionally used to also denote family structures. Moreover, they do not describe other key components of social systems, such as economics, religion, and education.
5. In their analysis of capitalism and socialism, Marx, and particularly Engels, noted what they called the first class oppression: that of women by men. But, except in some passages in Engel's *Origin of the Family* and an occasional paragraph in Marx's writings, they viewed this issue as a peripheral "woman question" rather than a key social issue.
6. Private communication from Peggy Reeves Sanday, January 30, 2002.
7. Eisler, R. *Human possibilities*.
8. Eisler, Loye, and Norgaard (1995). The nine measures used to assess the degree of gender equity were: the number of literate females for every 100 literate males; female life expectancy as a percentage of male life expectancy; the number of women for every 100 men in parliaments and other governing bodies; the number of females in secondary education for every 100 males;

maternal mortality; contraceptive prevalence; access to abortion; and based on measures used by the Population Crisis Committee (now Population Action International), social equality for women and economic equality for women. The thirteen measures used to assess quality of life, were: overall life expectancy; human rights ratings; access to healthcare; access to clean water; literacy; infant mortality; number of refugees fleeing the country; the percentage of daily caloric requirements consumed; Gross Domestic Product (GDP) as a measure of wealth; the percentage of GDP distributed to the poorest 40 percent of households; the ratio of GDP going to the wealthiest versus the poorest 20 percent of the population; and as measures of environmental sensitivity, the percentage of forest habitat remaining, and compliance with the Convention on International Trade in Endangered Species. In exploring the relation between the gender equity and quality of life variables with descriptive, correlational, factor, and multiple regression analyses, the authors found a strong systemic correlation between these two measures. These findings were consistent with their hypothesis that increased equity for women is central to a higher quality of life for a country as a whole, and that gender inequity contracts the opportunities and capabilities, not only of women, but of the entire population. The link between gender equity and quality of life was confirmed at a very high level of statistical significance for correlational analysis. 61 correlations at the .001 level with 18 additional correlations at the .05 level were found, for a total of 79 significant correlations in the predicted direction. This link was further confirmed by factor analysis. High factor loadings for gender equity and quality of life variables accounted for 87.8 percent of the variance. Regression analysis, also yielded significant results. An R-square of .84, with statistical significance at the .0001 level, provided support for the hypothesis that gender equity is a strong indicator of the quality of life.

REFERENCES

Dobzhansky, T. 1968. Cultural evolution. In *International Encyclopedia of the Social Sciences*, Vol. 5, Ed. Stills, D. L. New York: The Macmillan Company and the Free Press.

Eisler, R. 1987. *The chalice and the blade: Our history, our future.* San Francisco: Harper & Row.

———. 1993. Technology, gender, and history: Toward a nonlinear model of social evolution. In *The evolution of cognitive maps: New paradigms for the twenty-first century*, Eds. Laszlo, E. and Masulli, I., 181–203. Langhorne, PA: Gordon and Breach.

———. 1995. *Sacred pleasure: Sex, myth, and the politics of the body.* San Francisco: Harper Collins.

———. 1997. Cultural transformation theory: A new paradigm for history. In *Macrohistory and macrohistorians*, Eds. Galtung, J. and Inayatullah, S., *141–150. Westport, CT:* Praeger.

———. 2000. *Tomorrow's children: A blueprint for partnership education in the 21st century.* Boulder, CO: Westview Press.

———. 2002. *The power of partnership: Seven relationships that will change your life.* Novato, CA: New World Library.

———. 2003. Culture, technology, and domination/partnership. In *The great adventure*, ed. D. Loye, 166–202. New York: SUNY Press.

———. 2007. *The real wealth of nations: Creating a caring economics.* San Francisco: Berrett-Koehler.

——— 2013. Protecting the majority of humanity: Toward an integrated approach to crimes against present and future generations. In *Securing the rights of future generations: Sustainable development and the Rome Statute of the International Criminal Court*, Eds. Cordonier Segger, M-C. Goepel, M. and Jodoin, S. Cambridge: Cambridge University Press.

———. n.d. Progressive family values: A call for a pro-child, pro-democracy family agenda. www.partnershipway.org

Eisler, R., D. Loye, and K. Norgaard. 1995. *Women, men, and the global quality of life.* Pacific Grove, CA: Center for Partnership Studies.

Gimbutas, M. 1982. *The goddesses and gods of old Europe.* Berkeley: University of California Press.

Hausmann, R., L. D. Tyson, and S. Zahidi. 2011. *The global gender gap report.* Geneva, Switzerland: The World Economic Forum.

Hodder, I. 2004. Women and men at Catalhoyuk. *Scientific American* (January): 77–83.

Loye, D., Ed. 2003. *The great adventure: Toward a fully human theory of evolution.* Albany: State University of New York Press.

———. 2010. *Darwin's lost theory,* third revised edition. Pacific Grove, CA: Benjamin Franklin Press.

Marinatos, N. 1993. *Minoan religion: Ritual, image, and symbol.* Columbia: University of South Carolina Press.

Marx, K., and F. Engels. 1960. *Werke Vol. 8.* Berlin: Dietz Verlag.

Mellaart, J. 1967. *Çatal Hüyük.* New York: McGraw-Hill.

Min, J., Ed. 1995. *The chalice and the blade in Chinese culture: Gender relations and social models.* Beijing: China Social Sciences Publishing House.

National Research Council. 2000. *From neurons to neighborhoods.* Washington, DC: National Academy Press.

Niehoff, D. 1999. *The biology of violence.* New York: Free Press.

Perry, B. D. n.d. Aggression and violence: The neurobiology of experience. http://teacher.scholastic.com/professional/bruceperry/aggression_violence.htm .

Pietila. H. 2001. "Nordic Welfare Society–A Strategy to Eradicate Poverty and Build Up Equality: Finland as a Case Study" *in Journal Cooperation South,* 2: 79–96.

Platon, N. 1966. *Crete.* Geneva: Nagel Publishers.

Sanday, P. R. 2002. *Women at the center.* Ithaca, NY: Cornell University Press.

Schlegel, S. A. 1998. *Wisdom from a rain forest.* Athens: University of Georgia Press.

ENCOUNTER WITH A WIZARD

STANLEY KRIPPNER

Saybrook University, San Francisco, California, USA

My chance encounter with Ludwig von Bertalanffy in 1959 introduced me to general systems theory, and provided me with a perspective that has impacted my entire professional career. This article illustrates how systems thinking permeated my experimental and theoretical work with parapsychological phenomena, dreams and dreaming, and personal mythology. Without this perspective, these explorations of human consciousness would have been more simplistic and linear, and less holistic and complex.

When I was attending graduate school at Northwestern University, I had the good fortune to study social psychology under the tutelage of Donald Campbell, who was later elected president of the American Psychological Association. I had arranged for J.B. Rhine, the controversial biologist and parapsychologist, to give a featured address for an educational honors society, and Campbell was one of only two psychologists who disregarded the advisory letter from the psychology department's chair to boycott the event. Campbell remained skeptical concerning Rhine's claims that some phenomena seem to circumvent the ordinary constraints of time, space, and energy; nevertheless, he listened attentively and asked several penetrating questions following the lecture.

On May 29, 1959, I ran into Professor Campbell while on my way to a class in special education, my major field of study. He was accompanied by a man whose short stature and huge eyes reminded me of the German-born actor Peter Lorre. I assumed that Campbell was taking this wizard-like visitor on a tour of the Evanston campus. Campbell introduced me to his guest, Ludwig von Bertalanffy, and strongly urged me to attend his lecture the following day. I had never heard of von Bertalanffy, but decided to make the effort, repaying in a small way the courtesy that Campbell had demonstrated when I had brought Dr. Rhine to Northwestern University. It was a decision I never regretted.

Despite Campbell's advertising, the audience was slim. Nevertheless, von Bertalanffy's lecture was brilliant and it became my introduction to general systems theory. Originally, von Bertalanffy (1968) had used the German term *Allgemeine*

Systemlehre, which translates into "general theory of systems" or "general system theory." In English, the term became "general systems theory" or, more simply, "GST." Although a theoretical biologist, von Bertalanffy geared his lecture to his audience of psychologists and graduate students. He noted that both psychoanalysis and behaviorism viewed human beings as chance products of nature and nurture, a mixture of genes and accidental events from infancy to maturity. To the contrary, asserted von Bertalanffy, the world could better be seen as *organization;* he advocated an integration of the natural and social sciences to more fully understand this pattern. A *system,* he observed, is a pattern of two or more interacting components together with the relationships among them that permit the identification of a boundary-maintaining entity or process.

In 1968 von Bertalanffy proposed that GST, as a methodology, was applicable to all the sciences. For example, it encompasses the cybernetic theory of feedback that represents a special class of self-regulating systems. But he discerned a fundamental difference between GST and cybernetics since the feedback mechanisms of the latter are controlled by constraints while dynamical systems display the free interplay of various forces. I had learned about the heady promise of cybernetics from some of my enthusiastic friends in mathematics and engineering, but now I had discovered a perspective that highlighted similarities (or "isomorphisms") between cybernetic machines, living organisms, and social systems. In theory, at least, data from one scientific realm could be compared to another one.

At the time of his Northwestern University lecture, von Bertalanffy was a visiting professor at the Menninger Foundation in Topeka, Kansas. During that same year, the Menninger Foundation's director of research, Gardner Murphy, accepted an invitation from Northwestern's psychology department to give a lecture on his "biosocial" model of personality. This model, instrumental in Murphy's election to the presidency of the American Psychological Association, was a pioneering systems approach that described the interaction of individuals' biology and their social environment (Murphy 1947). Knowing of Murphy's interest in parapsychology, I wrote him and requested a meeting with a group of graduate students who shared this interest. Much to my surprise, Murphy graciously accepted our invitation.

Unlike von Bertalanffy's sparse audience, people were standing against the walls and sitting in the aisles of the colloquium room. After a dazzling presentation and stimulating question period, Murphy's hosts were surprised when he excused himself to join four members of his audience for a private seminar. Some of us had read his pioneering new book, *Human Potentialities* (Murphy 1958), and queried him about his integration of parapsychological data with concepts about the "self," noting his question of the difficulty discerning "where one person begins and another ends" (296).

Following our meeting, two of us drove Murphy to Chicago where he planned to catch a train back to Kansas. We moved slowly because of the snow, and Murphy remarked that this weather would be a marked contrast to what he hoped to experience in Honolulu the following summer where he would be a visiting professor at the University of Hawaii. I remarked that I would also be in Honolulu, participating in a friend's wedding; on the spot, Murphy invited me to be his teaching assistant.

The summer of 1960 was an educational bonanza. I had the opportunity of spending the day with Murphy and his wife, Lois Barclay Murphy, a noted developmental psychologist; our discussions ranged from world events to the origins of Hawaiian ukulele music. In addition, I was able to sit in on classes taught by two other visiting professors: S.I. Hayakawa and Anatol Rapoport. I had studied general semantics during my undergraduate years at the University of Wisconsin, using Hayakawa's (1949) text. My readings in GST later made me fully aware of Rapoport's (e.g., 1960, 1968) contributions, especially those in the areas of "game theory," conflict versus cooperation, and the mathematical modeling of systems. A former concert pianist, Rapoport had lectured on the semantics of music; at the University of Hawaii, he treated his audiences to a series of intellectual banquets that spanned a dozen scholarly disciplines. Indeed, in 1954 he, von Bertalanffy, and several others founded an organization that eventually became The International Society for the Systems Sciences. Later, I joined the organization and spoke at their conference in Pittsburgh in 2002 (Krippner and Combs 2002).

When summer school ended, and after the Murphys had left for India and the Society Union, I stayed in Honolulu to attend a meeting of the International Society for General Semantics. I delivered my first professional paper, demonstrating how expectancy set was responsible for an elderly couple's decision to leave their house once they believed it was inhabited by a "poltergeist" (or "noisy ghost"), when our investigation revealed that their grandson simply had been playing pranks. My co-investigator of this case was Arthur Hastings (Hastings and Krippner 1961), who had driven Gardner Murphy to the Chicago train station on that memorable winter's day. The general semantics conference was held at the famed Hawaiian Village Hotel, which was graced by a geodesic dome. Hayakawa and Rapoport both spoke on the topic, "Communication with Soviet Union," providing me with insights that I was able to utilize, years later, during my many trips to Russia during both the Soviet and post-Soviet eras.

DREAMING IN BROOKLYN

Following my graduation from Northwestern University in 1961, I served as the director of Kent State University's Child Study Center for three years. Most of my work was with children exhibiting learning disabilities; following Gardner Murphy's lead, I used diagnostic approaches that considered the potential biological, educational, and psychological aspects of their condition when planning remedial programs (e.g., Krippner 1968).

In 1964, Gardner Murphy recommended me for a position in Brooklyn, New York, where I would direct the newly founded dream research laboratory at Maimonides Medical Center. Murphy had obtained funding for the world's first intensive study of possible parapsychological effects in dreams, a field pioneered by Montague Ullman, the distinguished psychologist who headed the Center's department of psychiatry. With Ullman and our associates, dreamers were given instructions that would help them focus on their nighttime task: to dream about a post-card size reproduction of a piece of art that had been randomly selected once they retired for the night. Only a staff member in a distant room knew the picture's identity; any correspondences between the dream reports and the picture's contents would be anomalous, hard to explain in terms of mainstream science's concepts of space, time, and energy (Ullman and Krippner, with Vaughan 1989).

Outside evaluators judged these correspondences without knowing the actual matches; their results were evaluated statistically and the correspondences were so close that there was only one possibility in several thousand that the results could be due to coincidence (Child 1985). Research participants also made their own matches before they were given the correct identity of the "target picture." Their results were somewhat below those of the outside judges, but were still statistically significant (Child 1985).

For example, one night the research participant was a male psychoanalyst. Once electrodes had been glued to his head, and after he had entered the sleep room, a staff member threw dice and selected the sealed envelope corresponding to the randomly obtained number. The envelope was given to another staff member who took it to a distant room. Upon opening the envelope, and a second envelope that had been placed in the larger envelope, he discovered that the "target picture" for the night was Edgar Degas's painting, "School of the Dance," which depicts a dance class in progress. A female teacher leads the class and her students are girls wearing ballet costumes. The psychoanalyst was awakened each time the electroencephalograph indicated that he had been dreaming. His first dream report of the night involved "being in a class. Now, at different times, different people would get up for some sort of recitation or some sort of contribution." The themes of "school" and "class" continued throughout the night; his fourth dream report contained the statement, "There was one little girl that was trying to dance with me." Later, the outside judges had no hesitation in matching this night of dream reports with the Degas art print.

However, not every night contained direct correspondences, and not every series of experiments produced data attaining statistically significance. I recalled Donald Campbell's observation that there was no parapsychological experiment that could be repeated on demand by psychologists in different laboratories. He was right. Our team could not even guarantee similar results from experiments conducted in our own laboratory. My background in GST suggested that parapsychological phenomena represent a complex life system, a system in which there are many components, all of which are required to manifest the effect. There had been a number of studies suggesting that extraverts made the best research participants, that rapport with their experimenters was helpful, and that motivation and encouragement played vital roles.

Remembering that a "system" was a pattern of elements in mutual interaction, I suspected that we had overlooked crucial environmental conditions that play their role in the parapsychological system (Krippner 1975, 127), especially those that could be described as *fields*. For me, the term *field* refers to a region of influence, one presumed to exist in physical reality even though they may be observable only through their effects, rather than directly.

In 1970, I asked several of our student volunteers to collect data pertinent to three of these possible field effects, namely the lunar cycle, sunspot activity, and changes in the Earth's geomagnetic field. We detected slight relationships between each of these and a dream report's correspondence with the "target picture"; indeed, parapsychological effects seemed to be most robust on nights of the full moon (Krippner et al., 1972). By this time, however, our grant money was running out, I had a family to support, and—with regret—I left Maimonides to take a teaching job in San Francisco with the Humanistic Psychology Institute (which later became Saybrook Graduate School).

GEOMAGNETIC FIELDS AND ANOMALIES

I maintained my interest in field effects, especially after meeting Michael Persinger, a Canadian neuroscientist who was conducting research with geomagnetic fields that was much more sophisticated than my neophyte efforts. I invited him to write an article about his work for a journal I was editing. According to Persinger (1975), the geomagnetic field has several components. The Earth itself produces the main component, as if a huge bar magnet were running through its core. Regular daily and monthly variations occur, affected to some degree by weather conditions (such as electrical storms) but also by sunspot activity. The best known example of charged particles from the sun interacting with the Earth's magnetic field is the aurora borealis, or "Northern Lights," which I had witnessed several times during my visits to Canada.

Eventually, Persinger (1985) analyzed spontaneous reports of so-called "telepathic" and "clairvoyant" activity that occurred outside of a laboratory setting. In a typical "telepathic" experience, someone has an uncannily accurate hunch that a loved one is in danger and is calling out for help. In a typical "clairvoyance" experience, someone feels that a major accident is occurring at the time that it actually takes place. He found that these experiences were more likely to occur when the Earth's geomagnetic activity was significantly quieter than during the days directly before or the days directly after. About the same time, Marsha Adams (1986) found a positive connection between days with low geomagnetic activity and research participants' success in laboratory experiments in "remote viewing," in other words, "telepathy" and "clairvoyance" at a distance. Several parapsychologists (e.g., Tart 1988) revisited their data often discovering that geomagnetic effects were associated with "telepathy" and other types of so-called "extra-sensory perception."

Persinger (1989) referred to a day of sudden and large amplitude changes as a magnetically stormy day. After a survey of the parapsychological literature, he discovered a tendency for reports of spontaneous "psychokinesis" to occur on those days. Examples would include a ghostly shape seemingly "haunting" a location, or an invisible "poltergeist" purportedly moving objects around a room. If these instances are reported accurately, anomalies of *force* and *energy* are at work, rather than those of *time* and *space*. Once Persinger had published his report, several parapsychologists examined their data, discovering that experiments with "psychokinesis" were typically successful on stormy days (e.g., Braud and Dennis 1989) while experiments with "telepathy" and "clairvoyance" were characteristically successful on quiet days.

Persinger and I tested two hypotheses: (1) Nights on which parapsychological effects in dreams were strong would also be nights that displayed the more quiet geomagnetic activity compared to the nights immediately before or after; (2) Nights on which parapsychological effects were weak or absent would not demonstrate this effect. We tested these hypotheses in two ways. First, we examined the initial night that each of 62 research participants spent in our dream laboratory. For our analysis, we used the results of the matching made by the research participants themselves. Using the numbers assigned by research participants to the correct "target picture," we termed their matches "High Hits," "Low Hits," "High Misses," or "Low Misses." Persinger searched the archives to identify geomagnetic measures for the Northern Hemisphere for each pertinent night. There were too few "Misses" to yield data adequate for analysis, but a statistically significant difference was observed between "High Hits" and "Low Hits." The "High Hits" were more likely to occur on quiet geomagnetic nights when there was an absence of electrical storms or sunspot activity (Persinger and Krippner 1989).

Secondly, we tested these hypotheses with the matches made by a single research participant, William Erwin, the psychoanalyst who had spent more nights in our laboratory than anyone. It was Erwin who dreamed of the "little girl that was trying to dance with me" the night that Degas' "School of the Dance" was the "target picture." We assumed that using scores given by a single research participant would eliminate the problem of individual differences, a major source of variance in these studies.

The typical procedure followed during these sessions was to greet Erwin when he arrived at the laboratory, giving him an opportunity to interact with the staff member who would focus on the "target picture" once Erwin had retired for the night. Electrodes were attached to Erwin's head, he was led to a soundproof room, and the electrodes were plugged into an outlet near his bed. Two experimenters worked in shifts observing Erwin's brain waves and eye movements on the electroencephalograph machine. Near the end of each period of rapid eye movement activity, Erwin was awakened by means of a microphone and asked if he remembered a dream. He responded into a microphone near his bed, and his remarks were tape-recorded. In the morning, he was interviewed, giving him an opportunity to make associations to each dream report. The tapes were transcribed and sent to three judges who worked independently. The averages of their scores were used for statistical analysis.

Because almost all of Erwin's scores were "High Hits," Persinger made a direct statistical analysis of his matches. The most robust correlations between the scores and the geomagnetic activity occurred during the nights when geomagnetic activity was calm. The effect was most pronounced during the latter part of the night, the time when most of Erwin's dream reports were collected (Krippner and Persinger 1996).

PRECOGNITION AND PSYCHOKINESIS

In addition to putative "telepathy" and "clairvoyance," parapsychologists study another phenomenon that appears to circumvent the constraints of time and space.

It is referred to as "precognition," and involves time displacement between an experience and an event, as when, for example, on the basis of an intuitive impression someone cancels a train ride on a day when that train is involved in a serious mishap. Alan Vaughan was a research participant who obtained many "High Hits" in our studies of "telepathy" at Maimonides Medical Center. Since 1968, he had recorded his dreams after participating in a study about "precognitive" experiences. If a dream "came true," he entered a detailed description of the event in his diary; most of these premonitory dreams seemed to contain three or more exact details about the future event.

Vaughan sent another of my colleagues, James Spottiswoode, a physicist, the dates of 61 of these dream reports. Spottiswoode compared the geomagnetic activity of the nights of these dreams with those nights both before and after the dream report. The results were statistically significant (Krippner, Vaughan, and Spottiswoode 2000). Because Vaughan's dreams were not collected under controlled laboratory conditions, they are not as impressive as the other data we reported. Nevertheless, they indicate that "precognition" may involve similar field effects as do "telepathy" and "clairvoyance."

One of these dreams was recalled when Vaughan was living in Germany. He described the dream to me in a letter that I received on June 4, 1968. The dream contained many dramatic episodes involving the murder of Robert Kennedy who, at that time, was trying to obtain the Democratic Party's nomination for the presidency. On June 6, 1968, Kennedy was assassinated and some details of his murder resembled those described in the dream report (Ullman and Krippner with Vaughan 1989, 145).

Years later, I had the opportunity to investigate alleged psychokinesis in Brasilia, the capital of Brazil. In March 1994, I worked with a 7-person team studying the anomalous phenomena occurring in the presence of Amyr Amiden, events over which he claimed to have little conscious control. We spent several hours a day with Amiden, who joined us at the International Holistic University after his occupational duties had been completed (Krippner et al. 1996).

The settings for our work varied, but most of them were in an office where we sat in comfortable chairs around a table. Amiden drove to the Foundation, was met in the lobby by one or more team members, and was escorted to the office so that there could be no occasion on which Amiden entered the room prior to the session. In addition, several sessions were held in the campus Meditation House; I investigated this site each morning to be sure it contained no unusual objects which could later be labeled "anomalies." When the restaurant was the setting, Amiden entered and left with other group members. From the time that he arrived at the Foundation to the time that he departed, Amiden was in the presence of one or more members of the group.

When one or more team members felt that an unusual event had, indeed, occurred, a Brazilian physician and I took field notes. Periodically, three members of the team rated each of these events on a 5-point Anomaly Observation Scale I had constructed. It ranged from 1 (no apparent anomaly) to 5 (extraordinary degree of apparent anomaly). The mean of each set of ratings was used for comparative purposes. The research design stated that an event would have to have a mean rating of 2.1 or higher to be considered an "apparent anomaly," a non-ordinal number selected to divide events which were felt to be easily understandable from those that were ambiguous or difficult to explain.

For example, four black marks on a bedroom door were observed by another member of our team; this event was given a mean rating of 1.0 because someone recalled that a poster had been taped on his door a week earlier. While our group was seated in the office, a religious medallion appeared to drop on to the floor from a distant source; this event received a mean rating of 5.0, as did the similar appearance of another medallion a few minutes later.

Over a time span of eight days, a total of 20 sessions was held with Amiden; using a 5-point evaluation scale, 91 events were judged to have been "apparently anomalous" while 6 events failed to meet the predetermined criteria. On three of the eight days, a member of our group had taken geomagnetic readings in a nearby field (distant from electrical power lines) with the only magnetometer in Brasilia. There were 17 geomagnetic readings that had been preceded by "apparently anomalous events." The results were statistically significant; the higher the reading, the higher had been the score on our Anomaly Scale. On the other hand, 15 geomagnetic readings had been followed by "apparently anomalous" events; these correlations were not statistically significant. When the geomagnetic reading was paired with the anomalous event most contiguous in time (regardless of whether it was before or after the event), there were 16 pairs, and the correlation was statistically significant.

The two significant correlations between higher ratings on the Anomaly Observation Scale and elevated geomagnetic readings suggest that geomagnetic activity may be conducive to anomalous psychokinetic phenomena. These findings are in line with previous studies linking presumptive psychokinetic phenomena with heightened geomagnetic activity (e.g., Persinger and Cameron 1986).

The day on which the range of the magnetometer readings was widest was March 15, 1994, a day marked by rain and thunderstorms, and a day on which the ratio of "apparently anomalous" events was 1 such event every 13.71 minutes. The *Geomagnetic Indices Bulletin* for March 1994 lists March 15 as the most "magnetically disturbed" day of the month. The same bulletin lists March 20 as the tenth "most magnetically quiet" of the month. This was the "most quiet" of the days we worked with Amiden and the only day during which no events were judged to have been anomalous.

The results of our investigation were so provocative that plans were made for a more formal investigation utilizing sophisticated psychophysiological monitoring equipment. We also planned to have a Brazilian magician present because a clever sleight-of-hand artist could have performed several of the observed anomalies. Unfortunately, Amiden's health necessitated cancellation of these plans upon the insistence of his physician, who had observed an increase in Amiden's cardiovascular and gastrointestinal problems following our March 1994 visit. This was one of the greatest disappointments of my professional life. Nevertheless, the experiments we conducted at our Maimonides laboratory were rigorous enough to suggest the occasional presence of anomalies in dreams, and that a systems approach that includes environmental variables is needed to understand them.

HUMANISTIC PSYCHOLOGY

While at Maimonides Medical Center, I met Arthur Young, inventor of the Bell helicopter, a pioneer systems theorist (e.g., Young 1976) who was a volunteer research participant in our laboratory, to which he provided welcome financial support. In addition, I was invited by Julius Stulman to co-author an article about creativity and Eastern thought for his journal *Fields Within Fields* (Krippner and Arons 1973—1974). In was through Stulman that I met Ervin Laszlo, at that time directing the United Nations Institute for Training and Research. Laszlo had been credited by von Bertalanffy with writing the first book about "systems philosophy" and eventually produced a "grand synthesis" based on evolutionary principles (Laszlo 1987, 2000). I admired Laszlo's contention that evolution was now in humanity's hands, and that "only by becoming conscious of evolution can we make evolution conscious." Such a task was needed to "survive the awesome combination of highly evolved order and complexity in our brains and as yet immature and underdeveloped order in our societies" (Laszlo 1987, 149).

Similar concepts were being discussed by humanistic psychologists, and some of my colleagues and I pointed out the similarity of these concerns in an article titled, "Toward the application of general systems theory in humanistic psychology" (Krippner et al. 1985). In our paper, we cited several similarities between GST and humanistic psychology, for example, their portrayal of the human being as an "outward-striving open system," the way that feedback at various systemic levels (verbal, visual, hormonal, etc.) contributes to the human organism's organization, the importance of holistic perspectives in psychological therapy (e.g., monitoring mind/body interaction), and creativity's role in human beings' active mediation in their own existence.

The latter view was emphasized by Charlotte Buhler (1971), for whom individuals were open systems with certain "freedoms of operation" that allowed their potentials for growth. Buhler and I had worked together to organize several European humanistic psychology conferences (Krippner, Buhler, and Harari 1970), and she confided to me that her late husband, Karl, was interested in parapsychology and met regularly with a group of psychiatrists and psychological therapists to trade anecdotes and speculations about the ways in which telepathy and precognition seemed to appear in their client's dreams, imagery, and free associations. This was one of the reasons I was delighted when Division 30 of the American Psychological Association, in 1992, gave me its Charlotte and Karl Buhler Award. Years later, Ruth Richards (2000–2001), one of my colleagues at Saybrook, extended Buhler's ideas by placing several aspects of creativity within the framework of chaos theory.

I was also elated when Karl Pribram accepted my invitation to give the graduation address at Saybrook Graduate School. Pribram described his "holonomic hypothesis," and its potential for explaining many aspects of human consciousness (e.g., 1971; 1991). Pribram's laboratory data suggest that information and activity are spread out through the brain in a manner resembling a hologram. This view struck me as bold and broad because, for Pribram, brain organization and psychological organization are not simply multiple aspects of some underlying order but the actual embodiments of that order. Pribram holds that the consequences of activity change the brain even when those actions are considered "virtual" as when one brain system addresses another during attention, intention, and thinking.

In later talks, Pribram placed many of his concepts within the context of non-linear dynamics, especially chaos theory. Accordingly, one's future is dependent on initial conditions and the constraints operating at any moment. These determine the number of "degrees of freedom" or "attractors," something tantamount to "free will." Taking this a step further, Pribram noted that "spiritual experience" indicates that someone's conscious experience is attracted to patterns beyond his or her immediate daily concerns. This description resonated with me, because I have thought of "spirituality" as one's focus on, and/or reverence, openness, and connectedness to something of significance beyond one's full understanding, individual existence, and immediate daily concerns (e.g., Krippner, Jaeger, and Faith 2001).

Noting that consciousness is "relational," Pribram remarked that one can not hope to find consciousness by digging into the brain, just as one can not find gravity by digging into the earth's center. However, one can find out how the brain helps organize conscious experiences, just as one can dig into the earth to discover how its composition influences its gravitational force. If consciousness is relational, can telepathy be far behind? To his credit, Pribram is one of the few prominent neuroscientists I have found to be open to a discussion of this possibility.

Saybrook's graduation festivities also provided an opportunity to award honorary degrees, and one of the first went to my old friend Ervin Laszlo. In his acceptance address, he spoke about applications of systems thinking; much to my surprise, he included parapsychology in his panoply of new perspectives by postulating a "psi field" that complements other forms of perception. During my 1993 stay with Laszlo in his Tuscany villa, I met his son, Alexander. Within a few years, Alexander's wife, Kathia, had won a Fulbright scholarship to study at Saybrook and Alexander and I had been invited to write a chapter for a book titled, *Systems Theories and A Priori Aspects of Perception* (Laszlo and Krippner 1998). This chapter provided an opportunity for us to introduce the concept of "cognitive maps" (Laszlo 1990) as underlying patterns of conception and perception. We noted that their understanding would draw on "the sciences of complexity" to study systemic processes in both the biological and cultural realms (also see Butz 1997; Petraglia 2001).

I believe that these "cognitive maps" (or "personal myths" as David Feinstein and I [1997] have called them) are reflected in dreams. Christine Hardy (1998) finds that dreams often depict conflicts between two "chaotic attractors," for example, between dominance and cooperation, helplessness versus competence, activity versus passivity, or authenticity versus superficiality. These "cognitive maps" or "personal myths" can be thought of as "chaotic attractors," and a "mythological dialectic" is often necessary to manage or resolve the conflict. Hardy describes a dreamer whose reliance on social interactions based on authority and hierarchy was undermined by a powerful dream about cooperation and synergy. His reflection on "hierarchy versus cooperation" led him to adopt a new set of values, as well as different ways of relating to people at work and in social settings. In other words, there are practical implications to all this conjecture about "maps," "myths," and "attractors." Without a systems perspective, my work with personal mythology would have been too simplistic to deserve the application of "myth" and too linear to do justice to the complexity of the attitudes, worldviews, and schema that drive, often without one's awareness, decision making, behavior, and the interpretation of experience.

A JUNGIAN TYPOLOGY

Ian Mitroff was one of the other distinguished visitors who presented a seminar at Saybrook, where he discussed his systems-oriented typology of social scientists (Mitroff and Kilmann 1978). Borrowing Carl Jung's descriptive terms, they described the "sensing-thinking" type or "analytical scientist" as one characterized by precision, accuracy, reliability, exactness, and skepticism. In contrast, the "intuition-thinking" type or "conceptual theorist" is speculative, holistic, imaginative, and values the creation of novel conceptual possibilities. The "intuition-feeling" type or "conceptual humanist" admits to being interested rather than "disinterested," personal instead of "impersonal," and aware of personal biases rather than claiming to be "unbiased" when engaged in scientific activity. The "sensing-feeling" type or "particular humanist" holds that science does not necessarily occupy a privileged position but may be subordinate to literature, art, music, or even mysticism in approaching certain questions, a position later taken by many so-called "postmodern" thinkers. (However, I do not mean to criticize all postmodern writers; Karl Pribram has referred to Ervin Laszlo's 1993 book, *The Creative Cosmos,* as "a superb example of postmodern deconstruction at its very best.")

In an article applying this system to creativity research (Krippner 1983), I cited Paul Torrance as an "analytical scientist"; his *Tests of Creative Thinking* were breakthrough instruments in identifying and cultivating creative behavior. For my example of a "conceptual theorist" I selected J.P. Guilford, whose "Structure of Intellect" model (and its differentiation between "convergent" and "divergent" thinking) lent itself as an aid in developing curricular plans as well as serving as a diagnostic tool for individuals and groups. Rollo May was my example of a "conceptual humanist" because he used his background as a depth psychologist to portray the nature of human creativity, and his convictions as an existential psychotherapist to describe the "courage to create." For the "particular humanist," I chose Mildred Goetzel, whose case studies of 300 eminent creative personalities contained insights into their early life experiences and why, for example, they typically love learning but often dislike school. Finally, I proposed a systems model in which all four of these types could play an important role in identifying a problem, proposing alternative solutions, and implementing and/or evaluating the solution once it has been selected.

I had the opportunity to use Mitroff's typology again when I gave my presidential address to the Parapsychological Association in 1983 (Krippner 1984). For this occasion, I used J.B. Rhine, who brought quantitative, experimental, and statistical approaches into the field, as my example of the "analytical scientist."

The "conceptual theorist" I selected was E.H. Walker, who applied his work in quantum physics to the "hidden variables" that he posited were present in parapsychological interactions. My choice of a "conceptual humanist" was Lawrence LeShan, the psychologist who posited several "alternate realities" on the basis of his work with noted psychic claimants such as "mediums" and "healers."

To some extent, Louisa Rhine represented the position of the "particular humanist"; in time, it may be argued that her collection and analysis of over 15,000 anecdotal reports contributed insights to the understanding of parapsychological phenomena that equaled those produced by her husband's laboratory-focused approach. Ian Stevenson, the psychiatrist who amassed hundreds of case studies of "past life" reports, also shared many characteristics of the "particular humanist." However, both privileged formal science, and (probably to their credit) were cautious in applying their data to action-oriented movements such as "past-life therapy." For me, a better example of the "particular humanist" was Hans Bender, the German psychologist and physician who placed art, philosophy, and mystical insights on an equal footing with science, especially when he took an interest in the effect that his investigations would have on his research participants.

Again I pointed out the contribution that each type of parapsychologist could make to the advancement of the field. I noted that when the field originated, particular humanists were in the forefront of the movement; they gave way to analytical scientists when parapsychology began to utilize controlled settings and laboratory equipment. However, all four types are needed, and each has something to offer. I specifically mentioned the possibility that conceptual humanists might probe the psychodynamics of some psychic claimants who use sleight-of-hand and trickery. Indeed, during my presidency, the Parapsychological Association adopted a resolution underlining the necessity of collaborating with magicians and other specialists in legerdemain when working with psychic claimants, especially in conditions marked by minimal controls.

SELF-ORGANIZATION IN THE DREAMING BRAIN

I also applied this typology to the study of human consciousness (Krippner and Combs 1998). This time, my co-author and I used the biofeedback pioneer Joe Kamiya as our example of the "analytical scientist," the neuroscientist Karl Pribram as the "conceptual theorist," the depth psychologist James Hillman as the "conceptual humanist," and the psychiatrist Milton Erikson as the "particular humanist."

As an illustration of a "problem situation," we asked whether practicing meditation could enhance an individual's creative behavior. Knowing that the problem could be posed by any one (or combination) of the four types, we imagined that a "conceptual theorist" and a "conceptual humanist" would work together to formulate the research method. In our scenario, they decided upon Charles Tart's (1975) systems theory of states of consciousness to frame the idea that in meditation, a practitioner experiences a more fluid cognitive and affective process than in ordinary waking consciousness. The next step would be to formulate a specific scientific model. In our scenario, the "conceptual theorist" and "analytical scientist" worked together, choosing a type of insight meditation for the research participants to utilize, and outlining a set of questions that would tap the type of creative behavior that might be facilitated (e.g., satisfaction in work and personal relationships, involvement with a community theater, redecorating one's house). The "analytical scientist" then shaped the investigation utilizing an experimental and a control group, and selecting standardized tests, while the "conceptual humanist" prepared questionnaires and interview questions. The results were interpreted by the "conceptual theorist" while the "particular humanist" created programs to provide the benefits to the general public.

This article was co-authored by Alan Combs, a psychologist who I first met at the first convention of the Society for Chaos Theory in Psychology and the Neural, Human, and Social Sciences, held at Saybrook in 1991. I was instrumental in the selection of Saybrook as the host of this historic event, but even more credit must go to my colleagues Bela A. Banathy, Sr. and Arne Collen, both of whom have made far more contributions to GST than I could ever have attempted. From Banathy (e.g., 1996), I learned about "systems inquiry," an epistemology or "way of knowing" that is grounded in a systems view of the world, one that formulates theoretical postulates, conceptual paradigms, and such tools as "systems design" with its concern for the "goodness of fit" and its impact on future generations (35). From Collen (e.g., Minati and Collen 1997, 45–49), I discovered the difference between mono-disciplinarity (the typical, albeit fragmented approach to knowledge), multi-disciplinarity (the combination of several disciplines by one manager), inter-disciplinarity (the interaction among several disciplines by various specialists), and trans-disciplinarity (the attempt at a synthesis, but with "meaning and harmony" rather than "finding the ultimate truth" as a viable strategy). I have suggested that parapsychology has become a trans-disciplinary field because a common knowledge base is required to do rigorous work in this complicated field.

I gave a keynote speech at the conference, applying chaos theory to such areas of humanistic psychology as creativity, health studies, and the sleep cycle. I turned to my colleague Fred Abraham to help me refine this presentation for publication in the *Journal of Humanistic Psychology* (Krippner 1994). Combs (e.g., 1995) was another colleague who knew far more about chaos theory than I did, and volunteered to help me expand and extend my sketchy model of sleep and dreaming. Eventually, we proposed a model (Combs and Krippner 1998; Krippner and Combs 1998) that incorporates evidence that not all rapid eye movement activity is accompanied by dreams and, more important, episodes of dreaming occur during other phases of the sleep cycle. Thoughts, emotions, memories, and other components of conscious experience change from moment to moment during wakefulness as well as during sleep, as do the bodily hormones and neurochemicals with which they combine to produce various "mindbody states."

Combs and I have found evidence that there are great individual differences in the way that "mindbody states" fluctuate from day to day, even from hour to hour and minute to minute. Patterns are produced that can be called "chaotic," lending themselves to analysis by those "chaos theorists" who look for the underlying tendencies of such seemingly complex activities as weather patterns, stock market fluctuations, and the rhythms of the brain itself. Combs and I use the term "mindbody state" to describe such experiences as ecstasy, sadness, joy, and confusion. Each "mindbody state" exhibits a high degree of consistency; one does not have a sense of confidence and power while recalling past defeats and humiliations. These "mindbody states" are embedded in "states of consciousness," one of which is sleep, and during sleep, one's awareness is turned inward and sensations from the external world are prevented from reaching the higher brain centers. The muscular action and motor output is blocked so that one does not act out the scenarios of the dream. Only the motor output of the extremities are not affected; the dreamer's fingers can move, his or her toes move, and the eyes can move as well. Hence, rapid eye movements are a sign that a dream is very likely in progress. Nevertheless, dreams can occur during other stages of sleep, even though their content may not be as dramatic.

Dreaming can also be matched with the neurological activity that originates in the lower brainstem periodically during the night, traveling upward to those parts of the brain in which visual images originate. J.A. Hobson (1988), a psychiatrist, and his associates have proposed that lower brain activity evokes unstructured stimuli that are shaped by the higher brain into something meaningful. Chaos theorists refer to this phenomenon as "self-organization." Indeed, Combs and I have worked with David Kahn, a physicist (and an associate of Hobson) to describe how this self-organized activity often reflects the residues of daily life with its accompanying moods, concerns, and anxieties (Kahn, Combs, and Krippner 2002).

The part of the brain's cortex ordinarily involved in practical activity based on working memory, is less active during the night, giving other brain centers the opportunity to organize dream content. As a result, many of the resulting stories are bizarre, marked by abrupt transitions, quick changes of scene, and actions that would seem illogical in daily life. At the same time, as the chaos theorist Christine Hardy (1998) points out, dreams can provide "networks of meaning" that reflect "emotional intelligence," helping the dreamer to understand his or her personal feelings, especially about relationships with other people.

Combs and I proposed that there are two important qualities of the sleeping human brain that make the dreamer sensitive to subtle influences. The first of these qualities is the brain's susceptibility to what chaos theorists call the "butterfly effect"; very small alterations in the present condition of the brain, or of the weather, or of the stock market, can lead to major variations in its future status. A shift in the sleeping brain's neurochemistry can introduce a new image into an ongoing dream narrative, and the integration of this element into a dream story demonstrates, to Allan Hobson, the brain's incredible creative potential, even though the result might seem illogical, irrational, or unrealistic when the dreamer wakes up and remembers it.

The second remarkable quality of the sleeping brain is its capacity to respond to signals so tiny that the brain would not otherwise be affected by them. Known as "stochastic resonance" by chaos theorists, this effect has been noted in electronic circuits as well as in nerve cells. This quality of resonance keeps a system in motion following the signal where it follows the path of least resistance, rather than allowing the signal to disappear or get stuck. As a result, small, emotional residues of the day's experience may return during a nighttime dream. Several examples could be cited: a surprising scene from a movie, an intriguing face in the crowd, a sarcastic comment from a letter, or a poignant phrase from an overheard conversation.

In our opinion, the "butterfly effect" and "stochastic resonance" are qualities of the sleeping brain that make it susceptible to "telepathy" and other anomalous interactions. We suspect that dreams often begin as "chaotic attractors" that pull together diverse images, memories, and even some events distant in space and time that are attracted to the dream's forming vortex. Our colleague Ernest Hartmann (1999), a psychiatrist, has described how the brain's neural networks are open to greater novelty and emotional impact during sleep than during wakefulness, and that anomalous dreams often involve someone close to the dreamer with whom there is an emotional bond. In this manner, the self-organizing dream creates order from chaos, resulting in a unique story that may be a review of daily events, an attempt to resolve a life trauma, an inventive technological or artistic marvel, a metaphorical solution to a psychological problem, or a preview of an oncoming event in the dreamer's life.

The physicist David Bohm (1980) wrote about a subtle, underlying, inter-penetrating component of the universe that he described as order enfolded in chaos. Implicit within this order is a cooperative spirit and an inherent awareness that might be the foundation for anomalous effects such as dreams about distant and future events. Montague Ullman (1999) has suggested that the image-laden dreaming process is closer to Bohm's concept of this subtle, underlying order than the mode of waking consciousness. When dreamers work with their dreams, they can bring the implicit meaning of dream images and metaphors into explicit waking awareness. Incidentally, Hardy and Hartmann are open to the presence of anomalous effects in dreams; Hobson, however, remains doubtful.

In the meantime, Combs (2010) wrote a splendid introduction to a book I co-edited, *Mysterious Minds: the Neurobiology of Psychics, Mediums, and other Remarkable People* (Krippner and Friedman 2010). This book is systems-oriented in that it brings neurobiological data into the scope of the study of so-called psychics and mediums, thus providing a deeper understanding of what goes on in their brains and bodies while they conduct their purported work with spirits, discarnate entities, and the attempt to obtain remote information.

THE SHADOW SIDE OF SYSTEMS THEORY

Atomism (or mechanism) and holism (or organicism) are two different ways of un-derstanding the world. Both involve micro-construction and macro-construction. In atomism, the perspective of micro-construction gains detail but loses perception of the whole and an understanding of the interrelationship of parts. In holism, a holistic perception is gained, as well as an understanding of interrelationships, but detail is often lost.

GST is holistic in nature. It holds that systems are not intellectual constructions but occur naturally in one's perceptions. Development of wholes is a process of increasing complexity contributing to improved functioning; a homogeneity of structure alternates with heterogeneity, yielding transformation to more inclusive wholes. Holism describes entities as wholes having interrelated parts, where understanding the whole is prior to, and determines, description of the parts and their relationships. Interrelations of wholes qualify them as parts implying a greater whole. Relationships determine certain properties of parts, but there is always a residue of properties (especially emergent properties) of a whole that is not determined by the parts. An analytical description of parts implies some assumed understanding of a whole.

But this understanding may be a product of deduction rather than empirical induction. Deduced characteristics of whole and the methods by which they are deduced may be more metaphysical than physical. This potential dilemma has been highlighted by Morris Berman (1996), who feared that GST, in its quest for general principles, would ignore individual differences and aspirations, as well as social and historical contexts. The "order out of chaos" so fervently preached by GST advocates sounded, to Berman, suspiciously like the emerging global corporate economy with its demands for worldwide political stability.

Berman's first encounter with GST was quite positive; it provided him a framework to understand such complex historical events as the French Revolution, for which linear causal explanations had been contradictory and insufficient. He also found GST a helpful perspective for family therapists, ecologists, neuroscientists, and mathematicians, among others. But as GST was putting the last nail in "the coffin of the mechanical paradigm" (36) it may have laid the groundwork for a society where "the job of each part is to play its assigned role" (39). Instead of fostering freedom and diversity, Berman was concerned that GST could spawn corporate health managers, victims who blame themselves for their misery, and monolithic structures that pass themselves off as "complex systems" in which one dare not get out of line. He provided examples of where data from biology had been haphazardly applied to sociology, and where neurological data had been used as cultural dictates. GST enthusiasts, warned Berman, may project a paradigm onto nature—and then look for the data to justify their conclusions. Instead of stimulating change and evolution, Berman fretted, GST may find itself used to maintain an oppressive status quo!

Even if Berman has overstated his case, a worthwhile task would be to search for an antidote. Berman suggested that GST could avoid propositions that are unfalsifiable and that it would be well advised to build dialectical debate into its deliberations. From my perspective, these are worthwhile proposals. Falsifiability is an important reality check when dealing with anomalous phenomena, and the use of "cognitive maps" and "personal myths" requires a dialectical process to determine if the challenging narrative (the "counter-myth") is more functional than the belief system it attempts to replace.

Finally, Berman reminded his readers that there is nothing wrong with the mechanistic paradigm if it is simply used as a tool; after all, it performed a valuable function in liberating Western thought "from centuries of pedantic, Aristotelian dogma about nature" (46). The real culprit "is not holism or mechanism but 'ism'" (sometimes taken as an acronym for 'incredibly short memory'" (47). There is, Berman concluded, "a hierarchy of constraints involved in any system of reality"

(52), and that conclusion may be a point on which reflective advocates of GST can agree with Berman's critique.

In the wake of Berman's criticisms, I reviewed the proposition that wholes are organic unities; no part can be an independent, self-determining entity. Wholes are systems, not aggregates. Their "parts" are not directly experienced; instead they are perceived as "wholes." Oftentimes, phenomena are not directly experienced but are described metaphorically. As Hayakawa and other general semanticists remind us, metaphor is a useful tool; but metaphors must remain metaphors, not rules for behavior. When discussing anomalous phenomena, I consider such terms as "extra-sensory perception" metaphorical; I am extremely dubious that "telepathy," "clairvoyance," and "precognition" bypass the sensory apparatus of the person experiencing them.

Systems can be conceived as being, and containing, elements in a hierarchical structure that constitute relative wholes (Miller 1978). A "whole" is an ideal entity, presented to conscious awareness in different ways at different times for different reasons. These "wholes" are socially constructed synthetic products, but some GST theorists seem to write about them as if they were metaphysical entities. And here is the rub. One person's metaphysics is another person's dogma. Berman contrasted intellectual dogmatism with those spiritual perspectives that do not harbor a concept of heresy. In fact, he won an award from Saybrook's Rollo May Center that allowed him to write *Wandering God* (Berman 2000) in which indigenous spirituality was beautifully explored.

Not all elements of a system are defined by the same means: observations described in mechanical, physical, biological, and other terms may all play a part in the cumulative description. Elements not observed or explained may be assumed in anticipation of more data. Discoveries in one part of a system can not be haphazardly grafted onto elements in other parts of the system. For example, in my descriptions of various "systems of healing" (e.g., Krippner 1999), I faced enough of a challenge confining my discussion to the various terms used by allopathic and "alternative" medical practitioners, much less adding terminology from quantum physics, as is fashionable in some quarters.

Since its mid-twentieth-century conception, systems theory has held that the whole is *more* than the sum of its parts. More recent decades have added the dimension of complexity, giving birth to complex systems theory and offering the realization that the whole is also *different* than the sum of its parts (Petraglia 2001). In the meantime, chaos theorists speak of nonlinear and indeterminate "bifurcations," or transitions, between system states. Such bifurcations can reflect transformations in the development of individuals and societies. These changes may demand the creation of new and more appropriate cognitive maps, as well as revised personal and cultural myths. The field of "evolutionary systems design," at its best, can be a rigorous, future-creating, self-regulating arena of inquiry and action (e.g., Banathy 1996). Bifurcations have the potential of becoming emancipatory as new maps and myths emerge that offer a better "fit" to the newly emerging realities of individuals and their societies. It is the antiquated maps and myths that support those political, ethnic, and religious ideologies that are responsible for the three dozen wars that have raged since the beginning of the twenty-first century. If there are to be positive outcomes, they will depend upon the degrees of choice possible, and the determination of people to design their own futures.

Freedom is one potential outcome but, as Berman so eloquently pointed out, another possible result is authoritarianism in all its forms (e.g., cultism, fascism, even some varieties of globalization). Further, systems design (or any other aspect of GST) is only one possible approach to the world problematique; if GST theorists take time to reflect, they will realize the daunting efforts involved in modifying complex human and institutional systems. At best, GST can provide only one of several inputs needed to bring about systemic change.

Because they may yield hypotheses that can be tested and falsified, some implications of GST could be taken seriously by influential individuals and groups that are major "players" in science, technology, academia, the media, and government. For example, the self-organization phenomenon that operates in the dreaming brain (and elsewhere) honors nonlinear worldviews such as those of indigenous peoples and of Eastern philosophy. In the hands of an informed public, GST may contain insights that have the potential to help the human species re-vision itself in a way that will help its members to live a better life. Faced with the alternatives, this modest proposal is worth considering. Without a doubt, my encounter with a wizard enriched my life; but it also provided more questions than answers, more challenges than solutions.

REFERENCES

Adams, M. H. 1986. Variability in remote-viewing performance: Possible relationship to the geomagnetic field. In *Research in parapsychology 1985*, Eds. Weiner, D. H. and Radin, J. Metuchen, NJ: Scarecrow Press.

Banathy, B. H. 1996. *Designing social systems in a changing world*. New York: Plenum Press.

Berman, M. 1996. The shadow side of systems theory. *Journal of Humanistic Psychology* 36 (1): 28–54.

———. 2000. *Wandering God: A study in nomadic spirituality*. Albany: State University of New York Press.

Bohm, D. 1980. *Wholeness and the implicate order*. London: Routledge and Kegan Paul.

Braud, W. G. and S. P. Dennis. 1989. Geophysical variables and behavior: LVIII. Autonomic activity, hemolysis, and biological psychokinesis: Possible relationships with geomagnetic field activity. *Perceptual and Motor Skills* 68:1243–1254.

Buhler, C. 1971. Basic theoretical concepts of humanistic psychology. *American Psychologist* 26: 378–386.

Butz, M. R. 1997. *Chaos and complexity: Implications for psychological theory and practice*. Washington, DC: Taylor & Francis.

Child, I. L. 1985. Psychology and anomalous observations: The question of ESP in dreams. *American Psychologist* 40:1219–1230.

Combs, A. 1995. Psychology, chaos, and the process nature of consciousness. In *Chaos theory in psychology*, Eds. Abraham, F. D. and Gilgen, A. R., 129–137. Westport, CT: Praeger.

————. 2010. Foreword. In, *Mysterious minds: The neurobiology of psychics, mediums, and other extraordinary people.*, Eds. Krippner, S. and Friedman, H. Santa Barbara, CA: Praeger/ABC-CLIO.

Combs, A. and S. Krippner. 1998. Dream sleep and waking reality: A dynamical view of two states of consciousness. In *Toward a science of consciousness: The Second Tucson Discussions and Debates*, Eds. Hameroff, S., Kaszniak, W. and Scott, A. C., 487–493. Cambridge, MA: MIT Press.

Feinstein, D. and S. Krippner. 1997. *The mythic path.* New York: Putnam/Jeremy P. Tarcher.

Hardy, C. 1998. *Networks of meaning: The bridge between mind and matter.* Westport, CT: Praeger/Greenwood.

Hartmann, E. 1999. *Dreams and nightmares: The new theory on the origin and meaning of dreams.* New York: Plenum Press.

Hastings, A. and S. Krippner. 1961. Expectancy set and "poltergeist" phenomena. *ETC: A Review of General Semantics* 18:349–360.

Hayakawa, S. I. 1949. *Language in thought and action.* New York: Harcourt, Brace.

Hobson, A. J. 1988. *The dreaming brain.* New York: Basic Books.

Kahn, D., A. Combs and S. Krippner. 2002. Dreaming as a function of chaos-like stochastic processes in the self-organizing brain. *Nonlinear Dynamics, Psychology, and Life Sciences* 6:311–322.

Krippner, S. 1968. Etiological factors in reading disability of the academically talented in comparison to pupils of average and slow-learning ability. *Journal of Educational Research* 61: 275–279.

————. 1975. *Song of the siren: A parapsychological odyssey.* New York: Harper and Row.

————. 1983. A systems approach to creativity based on Jungian typology. *Gifted Child Quarterly* 27:86–89.

————. 1984. A systems approach to psi research based on Jungian typology. In *Research in parapsychology 1983*, Eds. White, R. A. and Broughton, R. S., 153–166. Metuchen, NJ: Scarecrow Press.

————. 1994. Humanistic psychology and chaos theory: The third revolution and the third force. *Journal of Humanistic Psychology* 24 (3): 48–61.

————. 1999. Common aspects of traditional healing systems across cultures. In *Essentials of complementary and alternative medicine*, Eds. Jonas, W. B. and Levin, J. S., 181–199. Philadelphia: Lippincott Williams & Wilkins.

Krippner, S. and M. Arons. 1973–1974. Creativity East, creativity West. *Fields Within Fields* 10:25–31.

Krippner, S. and A. Combs. 1998. A systems approach to studies of creativity and consciousness. *Systems Research and Behavioral Science* 15:81–91.

————. 2002. A systems approach to self-organization in the dreaming brain. *Kybernetes: The International Journal of Systems and Cybernetics* 31:1452–1462.

Krippner, S. and H. Friedman, eds. 2010. *Mysterious minds: The neurobiology of psychics, mediums, and other extraordinary people.* Santa Barbara, CA: Praeger/ABC-CLIO.

Krippner, S. and M. Persinger. 1996. Evidence for enhanced congruence between dreams and distant target material during periods of decreased geomagnetic activity. *Journal of Scientific Exploration* 10:487–493.

Krippner, S., C. Buhler and C. Harari. 1970, November. AHP's first international invitation conference on humanistic psychology: A joint report. *Association for Humanistic Psychology Newsletter* pp. 1, 6.

Krippner, S., C. Jaeger and L. Faith. 2001. Identifying and utilizing spiritual content in dream reports. *Dreaming* 11:127–147.

Krippner, S., A. Vaughan and S. J. P. Spottiswoode. 2000. Geomagnetic factors in subjective precognitive experiences. *Journal of the Society for Psychical Research* 64: 109–118.

Krippner, S., A. Becker, M. Cavallo and B. Washburn. 1972, Fall. Electrophysiological studies of ESP in dreams: Lunar cycle differences in 80 telepathy sessions. *Human Dimensions* 1 (1): 14–19.

Krippner, S., A. J. Rutenber, S. R. Engelman and D. L. Granger. 1985. Toward the application of general systems theory in humanistic psychology. *Systems Research* 2: 105–115.

Krippner, S., M. Winkler, A. Amiden, R. Crema, R. Kelson, H. Lal Arora and P. Weil. 1996. Physiological and geomagnetic correlates of apparent anomalous phenomena observed in the presence of a Brazilian "sensitive." *Journal of Scientific Exploration* 10: 281–298.

Laszlo, A. 1990. Cognitive maps and the energy-culture interaction. *World Futures* 30 (3): 8–13.

Laszlo, A. and S. Krippner. 1998. Systems theories: Their origins, foundations, and development. In *Systems theories and a priori aspects of perception*, Ed. Jordan, J. S., 47–74. New York: Elsevier.

Laszlo, E. 1987. *Evolution: The grand synthesis.* Boston: Shambhala.

———. 1993. *The creative cosmos: A unified science of matter, life, and mind.* Edinburgh: Floris Books.

———. 2000. *Macroshift 2001–2010: Creating the future in the early 21st century.* New York: ToExcel.

Miller, J. 1978. *Living systems.* New York: McGraw Hill.

Minati, G. and A. Collen. 1997. *Introduction to systemics.* Walnut Creek, CA: Eagleye Books International.

Mitroff, I. I. and R. H. Kilmann. 1978. *Methodological approaches to social science.* San Francisco: Jossey-Bass.

Murphy, G. 1947. *Personality: A biosocial approach to origins and structure.* New York: Harper and Brothers.

———. 1958. *Human potentialities.* New York: Basic Books.

Persinger, M. A. 1975. ELF field mediation in spontaneous psi events: Direct information or conditioned elicitation? *Psychoenergetic Systems* 3: 155–169.

———. 1985. Geophysical variables and behavior: XXX. Intense paranormal activities occur during days of quiet, global geomagnetic activity. *Perceptual and Motor Skills* 61: 320–322.

———. 1989. Psi phenomena and temporal lobe activity: The geomagnetic factor. In *Research in parapsychology 1988*, Eds. Henkel, L. A. and Berger, R., 121–156. Metuchen, NJ: Scarecrow Press.

Persinger, M. A. and R. A. Cameron. 1986. Are earth faults at fault in some poltergeist-like episodes? *Journal of the American Society for Psychical Research* 80: 49–73.

Persinger, M. and S. Krippner. 1989. Dream ESP experiments and geomagnetic activity. *Journal of the American Society for Psychical Research* 83: 101–116.

Petraglia, I. 2001. *Olhar sobre o olhar que olha: Complexidade, holistica e educacao* [Looking at the look that looks: Complexity, holism, and education]. Petropolis, Brazil: Editora Vozes.

Pribram, K. H. 1971. *Languages of the brain: Experimental paradoxes and principles in neuropsychology.* Englewood Cliffs, NJ: Prentice-Hall.

———. 1991. *Brain and perception: Holonomy and structure in figural processing.* Hillsdale, NJ: Lawrence Erlbaum.

Rapoport, A. 1960. *Fights, games, and debates*. Ann Arbor: University of Michigan Press.

————. 1968. General system theory. In *The international encyclopedia of social sciences*, Vol. 15, Ed. Sills, D. L., 452–458. New York: Macmillan/The Free Press.

Richards, R. 2000–2001. Millennium as opportunity: Chaos, creativity, and J.P. Guilford's structure-of-intellect model. *Creativity Research Journal* 13: 249–265.

Tart, C. T. 1975. *States of consciousness*. New York: E.P. Dutton.

————. 1988. Geomagnetic effects on ESP: Two studies. *Journal of the American Society of Psychical Research* 82: 193–216.

Ullman, M. 1999. Dreaming consciousness: More than a bit player in the search for answers to the mind/body problem. *Journal of Scientific Exploration* 13: 91–112.

Ullman, M. and S. Krippner, with A. Vaughan. 1989. *Dream telepathy: Experiments in nocturnal ESP* (2nd ed.). Jefferson, NC: McFarland.

von Bertalanffy, L. 1968. *General system theory: Foundations, development, applications*. New York: George Brazillier.

Young, A. M. 1976. *The reflexive universe: Evolution of consciousness*. San Francisco: Robert Briggs/Delacorte.

A CIGARETTE IS SOMETIMES JUST A CIGARETTE

ALBERT LOW

Montreal Zen Center, Montreal, Canada

In this short autobiographical account the author shows the evolution of an insight that he had in 1958 and that he has explored throughout his life. The insight is of an ambiguity that exists at the heart of the way we perceive the world. The ambiguity lies in our seeing ourselves simultaneously as at the center of the world and at the periphery of this same center. The author describes the effects that this ambiguity has in our lives and in the way we think about the world.

A Zen master held up his hand and declared, "If you call this a hand I will give you thirty blows of my stick. If you say it is not a hand. I will give you thirty blows with my stick. Now, what is it?" —A Zen koan

"So, what is it then?" We were sitting on the top deck of a London double-decker bus peering at a cigarette. "Um, a cigarette," she offered. We had only known each other for a short while, although she was destined to be my wife. At that moment, though, she no doubt wondered what she had got into. That was 1950, well before cigarettes were linked so clearly with cancer and I usually had a cigarette between my fingers. "That's the name we have given to it," I said. "Beyond the name, what is it? For example, one could say it is something white. But, science tells us, whiteness is what it is not. Whiteness is the result of light waves that have been reflected by the cigarette. It's similar with weight and smell. Weight comes from the pull of gravity. The smell comes form molecules that are no longer connected with it in any way." I repeated, "So what is it in itself?" We both looked somewhat glumly at the cigarette. I had only just encountered the question, which was really the question "What is reality?" and I was fascinated by it. The fascination has persisted throughout my life.

"What is reality?" has not just been an intellectual question for me. Several experiences I have had have shown that what we call reality is provisional, tentative. Probably the first of these occurred when I was about seven or eight years old. I had two precognitive dreams in fairly quick succession. I have not mentioned this to many people since, but I have no doubt that they were real precognitive dreams, and have wondered about them on and off throughout my life. Although many of the questions that life has posed have been put to rest, how one can possibly foretell the future, not in some vague way, but with specific detail, has remained a mystery for me. Given that they were authentic, and I have no doubt in my own mind that they were, then precognitive dreams show that reality must be quite other than we normally believe.

One of the dreams was about a propelling pencil that my grandfather had given me. It was one of those pencils that are used for promotion of some product. It was white and the writing black. I lost the pencil. Then I had the dream. In the dream a ginger-haired boy passed the pencil through the wire mesh of the fence that surrounded the school that I attended. I recognized the boy in the dream; he lived opposite the school. A few days later the boy with ginger hair who lived opposite the school passed the pencil to me though the wire mesh of the school. A writer, J. W. Dunne, an early aeronautical engineer, wrote several books on the subject of precognitive dreams. One was called *An Experiment with Time* (1929) in which he tries to account for them. He had a number of them himself and had collected examples of these dreams from other people. It was after reading that book that I really wondered about them.

Another experience, a pivotal one, has been at the origin of most of what I have thought about during the rest of my life. It occurred in 1957 when I was on a ranch in the northern Transvaal, in South Africa. I had gone there, with my wife and young daughter, to study for a degree. I was studying with the University of South Africa by a correspondence course. We lived in a partially completed house with a thatched roof, without electricity, phone or cooking facilities, and we had no car. My wife cooked on an open fire in the courtyard surrounding the house. Our nearest neighbor was six miles away and the nearest town 12 miles distant, although there was a Poste Restante about six miles away. Mail for the surrounding area was delivered here, and it was open twice a week for people to collect mail. I went there each time it was open to pick up and drop off assignments and books, doing the 12-mile round trip on foot. The area was a semi desert and only tough grass and stunted trees could grow there. The ranch was located in a hollow surrounded on all sides by low hills, and a strange but peaceful silence pervaded the whole area. It was an ideal place for deep meditation.

I was studying philosophy and psychology as main subjects, and at the time of the experience I was studying Kant's *Critique of Pure Reason*. Kant too had evidently been fascinated by the question of what is reality and he broaches the subject in that book. He says that what we know is the phenomenal world and this is a mixture of mental categories and sense perceptions. The categories act as a kind of mould that determines the shape, so to say, of our experience. But, he says, a noumenal world lies beyond the phenomenal world. The noumenal world moreover cannot be known. It is not simply unknown, but *unknowable*. The cigarette that I see is a collection of sense perceptions, whiteness, acrid smell, light weight and so on, molded by categories of time, space, causation, and unity. But beyond this world that I perceive lies the noumenal world.

What he said resonated with me. The two most common philosophical answers to the question "What is it?" are naive realism and idealism, and I felt that both were unsatisfactory. Naive realism denies any kind of mystery. A cigarette, a naïve realist says, is a cigarette and all questioning of that fact comes from an overwrought mind. Naïve realism is the common sense view of things. If we see a bus coming toward us, we step out of its way as fast as we can. The idealist says that all that we can know of the cigarette is what we *know* of it. This may seem tautological but it is not really so. For the naive realist the world is there and then I see it. For the idealist the seeing comes first and what I see is contingent. Both of these views are logically irrefutable and mutually exclusive. Now Kant comes along with a third view. His categories acknowledge the part played by the subject, and the sense perceptions acknowledge the part played by the object. But they both "come out of" the noumenal world.

That the noumenal world is neither a sense perception nor a category means that it cannot be known. This created a problem for me that could be roughly stated as, "How is it possible to talk about what cannot be known?" This is not quite the problem and it could also be stated, "How is it possible to know what cannot be known," or even, "How do we know we do not know." I am vague about the question because, in a way, it just cannot be formulated. In Zen Buddhism this same question became stylized into "What is Buddha?" or "Why did Bodhidharma (the first Zen Patriarch) come to the West?" The question was formalized in this way because, although very real, it is beyond the reach of the conceptual mind, and comes out of the nature of human existence itself.

I wandered around in something of a daze locked into this question that could not really be formulated, and so could not be answered, or at least could not be answered conceptually in a clear and distinct fashion. Suddenly everything became clear, in a moment of lightning insight. The nearest that I can come to saying what was revealed is that *I am at the center and at the periphery of the world at the same time*. How this related to my original puzzlement was not at the time either clear or important. For several months afterwards I lived in a clarity and lack of concern, even though I was stricken by tick bite fever, a particularly nasty kind of fever that comes from being bitten by a tick, and was harassed by a number of other difficulties, not the least of which was finding a job. As luck would have it the onset of the illness coincided with our decision to return to Johannesburg. In spite of this attack of tick bite fever, and of the difficulty in finding work that I had after I recovered, my sense of freedom and clarity persisted.

Since that moment of clarity I have been trying to communicate the import of what I saw. I have only very recently, forty-five years later, seen the connection between the way I have formulated the insight: "me-as-center/me-as-periphery" and the Kantian account of the noumenon. I will explain what I mean by this later on in this article. However, what I saw on that ranch revolutionized my whole way of thinking and it eventually drove me to practice Zen.

Let me try to elaborate on what I saw that day, but I must warn you that the exposition may not be easy to follow. The main difficulty comes from the fact that what I want to talk about lies upstream of consciousness. Indeed I am firmly convinced through my own experience and by the teaching of Buddhism, that what we call "I" and "consciousness" have evolved as buffers, so to speak, against its implications. This means that it is pre-verbal. It is also prior to logic.

One of the main outcomes of this experience is that I have had to evolve a new logic to talk about it and its consequences. I call this logic *the logic of ambiguity*. Another difficulty in talking about this experience is that our civilization has almost lost sight of the importance of the dynamic center. Some writers, such as Rudolph Arnheim, on art, Zuckerkandl on music, Jung on psychology, and above all Mircea Eliade on mythology, have recognized its importance, but in a limited way.

Let me start by talking about the dynamic center as indeed "conscious" life begins with it. I put the word "conscious" in parentheses as I use it provisionally for the moment. I will need to refine my vocabulary as we go on. Each sentient being is a dynamic center, a viewpoint. This means that you, the reader, are a viewpoint. If you were to be on an ocean liner far out to sea, or were in the midst of the prairies, you would understand immediately what I mean by saying also that you are a dynamic center. It would seem as though the whole world were a vast plate and you were at the center of this plate.

A soccer match can illustrate the difference between a dynamic center and a geometric center. The geometric center is marked on the field and is at the center of a central circle, which is equidistant from the two goals. This geometric center is fixed. The dynamic center is the ball. The center of gravity of the game is always in the ball. When the ball goes out of play a certain kind of tension leaves the field, which only returns when the ball is back in play. The dynamic center therefore moves around the field and a field of power surrounds the ball, which diminishes as one moves away from the ball.

When I say that you are at the center of the sphere, however, I am only giving half the story. The other half shows itself most clearly when you are with another person, particularly if you are also looking her or him in the eyes. Now, instead of being simply at the center of the world looking out at it, you are also looked at by another center of the world to which you are peripheral. In other words, *you are simultaneously at the center and at the periphery*.

Most people, under normal circumstances, find that they get somewhat tense if they look another in the eyes. Good manners dictate that one does not stare at another, but rather that one looks into his or her eyes and then looks away, then back again and so on. Sometimes one is even forbidden to look into the other's eyes. For example, when I was at boot camp as a sailor in the British navy the petty officer would yell, "Don't eyeball me sailor!" if one inadvertently looked him in the eye. This is done because the one who looks is in the position of power and the petty officer knew that he alone could have the power. Sometimes a contest will arise between people in which one tries to stare down the other and so determine who is the most powerful. Boxers for example will lock eyes while touching gloves before a fight begins, and the fight may well be determined at that moment. Macho men will often wear sunglasses, even though the sun is absent, because in this way they can look, but not be looked at, in the eye. What all this illustrates is that only one dynamic center is possible at a time. If two dynamic centers arise, and one will not yield to the other, then tension and even a fight will follow.

This encounter with another simply illustrates what I mean by me-as-center/me-as-periphery. My tension is not *caused* by the existence of the other, but is *triggered* by him. He triggers the tension, which lies dormant within me, a tension that arises because "me," the viewpoint, is divided in itself: me-as-center/me-as-periphery. This means that the original conflict is not between him and me, but *within me, the viewpoint itself*. The viewpoint is at the very source of my entry into the world, and so this schism or wound is at the very heart of my being. The viewpoint is the center, but the viewpoint sees itself as the center and in this way it is at the periphery of itself. This is often referred to as *awareness of awareness,* which, as most people know, is the basis of consciousness. The ancients depicted this as the oroborus, a snake that swallows its own tail. However, the situation is more complicated than this picture will allow as it cannot be determined which is the head and which the tail of the snake.

Is there any evidence to support what I am saying? I think that all kinds of evidence exist. For example, many different organisms—caterpillars, moths, frogs, and insects, fish—have false staring eyes "painted" on their bodies. These false eyes are perceived as threatening by would-be predators, and this gives the organism a greater chance of surviving. However, the eyes themselves have no power; they are simply patches of color in the shape of an eye. The power is derived from the conflict within the predator. Staring eyes are a cliché in horror movies and are used to evoke terror. The camera will suddenly switch to the staring eyes of a doll or a cat or a blind man. This will cause the audience to experience a thrill of horror, although the "eyes" are no more than shadows thrown onto a screen. Again they just awaken the schism dormant upstream of the conscious mind.

Because they do not create the fear but only trigger it, the eyes do not necessarily have to be physically present. You can have the *feeling* that another is watching you even though you cannot see another. You may have this feeling when alone in a strange house at night, a feeling that is often accompanied by frissons of fear. This "feeling" of another being present is a very well known mystical phenomenon and many accounts of it are available in the literature. Perhaps one of the most famous is Saul's encounter with Christ on the way to Damascus. Other accounts are given of people who experience a near-death experience during which some people "meet" a being of light, which, depending on their religion they might call Christ, Buddha, Krishna, or even God.

Frank Tipler, a physicist, suggests that computers will one day be perceived as being alive. He gives the following criteria by which you will tell if a machine is alive, and in doing so he follows the lead of Alan Turing, one of the early pioneers of the computer. He says, "if you talk to the machine—really talk to it, carry on a conversation with it just as you would with another normal human [sic] being—then the machine is intelligent. If after interacting for years with the machine it acts as if it has a personality, has consciousness, (and a conscience), then it really does" (1994, 20). But of course any young child could have told him that. The young girl nurses her doll, talks to it, feeds it and for her it is alive. One only has to remember the cartoon characters Calvin and Hobbes. But no sane adult will agree with the child. Is the child then mad? No, no more mad than Tipler. In both cases the other that they encounter is not the machine or the doll but the other half of "me-as-center/me-as-periphery."

All of this suggests that the other is not "out there," but the other half, so to say, of "me." I am not suggesting for a moment that the other is a product of my imagination or consciousness or anything like that. You and me come into existence at the same time; neither is dependent upon the other, both are equally "real," but neither is dependent on being "something"—a body, soul, or spirit—to exist. Many people have difficulty with this idea because they are convinced that they are an isolated "something" in a world that is simply a collection of somethings. Many go further to believe that they are simply the body and all that happens—imagination, thought, feeling, and so on—are but movements of matter. Others believe that they are a unique, independent soul. If any of these hear that the other is but the other half of the self then they immediately construe it to mean that the other is simply a product of my imagination and that I am condemning everyone to some kind of solipsistic isolation. On the contrary, what I am saying is a refutation of solipsism.

Another objection that may be raised is that looking another in the eyes, or the encounter with the other in a mystical encounter, does not necessarily create tension, but, on the contrary, may generate powerful feelings of love. In the film *Damage* that was shown in movie theaters a several ago, a father fell in love with his son's girlfriend. The moment of his falling in love was when he encountered her for the first time at a party and looked into her eyes. When the two held each other's gaze for a prolonged period of time was a dramatic moment in the film. But everyone knows that looking into the eyes of the one whom one loves arouses the feeling of love. Many love songs tell us about this. Furthermore the mystical presence of the other often brings very powerful feelings of love, feelings that are much more intense than the secular love that we feel for another human being.

This means that the context within which the "encounter" occurs is important. The same situation in two different contexts can provoke two entirely different reactions. But then is it not well known that love can turn easily into hate and hate into love? Not unusually, a mystic, after a period of intense ecstatic communion with the other, falls into deep anguish. The fifth-century mystic of Ireland, St Anthony, is an example of this.

At the time I had the experience I was not able to make sense of it in the way that I have written above. I knew at the deepest level that what I had seen into was of immense importance but it has only been after years of reflection and an intense meditation practice that it has come to be conceptually meaningful.

The next step in the evolution of my thinking came about seven years later. By this time I was living with my family in Canada. We had left South Africa in 1963 because of the political situation. This was the time of the Sharpeville massacre and the treason trials and the trials of Nelson Mandela when he was sentenced to life imprisonment on Robben Island. In Canada I was working for a utility company in Southwest Ontario and had the responsibility to set up wage scales for the company. In order to get ready for the task I read up on the latest literature about the subject and came across the work of Elliot Jaques.

Jaques was originally from Montreal and had graduated from McGill as an MD. He had gone on to Harvard and obtained a doctorate in social science and then went to England to work with the Freudian analyst Melanie Klein. After the '39–'45 war he joined the Tavistock Institute and was part of a team that researched ways to ease the transition from a wartime to a peacetime economy. He went to the Glacier Metal Industry and worked with the CEO, Wilfred Brown, who had been first made CEO at the age of' 33. The result of this partnership was quite remarkable. Brown was eventually made a peer of the realm for his contribution to British industry. The work that Jaques and Brown did attracted so much attention that in order to cope with it they set up the Glacier Institute of Management, which eventually became internationally famous.

I discovered that Jaques and Brown were to conduct a seminar at Illinois University. I attended the seminar together with my boss and another VP. During the seminar I had what one might call a psychological, subterranean explosion. On the surface nothing seemed to have changed but then I found that I was thinking quite differently about a company, what a company is, as well as about other things that had puzzled me for so long. For the next nine months I struggled to make sense of this. Eventually I sent what I had written to J. G. Bennet and he published a synopsis of it under the title of "The Systematics of a Business Organization," in a journal called *Systematics* that he published at his Institute at Coombe Springs, England (1996a). This was later expanded and became the basis of my book *Zen and Creative Management* (1966b).

Bennett was quite a remarkable man. He spoke many languages. He was a philosopher and a mathematician. He was also a student of Ouspensky and Gurdjieff. The Institute at Coombe Springs was originally dedicated to teaching Gurdjieff's methods and thoughts, but Bennett extended the scope of the Institute later in his life. I had first encountered Gurdjieff's work in 1949 when I read *In Search of the Miraculous* written by P. D. Ouspensky (1949). The work of all three of these men has influenced me very profoundly. The part that is particularly germane to what I am saying now is Gurdjieff's teaching of the "cosmos" and eneagram, and Bennett's adaptation of this in Systematics, which he wrote about extensively in vol. 3 of his work that he called *The Dramatic Universe* (1966).

Another writer whose work I have admired was Arthur Koestler. I had read his book *The Act of Creation* (1964) not long before going to Illinois. At Jaques's seminar, Koestler's definition of the act of creation, Jaques definition of work, Bennett's Systematics, and my own insight that we are the center and periphery simultaneously suddenly coalesced in my mind, although, as I have said, it took awhile before the result of this coalescence could be articulated.

I cannot give a full account of all that this implied. All the books that I have written since, with the exception of *An Invitation to practice Zen* (1989) are dedicated to clarifying the implications of this and the other insights that have come to me. What came to me was not simply a new view on the organization of a company but an insight into the nature and process of life itself. I saw particularly that creativity was basic to life, but it has taken years for me to grasp what this means.

The bare bones of what was revealed are the following. Jaques defined work as the exercise of discretion within limits in order to produce a result. Koestler said that creativity arises when a *single* situation or idea is perceived in "*two* self-consistent but habitually *incompatible* frames of reference" (1964, 33). I saw that Jaques's definition of work falls within Koestler's definition of creativity. He said that the most basic limits are cost and quality. Thus on the one hand quality must be the highest possible, but the costs must be kept as low as possible. The two limits are incompatible. But Jaques definition of work also transformed my understanding of creativity, because it shows that creativity always occurs within limits; it is not simply an arbitrary happening.

At a deeper level still we can see, using the same insight, that our life itself is an ongoing creative process. The two most basic incompatible frames of reference of Koestler's definition of creativity were me-as-center/me-as-periphery. These are also the limits within which subsequent creativity will occur. Because each of us is an individual, that which cannot be divided, each of us is a single force that arises in these two incompatible frames of reference. No entity is involved. The individual, me, is a viewpoint, something that is happening, not something that "is." Individuality is also not "something," and later I came to see that individuality comes out of a basic "dynamic unity." This means that each of us is creativity, a symphony that is unfolding, a creation in process. If we prefer to use Jaques's definition of work, then we are work in process; the limits are the same incompatible frames of reference, me-as-center/me-as-periphery. But what is the product or result that is being created or produced by this work?

Let me put what I have said in a slightly different way. As an individual I am single; as a viewpoint I am divided against myself. I am one yet two. The Sufis call this the *unoambus*. All our joys and agonies arise from this impossibility for the following reason. I pointed out that when two men look each other in the eye a contest is likely to break out about who is the dynamic center, who has the position of power. If they are equally matched and if neither can give way to the other, then the contest is likely to escalate into a fight. The fight could be a fight to mutual destruction. In the divided viewpoint two equally matched centers arise, neither of which can give way to the other because both are "me." Me, the center, is the same me that is periphery. But, in that they are both me, which me is the center and which periphery? This is as though you were the actor on the stage and a member of the audience *at the same time*. The upshot is that me is in contest with me for dominance. This leads to a vicious circle and the various emotions arise out of this vicious circle.

We are all aware of what this means. We become anxious. We then get anxious about being anxious. This builds up until we begin to panic because we are so anxious and then we panic because we are panicking. Or we are angry. We get angry about being angry. This builds up until we are in a rage about being angry and then in a rage about being in a rage. The same cycle can be found to exist for depression and for joy. The emotion comes from me separating myself from myself. We have the expression "I was beside myself with anger or anxiety or fear" and so on.

An opposite cycle builds up with love. In love we yield the center to the other, while the other yields the center to me. This encourages me to yield further encouraging the other to yield further and so the love increases in intensity. Whereas the first cycle leads to the feeling of me being swallowed by me, in love the feeling is of me becoming one with me. Mystical states, the feeling of a beloved being present and of a loving light, or being of light as it is also called, being present can be understood in this way.

A moment ago I said that we are work in process and then I asked what is the product or result created or produced by this work? Just after the Jacques seminar I saw also that a product is *an idea in a form with a demand*. This perception itself was a creative leap.

At that time management by objectives was the managerial mantra, and it seemed to me that this was very much management by pie in the sky. If work really was the exercise of discretion within limits to produce a result, the result is a product. This meant that each role in the company was there to produce a specific product or number of products that would be in demand by other parts of the company and eventually by the company product. This also meant that the way roles interacted within a company could be clearly defined according to the product of a role and its relation to that part of the company that needed the product. This offered a new way of looking at a company, which among other things would supercede the old staff-line way of seeing a company.

But it also offered an answer to the question, "What is being created by the work in process that I call my life."

Before I explain what I mean by this let me repeat, creativity arises when a single idea brings about a resolution of the tension inherent in two incompatible frames of reference. The resolution takes the form of a new unity. Perhaps the best illustration of the tension being resolved in a creative act is given in humor, because we are all familiar with the explosion of laughter that often accompanies a joke. The following joke gives an example of what I mean.

Two hunters were out hunting and one of them suddenly collapsed. The other, fearing his friend had died, took out his cellphone and, in a panic, called 911. The operator, wanting to get some control over the situation said, "Look, please calm down. Just make sure that your friend is indeed dead." There was silence on the line for a few minutes. The operator heard a shot and then the caller said, "Right, what's next?"

"Just make sure that your friend is indeed dead" can be understood in two entirely different and incompatible ways. As each way has equal call on us we are faced with two incompatible frames of reference in which we have to find a single understanding. In a joke the tension is released in laughter. Many doctors recognize the curative power of laughter because the release may not simply be the release of the tension induced by the two incompatible statements, but the release could be of tension induced at a much deeper level, the level of me-as-center/me-as-periphery. This tension, in the extreme can be felt as terror, horror, uncontrollable rage, and so on. Most frequently, however, the tension is controlled and we feel it as a grumbling sense of dissatisfaction, remote emotional pain, a feeling that something valuable escapes us.

The control that I speak of is maintained by the "product" that arises from the creative tension generated by the basic wound. We call the product that is created, the "self," "personality," "experience," "I," and so on. Furthermore, with the aid of language, consciousness evolves, and the threat from the basic schism is controlled even more. This is why I said earlier that "I" and "consciousness" are buffers protecting us from anguish. But, they are also creations.

Nevertheless the threat, although under control, remains. Periodically the stability of the ego is shaken and anxiety, anger, depression, or fear asserts itself again. Buddha said that life is suffering and the word he used for suffering was *duhkha* dualism, twoness.

Me-as center/me-as-periphery, therefore, can be understood not only as the cause of suffering but also as the basis for the creativity of life. One can see how far life is from being a mechanical process, and how far organisms, including human beings, are from being simply machines. One can see that life is essentially an ongoing creative process and organisms themselves are essentially creativity.

One aspect of the product I, or what is known pejoratively as "ego," must be mentioned because it plays such a dominant role in our lives. Each viewpoint sees itself as unique, special, apart, and superior. The famous saying that comes from Yorkshire, England sums it up well. "All the world's a bit queer except thee and me. But sometimes I'm not too sure about thee." Evidence for saying that each viewpoint sees itself as unique abounds. Nationalism, competition in industry, in sports, in fashions, in academia, as well as the need to be the first or the only one are examples of what I mean. The Guinness Book of Records tells of the extent which we will go to be the first in something, unique in some way. That periodically we come to the brink of destroying the world shows how important it is for each of us to feel that he or she is unique, the only one. The reason for this is obvious. We are individual, One. We suffer because we are divided against ourselves. We seek to overcome the suffering by discovering a new unity, uniqueness.

That I am unique is not enough. I must be known to be unique by others. In other words, the product must have a demand, it must be linked into a wider context, which in a company is called a market. We look for praise, acknowledgment, and recognition. We seek after certificates, honors, degrees, medals, and rank. We also invest this uniqueness in a flag, a country, another person, an ideology, or what have you, and then claim that country, flag, ideology and even "the Fuhrer" to be "mine."

I met Jaques and Brown at Illinois in the spring of 1965 and for the following year I was struggling with what I had seen into. It was during this year that I wrote "The Systematics of a Business Organization" and that I started talking to the management of the company about these ideas and trying to find some way to use them in practice. I received great encouragement from the president of the company to whom I had given an outpouring of thoughts and ideas that lasted over an hour. I do not think he understood much of what I was talking about, but he obviously was infected by my enthusiasm and encouraged me to talk to the rest of management. I was to do this for the next six years on and off with varying degrees of success.

In the autumn of 1966 my wife and I met the Japanese Zen master Yasutani roshi and we began formal Zen training. I had been sitting in meditation regularly since the spring of 1964 and even before that had sat in a desultory fashion since 1961. The encounter with Yasutani had a dramatic effect on my health and on me. My blood pressure shot up and I was to suffer long periods of insomnia and my life became a constant struggle with anxiety. I had no doubt that in Yasutani and in the practice of Zen I had found what I had sought for years so ardently. I remember the sheer elation that I felt after attending a weekend workshop with Yasutani in a holiday resort that was rented north of Toronto. My wife and I followed this with a four-day retreat near Rochester, New York. We then became members of the Rochester Zen Center where we practiced for the next twenty years, and for three of these we were residents at the Center. Yet with my meeting with Yasutani it was as though a dam had burst and I had difficulty keeping everything in balance. Fortunately I had a very understanding wife, three very bright children, and a very challenging job, all of which anchored me solidly to the ground. I continued working on the ideas of organization and, with my wife, practiced three hours of meditation a day: two in the morning and one in the evening.

Unfortunately, for him but also for me in a far less terrible way, the president of the company where I was working contracted Parkinson's disease and was forced to retire. His replacement was a much younger man who was full of good ideas on how to modernize the company. He did not agree with what I was doing and felt that it was more suited to a university and stopped all of the work I had undertaken. This was in 1972. I then decided that I would have to leave the business world and do something to promote Zen.

I started to write a book, although I did not feel that I had really resolved the practical issues of the theory. I had seen that the principal products that most people made within a company, certainly those at the supervisory and foreman levels and above, are decisions, and the company therefore is a network of decisions. I tried to come up with decision tables to show how this network was linked. This was a very crude idea but the new president did not give me the time to refine it into something more worthwhile. Had personal computers been as available as they are today, I think I could even so have made something worthwhile of the theory. We were working with IBM 360s and it took two to three days to get documents processed, documents that these days would be processed in two to three seconds.

Another big obstacle to a decent theory of management and organization is that a company is not simply a decision-making structure, which would be dependent on a structure of perceived authority. It is also a power structure. Authority is exercised within limits and is a property of the role, whereas power has uncertain limits and is a property of the person exercising it. Whereas the decision structure is ultimately centered upon the company product, the power structure is centered on particular individuals and the relation that these have with other centers of power in the company. I could see that a whole new kind of research would have to be conducted to determine whether ways could be found to identify the power structure, and then perhaps to limit its deleterious effects on the decision structure.

On a retreat at Rochester in December of 1974 I came to awakening. This eliminated in one stroke all the anxiety and oppression with which my life had been encumbered for so long. I had a freedom of spirit that could have hardly been imagined possible just days before the awakening. My understanding of course also underwent a further development.

One of the first things that became evident was that things are "empty." One metaphor that is used in Zen to explain what this means is the metaphor of the mirror. We see reflections in the mirror; we do not usually see the mirror. Analogously the world is the reflections; the mirror is the "knowing." We usually say, "The sun is shining" or "the house is over there," or "the flowers are blooming." In other words we make statements about the world and imply by those statements that the world is separate from us, "over there" so to say. Science is based on this belief in the independence of the world. This is the objectivity of science as well as the objectivity of naïve realism.

However, the statement "the sun is shining" is a shorthand statement, and is really incomplete because we ignore the "mirror." The full statement should be "I know the sun is shining." "I know the flowers are blooming." And so on. The "I know" is usually dropped because it is taken for granted, and it is taken for granted because the "I know" is always the same, always constant. Earlier, when speaking of the naïve realist and the idealist, I said that as a naive realist I would believe that the world is there and then I see it. As an idealist I would believe that the seeing comes first and what I see is contingent. Both of these views are logically irrefutable and mutually exclusive. Using the language that I have now introduced I could say that for the naïve realist "[I know] the sun is shining" would be "I know [the sun is shining] for the idealist. Each would claim that what is in the brackets is dependent upon what is not. In truth each part, the knowing and what is known, is equally important; neither is more dependent than the other. This means that contrary to scientific objectivity, knowing is as important as what is known. Knowing is not, in other words, derived from matter however complex the matter might be, because matter is what is known. Quantum mechanics acknowledges the equal importance of the observer and the observed, although a number of scientists object to this and feel that to admit that they have equal status indicates a shortcoming in the theory and not a fact that must be taken into account.

One could refer to a realm of being. This is the realm where everything *is*. Rocks, trees, fields, mountains, houses, roads, cars, all "are." However, the realm of being is not the only realm. Another, equally important, realm is the realm of knowing. If the realm of being is the *objective* realm, the realm of knowing is the *subjective* realm. Science looks askance at subjectivity. Part of the reason for this dislike is that the word "subjective" is ambiguous, as is the word "objective." Subjectivity can mean colored by my desires, hopes, fears, prejudices, and so on. But it can also mean belonging to the realm of knowing. Objectivity likewise can mean not colored by my hopes, fears, and so on or belonging to the realm of being.

Yet even so, to get some scientists to accept that the subjective and the objective have equal validity is very difficult. As I said, many physicists object to the notion that in quantum mechanics an observer is as essential as what is observed, and they still make great efforts to eliminate the need for the observer in the equation. In the field of evolution also the lengths that biologists go to exclude knowing from the study is extraordinary. Neurologists who study the brain and mental processes perform the same mental gyrations. Many scientists now take it for granted that knowing, or what is more generally called the "mind," is the result of the complexity of matter. Researchers in the study of artificial intelligence also take for granted that once computers are sufficiently complex, "consciousness," or what I would call knowing, will emerge.

Not only do knowing and being have equal status, but also one cannot have the one without the other. Although one does not have to know something to be, or be something to know, nevertheless knowing and being are inseparable as knowing/being. In Zen this is summed up in a famous statement: "form is only emptiness/emptiness only form." At the level of experience this means that the world and I are one. Zen master Bassui put it this way, "The universe and you are of the same root, you and every single thing are a unity. The gurgle of the stream and the sigh of the wind are the voices of the master. The green of pine, the white of snow, these are the colors of the master, the very one who lifts the hands, moves the legs, sees, hears. The One who grasps this directly without recourse to reason or intellection can be said to have some degree of inner realization" (quoted in Kapleua 1996, 183).

One wonders why scientists fight so hard and deny knowing, or subjectivity, at all costs. One only has to read the absurd excesses of so called evolutionary psychology to realize how this denial is pushing us away from scientific integrity into the realm of ideology.

The reason for all this, apart from the confusion about the word subjective, is that the realm of knowing and the realm of being are two incompatible realms. This means that according to the principle of the excluded middle of classical logic, either knowing is dependent on being or being is dependent upon knowing; hence the two schools of philosophy—idealism and realism.

At the time of the awakening I had no inclination to subject emptiness and its implications to any kind of analysis. I was more aware of the freedom and openness that accompanied it. But later I wondered about emptiness and how it could be understood in Western terms.

In 1976 I finally left the company and, our three children having left home by then, my wife and I went to Rochester to live at the Zen Center. We stayed there for three years and lived a semi-monastic life. However, each person had a job to do and for most of the time I acted as editor to the Rochester journal, while my wife was in charge of the sewing room making cushions and robes.

During my stay at Rochester I had another major breakthrough. It occurred half way through a seven-day retreat. I saw all is One. I know how corny that sounds. All is One is a New Age mantra. It was also a mantra of the German Idealists and has a long history of effete philosophy. But for me it was not a philosophy. I looked at everything in wonder. Everything was it; everything was the one. I remembered reading Plotinus saying, "It is by the One that all beings are beings. (If) not a one, a thing is not. No army, no choir, no flock exists except that it be one. No house, even, or ship exists except as the one" (quoted in Turnbull 1976, 188). I knew that he and I were saying the same thing. But how to convey what I had seen?

It so happened that I was invited to give a talk at an art school in New York shortly after this new awakening. At the time it was so obvious to me that I felt all that I had to do was say to people, "Everything is the One; all is one and One is all!" and they would immediately understand. I know that that may well sound naïve, but what I had to say was, and still is, so obvious, but so very important, that I tried to say it in various ways to a group of about 50 young and eager people. I could see that after a very short while I was losing them. They became restless; they started to look at one another. Those at the back started to creep away, and within an hour I had lost at least half my audience and thoroughly confused the other half. What I wanted to say is too obvious, too simple. Gradually I have come to realize that this is true of all that is worthwhile saying and I have grown to have enormous respect and admiration for the old Zen Masters with their *mondos* [dialogues] and koans, those enigmatic statements and actions of the old masters. These are ingenious methods by which one is able to speak about the unspeakable, think about the unthinkable.

Once one sees that everything is the One, not in an abstract theoretical way but concretely and immediately, it becomes obvious that oneness is not simply what is left after all the other qualities have been drained away, it is not an empty concept but a dynamic power, or, rather, *the* dynamic power. It makes the world; the forces that hold the world together are its immediate manifestation. In physics we have recently learned that forces hold the world together: electromagnetic, gravitational, weak, and strong forces. We have come to see dramatically the enormous power held in equilibrium in an atom, and we now realize that matter can be converted into energy. The universe we are told began with an explosion of immeasurable force flinging out what was to become the galaxies, stars, and planets in an accelerating rate of acceleration. In other words, the new picture of the world that has been emerging over the last 150 years is of immense forces in equilibrium. In biology also Darwin showed that organisms are not static species but that all life is evolving, moving forward into greater and greater complexity. More recently it has become evident that the environment is also reciprocally evolving. Henri Bergson (in Mitchell 1994) suggested that this forward evolution comes out of an *élan vital,* which in a book I have just completed on evolution may be seen as another name for dynamic unity, and dynamic unity is also manifest in the forces of which the material world is made.

These forces, including energy itself, are unknowable. All that we can know are their effects, not what they "are." Quantum physics has also come up with an unknowable called the *non-local domain*. Although unknowable, nevertheless it is the source of all material manifestations. In the book *Intelligent Evolution: The Evolution of Intelligence*, published as *Creating Conciousness* (2001), I have suggested that the non-local domain, the noumenon of Kant, what I am calling dynamic unity have something in common and are either related in some way or even are different ways of talking about the same unknowable.

About 1980 I first began to feel that we had to find a way out of the limitations imposed by classical logic. I had read Korzybski's book *Science and Sanity* (1993) a long time ago in the mid fifties and had been aware of his objections to classical logic. He saw quite clearly that the map was not the territory, that the word is not the thing. He saw too what Bergson had seen: that things do not change; *things are change.* The principle of identity, $A = A$ obscures this truth. It gives the appearance of there being static things—things that change into other things, and other things that cause the change. Korzybski's solution was to index names. For example an apple at 8.00 a.m. is not the same apple as the apple at 5.00 p.m. Thus strictly speaking one should speak of apple 8.00 a.m. and apple 5.00 p.m.

However, this, apart from being clumsy and impractical, would not take ambiguity into account, particularly the kind of ambiguities given by me-as-center/me-as-periphery and knowing/being. Classical logic refuses to recognize ambiguity,

Figure 1. An illustration demonstrating ambiguity.

declaring it to be a failure of thought. Classical logic, dependent as it is upon clear and distinct ideas, demands that one datum has one concept: X is either A or not-A. However our thinking is plagued by dichotomies brought about by this either/or kind of thinking. Knowing or being is the most basic of these dichotomies, with its better-known variant of mind or body. But some of the others that haunt our thinking are "nature or nurture," "structure or function," "reductionism or holism," "mechanism or vitalism," and so on.

Quantum mechanics has discovered the wave particle dichotomy. I mention this because quantum mechanics has a great deal of experimental support and so its findings are somewhat more telling than philosophical difficulties of the kind that Korzybski was dealing with. The wave–particle antinomy does not, it seems, come from the way we talk about the world, but from the way the world is when subjected to our experimentation. Neils Bohr, one of the early pioneers of quantum mechanics, suggested a principle of complementarity to account for the wave particle dichotomy and two physicists, Nadeau and Kafatos, suggested three criteria, which would help determine when the principle of complementarity could be used. These criteria are "(1) the situation consists of two individual and whole constructs (2) the constructs preclude one another in a description of the unique physical phenomenon to which they both apply (3) the complete situation cannot be reached through an addition of the two constructs"(1999, 95).

Let us apply these criteria first to the principle of complementarity then to the logic of ambiguity. We will find that these criteria, which were designed to make the principle of complementarity into a legitimate logic, in fact, negate the value of that principle. On the other hand they do support the use of the logic of ambiguity. Before going on however, let me be clear about what I mean by "ambiguity." I do not mean vague. Ambiguous often means unclear, vague, and not immediately obvious. For example one is walking in a woods at night and ambiguous shapes and shadows surround one. I do not mean this kind of ambiguity.

The word ambiguous is derived from the word *ambi* that means two: ambidextrous, ambivalent are two other uses of ambi.

This is one but two pictures: a picture of a young lady and of an old lady (Figure 1). What makes it an ambiguity is that although it is two pictures they occupy the same space, and therefore it is only one picture. Although you can only see one at a time, both are simultaneously present. If you see the old lady you do not see the young. If you see the young lady you do not see the old. Music gives an even better illustration of the ambiguity because in music we hear both aspects simultaneously. Indeed tonal music at least is based upon ambiguity. Leonard Bernstein in 1974 gave the Eliot Norton lectures on just this theme. I would also refer the reader to the last chapter of *Creating Consciousness* (2001) in which I discus ambiguity and music at considerable lengths and show the relation between the ambiguity of music and the ambiguity me-as-center/me-as-periphery. I show further how music and emotions are intimately connected through these ambiguities.

Ambiguity as I have described it is different from a duality and a complementary pair. A typical complementary pair is a nut and bolt. They are always present together at the same time; they complete each other. One can throw away the nut and still have the bolt. But one cannot throw away the old lady and still have the young. The nut and the bolt occupies its own space. Furthermore a nut is incomplete without a bolt and a bolt is incomplete without a nut. Together they make a whole.

Let us now apply the criteria suggested by Nadeau and Kafatos to the principle of complementarity illustrated by the nut and bolt, and then to the logic of ambiguity illustrated by the young and old lady.

The first criterion says *the situation consists of two individual and whole constructs*. This not true in the case of the nut and the bolt. As I said the nut needs the bolt and the bolt the nut to be whole. With complementarity the situation consists of two half constructs, which, joined together make a whole. It is however true of the young and old lady. Each of these is individual, and each accounts for the whole situation.

The second criterion says *the constructs preclude one another in a description of the unique situation to which they both apply.* This is not true of the nut and bolt, which, as I have said, need each other. The young and old lady do preclude one another: if you see the young lady, you do not see the old lady and vice versa.

The third criterion is *the complete situation cannot be reached through an addition of the two constructs.* Again this is not true of the nut and bolt. On the contrary the complete situation requires the nut to be added to the bolt. It is true of the young and old lady. But why I say it is true needs some explanation, an explanation that will enable me to give a more complete picture of the logic of ambiguity.

What is the complete situation illustrated by the young and old lady? As I said, both young and old lady represents the whole picture, but neither represents the complete situation. Each rejects half of the situation. The old lady rejects the young, and vice versa. The complete picture is the black and white shapes. Both the young and the old lady are potential in, and "come out" of, the black and white shapes. The black and white shapes are a unity; they are not ambiguous.

The logic of ambiguity can be described in the following way. There is a situation one face of which is ambiguous; the other face is not. This means that the situation contains not one but two ambiguities. The first ambiguity is the young and old lady: when you see the one you do not see the other. The second ambiguity is the black and white shapes and the young/old lady. When you see the black and white shapes you do not see the young or old lady. I use the (/) to indicate ambiguity. Generalized this is One/(young/old lady.) Bohr's principle of complementarity was suggested to account for the wave–particle duality. However, this duality is an ambiguity; it is not a complementarity relation. If a wave then not a particle; if a particle then not a wave.

Being and knowing are ambiguous. One could define knowing as that which is not being, and being as that which is not knowing. But if you do not have being you cannot have knowing; if you do not have knowing you cannot have being. The unity from which they are derived is the unknowable dynamic unity that I referred to above, and which in the old/young lady illustration is the black and white shapes. One/(knowing/being). Likewise me-as-center/me-as-periphery are ambiguous. The unity from which they are derived is the viewpoint, me, and the viewpoint is dynamic unity in action.

According to the principle of the excluded middle, X is either A or not A; X cannot be both A and not A. Me is either me-as-center or me-as-periphery; me cannot be both. According to Koestler, creativity arises when a *single* situation or idea is perceived in "*two* self-consistent but habitually *incompatible* frames of reference" (1964, 33, emphasis added by author). This means that if we say that X is the single idea, and A and not A are the incompatible frames of reference then X is both A and not A. But because A and not A are incompatible X is either A or not A. Unfortunately, as I have said the illustration that is given above of the logic of ambiguity may be misleading because both the old and young lady are present simultaneously, although one can only now see one and now the other. I emphasize this because one of the ways that we evade ambiguity is by alternation: now I see the young lady, now the old and no ambiguity results. This is what consciousness allows us to do with me-as-center/me-as-periphery. We are then either the participant (me-as-center) or the observer (me-as-periphery), or even, conceptually divide the ambiguity into subject and object.

The logic of ambiguity is the logic of creativity. Because classical logic cannot take account of creativity, it will necessarily follow that those for whom classical logic is the only possible logic will favor mechanism over vitalism. This tendency will be enhanced by another tendency that also follows from classical logic, and that is the tendency towards reductionism. Reductionism is a necessary consequence of the need for clear and distinct ideas: that is one concept for one datum. If life is essentially creative, then as long as we only have classical logic we can never have an adequate scientific theory of living organisms and their evolution.

A serious objection might be made that one cannot simply reject classical logic, as I seem to be doing. On the one hand modern technology, including the amazing advances that have been made recently in computer science and artificial intelligence, and, on the other, the long history of use of classical logic in philosophy, theology and science in general, give proof of its extraordinary heuristic value.

For the sake of completeness, therefore, I must add a further refinement to the definition of the logic of ambiguity and in this way I shall show how classical logic fits into the overall picture.

Unity itself is ambiguous. There are no absolutes in the world. When one speaks of Unity, or Oneness, then one most often thinks in terms of the mystical One. While I appreciate that the positivist may well snort in disgust at my bringing the mystical one into serious discussion and so be inclined to dismiss any further argument, nevertheless the world's religions and philosophies abound with references to the One. To reject all of these references as being the product of overheated minds or even madness would be unfortunate. Science too has many references to Unity as a cohering principle. When Einstein said that God does not play dice, he was not, I believe referring to the God of the Catholic Church but to this principle of unity that pervades everything. The very word "universe," whose etymology means "turning to the One" is itself evidence of how deep this intuition of an all embracing unity is in our minds.

In addition to this "inclusive unity," is the exclusive unity of the law of identity. If the ultimate of the all-embracing unity is the Universe, then the ultimate of the exclusive unity is the dimensionless point or singularity. Both the inclusive and exclusive unity are the one. So which is the one? Again we encounter ambiguity.

Unity is unity, how can it possibly be ambiguous? This objection comes from those who believe that everything can in principle be explained and understood. Logically, and that of course means according to classical logic, Oneness cannot be two. But logic aside, existentially one cannot possibly be two. Although impossible, yet it is so. The creativity of unity explodes out of that very impossibility. Exclusive and inclusive unity are mutually exclusive and incompatible. The unity of which I speak is dynamic, vibrant and creative. Yet we are talking about unity and we see in this the original application of Koestler's definition of creativity. One is the single idea, the exclusive one and the inclusive one are the two incompatible frames of reference. This seems like a variation of the old physics conundrum of what happens when an irresistible force meets an immovable object.

Inclusive unity is the Unity of religion and mysticism; exclusive unity it the unity of classical logic, the exclusive unity of either/or, of this is this (A = A). The full rendition of the logic of ambiguity would now be: there is an ambiguity, one face of which says there is no ambiguity; the other face says there is an ambiguity. The face of no ambiguity is not itself unambiguous. Put more succinctly: *the logic of ambiguity has one face that is ambiguous in principle but unambiguous in expression; it has another face that is unambiguous in principle but ambiguous in expression*. However, as a whole, the logic is one ambiguity in principle but two in expression.

I have traveled a long way since asking the question about the cigarette, through fifty years of doubt and sorrow, discovery and joy. Where have I arrived? We could change the wording of the koan I used as the epigraph to this article and say, "If you call it a cigarette I will give you thirty blows of my stick; if you say that it is not a cigarette I will give you thirty blows of my stick. So what is it?" To say it is a cigarette is to take the realist stance; to say it is not a cigarette is to adopt the idealist stance.

But why the koan? Why do those who practice Zen work long years on koans? I worked for eight years before penetrating the first koan and another 12 years working on subsequent koans. By work I mean several hours a day in formal meditation and retreats each month of three, four, and seven days. Even now, as a teacher, I still work on these koans, either with individuals as their teacher, or in talks that I give to groups of students on retreats that we have at Montreal.

Perhaps some clue is given by a commentary that a Zen master, Mumon, made on one particular koan. He said, "In order to practice Zen you must pass the barriers set up by the patriarchs" (quoted in Low 1995, 25–26). The barriers of the patriarchs are the koans. He goes on, "To reach subtle awakening you must cut off ordinary ways of thought." The ordinary ways of thought are thinking logically in a linear way, and using reason and cause and effect. Another teacher said that one must think the unthinkable. When asked how one could do this, he said, "Without thinking." That is without the use of concepts, ideas, memories, even without intuition. These ways are adequate when we can address a closed system, when we can define our terms, have clear and distinct ideas.

But what is this thinking without thought? This is the question to which all the koans, and Mumon in his commentary are calling us. To answer this question we must, as Mumon says, "Arouse our entire body with its three hundred and sixty bones and its eighty four thousand pores; summon up a great mass of doubt and pour it into the koan day and night without ceasing. Question it day and night." *We must think with our muscles*. The thought without thought then becomes a question without form. By arousing ourselves in this way the whole body and mind becomes the question. With this we go beyond the conflicts of inside and out, yes and no, this and that and become simply the full and complete manifestation of dynamic unity.

One might think it overkill to ask the question, "What is a cigarette?" with that degree of intensity. However a Zen master said that if you see through a speck of dust you see through the whole universe. The cigarette or the hand or stick or whatever are just the focus of the questioning. They are not what is important but the questioning itself. Mumon goes on to insist, "All the delusive and useless knowledge that you have collected up to the present—throw it away. After a period of time, this striving will come to fruition naturally, spontaneously giving way to a condition of internal and external unity."

Let us remember that to say, "That is a cigarette," is only half the truth. The full truth is "I know that is a cigarette." We also know that knowing and being are mutually exclusive. We normally overcome this problem by saying that knowing is "internal," the cigarette "external " and everyone knows that these are mutually exclusive. Everyone "knows" that we have a private life, and that the cigarette exists in the outer world. The scientist in the search for unity then says, "Oh, so you think you have a mind and it is inside. I cannot find it when I look for it in your brain!" But of course the brain is what he knows. He cannot know the knowing in this way. The only way he can know the knowing is by deep meditation.

Mumon says that if you really apply yourself you can go beyond this dichotomy of inside and out. He says, "After a period of time, this striving will come to fruition naturally, spontaneously giving way to a *condition of internal and external unity.*" I have emphasized this last phrase because it is a key phrase. As I said just now, what we thought was an outside world and an inside world turns out to be one world, an inconceivable and indescribable world. He says, "You will know this, [one world] but for yourself only, like a dumb person who has had a dream." As I say, it is indescribable.

He then goes on to say, "Then suddenly it will all give way in an explosion and you will astonish the heavens and shake the earth. It will be as if you have seized the great sword of Kan-u. If you meet the Buddha you kill the Buddha; when you meet the patriarchs and masters you will kill the patriarchs and masters. On the brink of life and death you have the Great Freedom." The freedom is the freedom from the dichotomies, from "it is" and "it is not" If you held out a cigarette in front of me and asked "What is it?" I would take it in my hand and crush it into a thousand pieces, or even, if I still smoked, light it up and smoke it.

But as Mumon says, one must earn the right to do this. He says, "Every ounce of energy you have must be expended on [the question.]" But "If you do not give up on the way another Lamp of the Law will be lit."

A monk on coming to awakening said,

> The moon's the same old moon,
> The flowers are not different,
> Yet now I see
> I am the thingness of things (quoted in Stryk and Takashi 1965, 15)

REFERENCES

Bennett, J. G. 1966. *The dramatic universe, Vol. III*. London: Hodder & Stoughton.

Dunne, J. W. 1929. *An experiment with time*. London: A & C Black Ltd.

Kant, I. 1998. *Critique of Pure Reason*, ed. P. Guyer and A. W. Wood. New York: Cambridge University Press.

Kapleau, Philip, ed. 1966. *The three pillars of Zen*. New York: Harper and Row.

Koestler, Arthur. 1964. *The act of creation*. London: Pan Books.

Korzybski, Alfred. 1933. *Science and sanity*. Lancaster: The International Non-Aristotelian Library Publishing Company.

Low, A. 1966a. The systematics of a business organization. *Systematics* 4 (3), 248–281.

———. 1966b. *Zen and creative management*. New York: Anchor Books.

———. 1989. *An invitation to practice Zen*. Tokyo: Charles E. Tuttle.

———. 2001. *Creating consciousness*. Oregon: White Clod Press.

————. 1995. The world a gateway: Commentaries on the Mumonkan. Tokyo: Charles E. Tuttle. p. 25–6.

Malle, L., Director. 1992. *Damage*. USA: New Line Cinema.

Mitchell, A., Trans. 1944. *Creative evolution*. New York: Modern Library, Random House.

Nadeau, R., and K. Menas. 1999. *The non-local universe: The new physics and matters of the mind*. New York: Oxford University Press.

Ouspensky, P. D. 1949. *In search of the miraculous: Fragments of an unknown teaching*. New York: Harcourt, Brace.

Stryk, L., and I. Takashi, Eds. and Trans. 1965. *Zen: Poems, prayers, sermons, anecdotes, interviews*. New York: Doubleday.

Tipler, Frank. 1994. *The physics of immortality: Modern cosmology, God and the resurrection of the dead*. New York: Anchor Doubleday Books.

Turnbull, G. H., compiler. 1976. *The Essence of Plotinus*. Westport: Greenwood.

BRINGING FORTH THAT WHICH IS WITHIN: HOW AN INVISIBLE HAND LED ME TO A LIFE THAT "FEELS LIKE MY OWN"

S. J. GOERNER

The Integral Science Institute, Chapel Hill, North Carolina, USA

I did not plan or even expect the life I now lead and see as my own. Instead, it emerged from a series of dark nights of the soul, followed by sudden break-throughs, synchronicities, and epiphanies that, in retrospect, all seemed designed to "bring forth" an authentic Self that already existed within me and that had a purpose in this world. Ironically, the scientific framework that emerged from this volatile process helped me see that I was experiencing the classic, spiritual learning journey. The science also clarified how and why the process worked as it did, while also making the process and the Grand Invisible Hand that prodded me through it altogether more real, practical, and daily than my traditional modern mind could have imagined. This article, therefore, is dedicated to the "bringing forth that which is within you," which Jesus describes in the opening quote. I am now a grateful participant in my own unfolding and a thankful true believer in the Great Ordering Oneness, which envelops and guides all things.

ORDINARY LIFE AND THE NEW SCIENTIFIC STORY

If you bring forth that which is within you, what you bring forth will save you. If you do not bring forth that which is within you, what you do not bring forth will destroy you.

—Jesus[1]

The tale of how I came to Systems Science and my life's work, integral science, can be told either as a mundane story or a spiritual one. I will explain both versions starting with the mundane.

In the ordinary version of my life, I grew up in the American Midwest with equally strong interests in psychology, engineering and the human condition. Throughout my life I have oscillated between these interests becoming, in turn, an engineer, a psychologist, a mathematical physicist, and a system scientist with a central focus on integrating all of the above. In the process, I acquired advanced degrees in three of these fields and have been a practicing professional in all of them. I now lecture, teach, sponsor practical projects, and write books and articles on how the new scientific framework clarifies the human transformation and unifies the practical changes already taking place in virtually every sphere: education, medicine/health, business, economics, spirituality, community, and so on.

I discovered System Science during a quest to reconcile my diverse passions in a way that made sense to my engineering mind. I was happy being an R&D engineer, but it was not my passion. Having become seriously disillusioned with the state of science in psychology, I began a new quest with the question: "Why isn't psychology a science?" When I discovered Chaos Theory in the mid-1980s, my focus shifted to: "What is science?"

Through the unplanned process I describe below, I eventually learned that a combination of scientific breakthroughs–including Chaos Theory, Systems Theory, and General Evolution Theory–were all part of a much more comprehensive scientific metamorphosis. As the scientific facets came together, I saw that the lens they formed provided a more accurate picture of how human vicissitudes and how they emerge from and reflect the laws of a comprehensively connected, energy-driven universe. It looked like the resulting, *integral* scientific framework might resolve my quest by: (1) providing a cogent explanation for why mechanistic science was inadequate for understanding complex phenomenon like human beings; and (2) offering a vastly superior alternative. Integral concepts and methods were clearly more scientifically powerful and pragmatically useful, while being more emotionally appealing to boot.

Integral science, for example, painted a picture of the cosmos as a single unified energy web (network) that housed amazingly intricate order at ever level of its dynamic, developmentally unfolding Being. Here, for example, the similar patterns of organization and development found in vastly different systems–galaxies, organisms, ecosystems, societies, and so on—that the Greeks called "sacred geometries," emerged from the natural, self-organizing dynamics of energy-flow webs. Human societies were moved by the same invisible hand of "web" dynamics, predictably and even *measurably* so.

The model suggested that global civilization was in a transition phase, at the cusp of a make-or-break developmental transition. Furthermore, the new pattern of civilization struggling to be born would be the product, not of few geniuses or highly placed elites, but of our collective societal mind, in this case, a vast planetary brain made up of the quiet brilliance and endless local choices of billions of diverse human minds grappling with pressing problems right in front of them. This same process has happened before, with the medieval to modern transition being the last example of what I now call, great change.

Throughout the 1990s and early 2000s I traveled the world giving talks on how this new Dynamic theory of evolution provided a much more empirically accurate, pragmatically powerful, and emotionally satisfying explanation of human behavior and societal evolution than the selfish survivalism that neo-Darwinism proffers. This travel also served as my apprenticeship in the validity of the model. During this time, I was giving talks to every kind of group imaginable: advertisers, educators, artists, economists, doctors, political groups, religious groups, urban planners, and consciousness study groups. And, after every talk, a few people would come up to me and tell me how some folks in that field were already reinventing their discipline along lines that fit the framework I had just explained. Each field had its own issues, history and language, of course, but the same patterns could also be seen clearly beneath.

As I saw it, the unifying theme was: a healthy *human* ecology and their field's role in creating one. Successive groups taught me how their field was working toward:

- *A Healthy Learning Society/Knowledge Ecology:* Some educators were discovering that the human brain (and the children who owned them) worked best in collaborative learning teams, which valued the natural diversity of talents, perspectives and roles and had plenty of opportunity to learn win-win problem-solving and common-cause skills from meaningful, hands-on, experiences.
- *A Healthy Economic Ecology*: At least some economists were realizing that today's global economic instability was the result of letting predatory, multinational corporations do whatever they wanted to make the biggest personal profit possible, *regardless* of the devastation this caused to people, small businesses, local and regional economies, and the environment. This violated the first rule of economic ecology: maintain diversity and the balance between big and small lest the big predators eat so much that the whole collapses.
- *A Healthy City Ecology:* At the same time, urban planners were learning how the built environment could make or break a human ecology by either catalyzing or crushing crucial exchanges at different scales, from community interactions and business opportunities for small and medium sized companies to high-speed rail and large-scale industry.
- *A Healthy Marketing and Production System*: Even Madison Avenue advertisers were discovering that the only way around public cynicism built from decades of manipulative, slick-Willy salesmanship was to build high-quality, trustworthy products by *pushing back on producers* to create them. Oh the irony! One Strategic Planning group I talked with gives their clients a "Noble Purpose Worksheet" to get them back in touch with the honest passion that once guided their business.

It eventually struck me that all of these people, in all of these fields, living all over the world were acting like a vast societal mind, moving independently but consonantly toward a convergence, as if guided by some invisible, directing hand. This was the reality of great change staring me in the face in the form of educators, economists, and little old lady church groups all making their own choices and yet moving in a common, *predictable*, global direction.

I began to sense that I too was being moved. I also seemed to have a role to play, which appeared wound up with using integral science to support the broader societal transformation already afoot. My Midwestern mind recoiled at the grandiosity of this role, but the model reminded me that it was only a niche.

It was no better or worse than anyone else's role, it was just mine. At some deep level I began to comprehend that if I stayed true to this role, to my calling, that I would feel satisfied at my core *regardless* of whatever conventional successes or failures I might experience. Highs and lows were ephemeral; it was the profound meaningfulness of staying in integrity with the calling that mattered.

FIERY TRIALS AND CYCLICAL REFINEMENT: S-CURVE LEARNING

> When through fiery trials thy pathway shall lie,
>
> . . . The flame shall not hurt thee. I only design
>
> Thy dross to consume and thy gold to refine.
>
> —Church hymn, "How Firm a Foundation"[2]

The more I followed the parallels between integral science and the mysteries of the human condition, the more I also began to realize that the world integral science portrays was not a new invention, but a rediscovery of insights and realities described by saints and sages across the world and throughout time. Integral science merely provides a more commonsense, rigorous explanation for why these beautiful, inspiring, and sometimes enigmatic ideas accurately reflect *physical* reality as well as spiritual and human truths.

Consequently, until ten years ago, I only told the mundane version of my life because that was all I saw: I was an engineer, a psychologist, and now a scientific lecturer, consultant, and writer. I did not know enough to recognize that the many struggles, confusions, and crises I was experiencing fit the classic pattern of a life-long journey *to discover and develop one's authentic (higher) Self as part of discovering one's service to the greater Oneness.*

In contrast, I opened this article with the quote from Jesus because it now epitomizes my view of a learning journey we all face. Although there seems to be a cultural taboo against saying so, we are all struggling to bring forth our own unique "spark of the Divine," our internal "diamond in the rough." Each of us *needs* to do this for both ourselves and the greater whole.

The spiritual sages understood centuries ago, of course, but I originally found their explanations impossible to follow. I also tended to assume spiritual insights applied only to great people, not to me. Then too, I could not reconcile these intuitive accounts with either my Midwestern upbringing or my modern conception of the world. In effect, until my understanding of the science came together, I simply did not have a realistic framework that could reconcile my intellectual assessments with the deep, desperate feelings and wild, instinctual search that formed the true story of my life underneath.

In retrospect, I did not have faith in the cosmos or myself because nothing accessible explained what a purpose-seeking life journey would feel like and how it would unfold. This left me simply unable to believe that the key to my salvation lay in learning to love my authentic self and accepting that I too have a role in the cosmic plan unfolding in this moment in time.

Integral science changed all this by freeing me from my limited cultural cocoon, and showing me how I *personally fit* in a world that was scientifically sound, emotionally satisfying and spiritually consonant at the same time. The S-curve of development provides an example of how it helped.

The early stages of my journey were fairly typical of what happens when one walks in ignorance of the Greater Plan and Process. My early life was filled with pain because, in conventional terms, I am a very odd duck. I grew up in a wholesome, but exceedingly conventional and restrictive culture. Being a Midwesterner, I tried hard to be what I was "supposed to be," as defined by my culture: a nice, sweet, dutiful girl. Unfortunately, some parts of my intrinsic nature simply did not fit into this role-jacket, in large part because I have very strong proclivities in arenas that the modern mind sees as both contradictory and unsuitable for girls. For example, I am seriously scientific and concerned with realistic solutions, AND I am profoundly intuitive, psychologically minded, and warm-hearted. I like sports and working on cars AND cooking and mothering. Most of all, however, I was born female with a high IQ in the highly conventional heartland of America.

Neither my family, nor anyone on either side of the usual scientist/humanist divide, was prepared for this combination. My family was concerned that I would never find a husband because I was too smart, aggressive, and nerdy. As an adult, my fellow scientists and engineers tended to discount me as warm, fuzzy, and female, while psychologists and new-agers tended to react badly to a female who insists on maintaining scientific rigor. I ended up being defensive on both sides of the aisle as talents and traits that were valuable in theory tended to constitute obstacles to acceptance in reality.

My constant failure to fit then drove me back and forth searching for a compatible home in the different camps. Being a deeply sociable person, this inability to fit caused me extreme pain. Indeed, despite a great deal of conventional success in terns of money, career, marriage, and so on by my late twenties I was in so much psychological pain that I became seriously suicidal.

In retrospect, this desperation forced my hand. At the very bottom of my despair, when I was seriously considering killing myself, a little voice inside suggested an alternative. It said, "If you are going to kill yourself, why not try to live life that feels like your own?" Mind you, I did not have the foggiest idea what "a life that felt like my own" might be, but I had to agree that, if I was going to throw my life away, I might as well try to figure it out.

This decision to let go of what I thought I "*had* to be" and to try to follow that inner voice changed my life forever. My life did not become instantly easier. I remained seriously anxious, depressed, and defensive for at least another decade. But, in the week following my decision, the cosmos gave me a reason to believe. Synchronicity struck! For one amazing week, a large number of uncanny connections popped up everywhere and they all seemed to point in one, obscure, improbable direction. In this case, they seemed to confirm a choice that I was contemplating about graduate study at the Saybrook Institute. At the time there was no logical reason to believe pursuing another degree, this time from a small, maverick-loving institution, would give me a new path, but in retrospect, the synchronistic nudges I was experiencing tilted me toward the path and the life that *does* feel like my own.

In the years since, my life has gotten steadily better—sometimes dramatically so–because I learned that there *was* a pattern to the process. Realizing that there was a pattern gave me a sense of what to expect during the crises that still pop up to this day.

After my first "dark night of the soul" experience, I began to sense that, at least for me, struggle and crises were part of a learning cycle that moved me forward on my path. The pattern was pretty straightforward: when my mundane self–my "ego" if you wish–was in the depths of despair, it found the pain unbearable and could see no way out. It wanted to die; it merely needed to let go. I discovered that, if I had faith in the process and kept an ear out for my honest inner voice, then at some point the darkness would break. The internal beliefs that made some choice or direction seem impossible would dissolve, or I would find the courage to move forward anyway. My little ego would break out into a new level of learning. Then synchronicity would appear! The world would be utterly magical for a moment, and I would feel a flash of inexplicable clarity, and a deep sensation that my life had a purpose and a direction that I needed to follow.

In some cases, I would also realize that I had learned some lesson, reconciled some internal conflict or let loose of some false desire or belief. I almost never had any sense of what lesson I was trying to learn before the fact, but I discovered that it did not matter if my conscious mind understood or not. My inner voice clearly knew much more than my conscious mind did and it could be trusted. "It" knew what I needed to learn better than "I" did. All I had to do was have faith in the process; the courage to push blindly into the darkness; and the willingness to listen to my gut, which is the usual form It took in talking to me.

Over time, I also came to understand that no breakthrough was final. Each step was just another stage. Life would be better for while and then some new crisis would appear. The crisis would build to a breaking point and the process would start all over again.

As I became comfortable with the process, I also began to realize that it fit spiritual descriptions from a wide variety of faiths. One friend, for example, pointed to the Christian Hymn describing God's use of fiery trials to burn away the "dross of sin and self-will" in order to refine one's inner gold (see opening quote in this section).

I began to re-read spiritual accounts, now seeing how their strange words fit my personal experience. I began to use my internal guide to help my conscious mind figure out what I should do next. What offers should I accept? Which ones should I decline? I began to notice that some people, places and events seemed to have some "significance" beyond anything apparent to my normal intellect. It might take days, months, or years to discover what that significance was, but eventually it always became clear, sometimes bizarrely so.

Eventually, integral science's S-curve cycle of development gave me a ground-ing visual image of the process (see Figure 1). In this view, my authentic Self

Figure 1. S-curve vision of the learning journey, by the author.

was unfolding through a series of onion-peeling, developmental cycles that went something like this:

1. A "dark night of the soul": a depression, crisis, or other precipitating event;
2. A need to "let go, and let God";
3. A sudden, though sometimes subtle, change of vision or heart;
4. Meaningful synchronicities that hailed a new tack in the journey;
5. A renewed sense of direction that settled into a new normalcy; and
6. A new limit, marked by a new, dark night.

Understanding the cycle made the journey much faster and less painful. If I relaxed, noticed, and did not worry, then I was happier and the pieces came together faster than if resisted and I tried to make something happen. Instead of attempting to use my puny ego to predict and control, I started to learn to listen to my gut, go with the flow and let the cosmos direct my path.

DIVINE UNITY AND THE PHENOMENAL SELF

There is a force within which gives you life. Seek that.
In your body lies a priceless gem. Seek that.
O wandering soul, if you want to find the greatest treasure,
don't look outside. Look inside, and seek that.—Rumi (cited in Shiva 2000, 75)

The synchronicities that sometimes appeared also gave me a tangible awareness of my own development as a purposeful part of a vastly larger, invisibly ordered evolution of spheres from country, species and planet to cosmos. About 10 years ago, I stumbled on an introduction to the *Bhagavad-Gita* written by Aldous Huxley (1954) that helped me understand my own unceasing pull toward and guidance from my Authentic Self as part of exactly such a greater process, an underlying striving toward unity with the Divine.

According to Huxley, a Perennial Philosophy, a kind of common archetype, lies at the root of all the world's great religions. Articulated in various places and to varying degrees for over 2500 years, from the Logos of St. John to the Kabala and the *Bhagavad-Gita* itself, Huxley describes the Perennial Philosophy as consisting of four fundamental doctrines:

1. The world of all things, animals, and humanity are manifestations of a Divine Ground within which all partial realities have their being and apart from which they would be nonexistent.
2. Human beings are capable not merely of knowing *about* the Divine Ground by inference, they can also realize its existence by direct intuition, which is superior to discursive reasoning. This immediate knowledge unites the Knower with that which is Known.
3. Human beings possess a double nature, a phenomenal ego and an Eternal Self, which is the inner person, the spirit, the spark of divinity within the soul. It is possible for a person, if they so desire, to at identify themselves with the spirit and therefore with the Divine Ground, which is of the same or like nature with the spirit.
4. Human life on earth has only one purpose: to identify oneself with one's Eternal Self and so come to unitive knowledge of the Divine Ground.

Huxely's frame helped me understand that what I experienced as my "inner voice" or "my gut" was the voice of my Eternal Self talking to my phenomenal self. My sense that my internal guide was smarter than "I" seemed a logical result of my Eternal's Self's connection to the ineffable fullness of the Divine Ground. It seemed natural that listening to my Eternal Self would help me go with the flow of the Invisible Hand as it guided me along a Divine Plan that is infinitely more complex than any mortal mind could comprehend.

Medieval theologians have used these kinds of words for a thousand years. Now integral science helped me see how their words fit a physical understanding as well as a spiritual one. To give you a better picture of what I mean, let me take a moment to flesh out integral science's portrait of a cosmic-level Great Ordering Oneness that acts like a Divine Ground and an Absolute Mind.

INTEGRAL SCIENCE AND THE GREAT ORDERING ONENESS: HIGHER POWERS AND PLANS

First the basics: Integral science is best thought of as a new *stage* of science, that is, a new stage of the same old rigorous, empirical, mathematical quest for understanding the world that we all know, and at least some of us dearly love. This new stage is being made possible by new, more powerful scientific tools, particularly the high-speed computer. The greater scope and empirical power these tools afford is producing a much more massive change in vision than most practicing scientists currently understand.

The easiest way to differentiate Integral stage science from its Modern forbearer is via their strikingly different, root metaphors. Modern science, like modern society, is built around a "machine" metaphor: a logical system of separate, streamlined material parts connected by mechanical cause and effect. Unfortunately, in this system, anything resembling a human heart or intelligence appears as an incongruous epiphenomenon. Happily, where modern thinkers once believed everything from factories to the human body worked like sterile machines, now integral thinkers are beginning to recast all things as complex ecosystems or networks, bound up in bigger webs. Already visible in images of environmentalism, global economy, global village, holistic health, and the World Wide Web, every facet of our society—from business and education to science and spirituality—is being re-colored in kind.

Scanning current events through the "web" lens makes the term *integral society* more understandable. Integral means whole. The integral age is a time when human beings reconnect, heal schisms, and begin reweaving civilization in harmony with the natural world and its principles. So, instead of a clockwork universe of separable, streamlined parts, integral thinkers envision a web-world, One Planet in which all things are inseparably linked.

Yet, metaphor is not all that changes. New *mathematics of networks* and webs (particularly Chaos and Complexity Theories) has discovered awesome, intricate, virtually endless "order" in what was previously assumed to be a chaos of complex systems. At the same time, expanded understandings of how *energy* moves, shapes, and "self-organizes" all things, from the first bits of matter to the wonder that is life, is forcing scientists to replace the simplistic Darwinian notions of life as a cosmic accident proceeding through a nature red in tooth and claw, with a vastly more logical and useful understanding of life proceeding through the universal patterns of growth, development, and learning and born of the natural workings of a dynamically developing, energy-web cosmos. The human upshot here is a more emotionally appealing understanding of a family of Being—including individuals, societies, and economies—emerging from the invisible hand of a self-organizing cosmos and still inseparably woven into its encompassing fabric. Add energy's role in information, and even intelligence, mind and consciousness become natural too.

From Ecological Economics and fractal urban planning to the Gaia hypothesis, the practical but often surprising implications of these "web" revisions are already rippling through virtually every discipline, changing scientific views, not just metaphorically, but with quantitative precision. The term *integral science* refers to the union of these web insights, now fused into a logical, working whole (see Table 1).

This wholesale change of scientific vision comes with a particularly radical revision of our human story. Here humanity is quite literally a *collaborative learning species*[3] and civilization is a knowledge ecology, a learning web struggling to learn how to live wisely and well. This human narrative dovetails neatly within a fully empirical account of an all-embracing Great Ordering Oneness (GOO) that invisibly guides and creates all things.

Table 1
The Four Underlying Shifts that Give Rise to Integral Science's Wholesale Change of Vision

Core View of...	Modern Science (A Machine)	Integral Science (An Energy-Flow Ecology)
Fundamental Substance:	Matter	Energy
All things are...	Separable	Inseparably Entwined
Causality is...	Simple, Sequential	Complex, Interconnected
The Universe's Underlying Nature:	Random/Disordered	Filled with Intricate, co-evolving Order

This combination of learning humanity and Divine backdrop provides a matter-of-fact foundation for the Perennial vision. Plato coined the phrase "Great Ordering One" to describe THE omnipresent force and all embracing web that shapes, creates, guides, and even learns and evolves through all things. It is "in us, of us, and more than us," as the sages say. Humanity develops and history unfolds according to its laws; it functions like a Cosmic Mind; and modern science has profoundly misunderstood its nature. Integral science suggests that it is physically real, and that its invisible hand acts through the invisible, ordering forces of energy flow and web dynamics.

The easiest way to understand how the new human narrative fits within the Ordering Onenessis via the Evolutionary Braid, that is, the weave formed by three inter-locking threads: cooperation, intelligence, and structure/organization.

- *Organization and Structural Development*: All organization emerges from the hidden, ordering forces of energy flow and web dynamics.
Researchers have been exploring energy's penchant for creating organization and driving ongoing, developmental change (evolution) for over a century.[4] The most dramatic breakthrough came in the 1970s when Noble Laureate Illya Prigogine identified and explored the workings of a process he called *self-organization*.[5] In this view, the entire tapestry of creation, from the first bits of matter to the latest cycles of civilization, is the natural product of the self-organizing properties of energy-flow webs. Energy pressures and the shaping properties of web (nonlinear) dynamics successively fused plasma into subatomic particles which then fused into atoms, molecules, gases, dust, galaxies, and stars. Stars baked dense molecules and then tossed off burnt chunks of matter called planets. On early earth, the fiery chemical soup created vast chemical chains and networks that circulated matter and energy from the smallest cranny to the largest sphere. These self-organizing chemical networks then coalesced into the precursors of life—membranes, metabolism, amino acids, DNA, hormones, and so on–which in turn came together in the first living cells. (Note: this means life was born already linked into the vast chemical networks that span the globe and connect us to all life on earth.) Cells joined together to form multi-cellular organisms, which eventually joined to form families, herds, and societies. This process of building more complex systems

by linking simpler bits is moving inexorably toward ever-more synergetic, intelligent, and intricate wholes.

- *Intelligence, Mind and Consciousness*: Intelligence is a natural part of the energy-web dance because energy trails give rise to information. Because information has an energy base, it is also capable of physically interacting with organization in subtle, directing ways. Because energy is behind organization and information, mind and body–that is, information processing and material organization—are inseparable.

  In the energy view, the first cells were little more than metabolic processes taking place in gelatinous sacks. The metabolic activity gave cells enough energy to move, but to survive for long, cells had to find new energy sources (food) whenever the current supply ran out. The first living cells began responding to hints (information) about where food might lie. Since these hints originally came from little trails of patterned energy, perhaps a few photons of light (seeing) or a few energized chemical molecules (smell or touch), it is easy to imagine how intelligence could have evolved. Metabolism already gave cells enough energy to move and gulping down a photon, for example, could easily have triggered a slight movement this way or that. If that movement propelled the cell toward food, then natural selection would take its course. Cells that happened to respond appropriately to the nudges of incoming information would survive, while all others would starve. Biologists Umberto Maturana and Francisco Varela (1987) summed up the primal connection between survival and functional response to information, saying: "To live is to cognize." Responding appropriately to energy trails, the primordial form of information, marked the first step in the march toward intelligence.

- *Cooperation:* Cooperation, the balanced give-and-take arrangements that help multiple parties survive better together than apart, forms the connective tissue and major means by which living organisms become more complex. Cooperation is a byproduct of GOO's drive for increasing intricacy, that is, lace-like networks of small, synergetic circles linked in complex patterns of Being.

  As always in energy-driven evolution, living organisms became more complex as time progressed. Separate cells began to gather in enclaves. Those that worked together survived better because they had the power of many hands. A new theme arose: specialize and integrate! The best way to grow and thrive is for individuals to find a special task in-service to the whole (a niche) and band together with other specialists to create a new unity, a synergetic organization that is (quite literally) more than the sum of its parts. Multi-cellular creatures such as ourselves are a tribute to this theme, as are supra-living systems such as societies: Living systems get more complex through cooperating.

The literal understanding of humanity as a collaborative-learning species and civilization as a knowledge ecology, a wisdom-weaving web, emerges easily from these threads. Cooperation, intelligence, and increasingly complex structure all played a role. Since any advance in intelligence improves survival by definition, evolutionary pressures drove an incredible progression of information processing and effective response from the first knee-jerk cellular response to nerves, brains, vision, and scientific theories. At the same time, as multi-cellular creatures became more complex, internal communication between distant parts of the cooperative endeavor became crucial for coordination and from there for survival. (Lung cells, for example, must get timely accurate information from leg cells in order to breathe harder and take in more oxygen when running.) Nerve cells, for example, emerged to circulate internal information. Brains eventually emerged to coordinate sectors and find crucial patterns in the complex flows and use them to improve response. The pattern then repeated at the herd level.

As multi-cellular creatures joined into families, herds, and eventually civilizations like our own, the needs for internal communication and integrative information processes gave rise to yet more amazing innovations along parallel lines. Human groups exchange information by talking and eventually by writing. We also pool information, find patterns, and forge shared mental maps about how the world works, which we then use to change our responses/behavior. We have done this so well that we are now the cutting edge of collaborative learning and intelligence on the planet.

Unfortunately, societies do not always learn in a timely, effective manner, and when they do not, they become prone to collapse. This is the problem we face today. We have become so locked in the current modern map of the world that we seem unable to imagine, much less forge a better chart. The momentum of our economic, political, media, and governmental institutions has become so powerful that even those running the treadmills cannot stop it. We have reached the limits of our modern pattern of life and we face a dangerous dark night of the soul from which we may not emerge.

Still, the model says that, with luck, the Integral Age emerging before us will simply be the next step in a grand journey of humanity, civilization, and the cosmos, all developing by consuming dross and refining gold. I know from personal experience that all over the world, every field is already reinventing itself along more effective and healthier integral lines. All the answers we need are out there and new crises keep pushing us toward our next stage of life.

The only question that remains is whether we will break out of our old cultural cocoon and come together in a new synthesis before the failures of the old pull us under. Understanding our cooperative learning nature can help–so too might the physical (energetic) understanding of the Great Ordering Oneness that forms the Divine Ground of all life.

We now know that energy running through every vein of the universe makes all things One. But, this grand unity is constantly organizing and reorganizing itself into endless forms of Many. Everything is connected; everything co-evolves; and underneath all vicissitudes lays an unfathomable degree of order as well as a powerful drive toward development. Because energy is also the basis of information, the Great Ordering Oneness is a sea of information and intelligence as well as self-organizing system of matter. This invisibly ordered sea is constantly refining its own internal Self through "us," meaning the entire wondrous web of Being. This refinement, learning, and searching for better patterns of Being makes it a kind of Cosmic Mind as well.

Here Huxely's Divine Ground can be imagined as a kind of Cosmic Body, a unified Field/Force/Energy backdrop from which all things emerge and into which all things recede. At the same time, we also have new reason to believe this Ground embodies a kind of an Infinite Cosmic Intelligence or Mind as well. From the Logos of the early Greeks to Hegel's Absolute Mind unfolding through History, sages throughout time and place have suggested as much.

Parallels to esoteric descriptions abound.

- We live in: a Web that has no Weaver; a Design that has no Designer; a sea of energy that organizes itself; an inseparable, co-evolving, mind-body Unity.
- The One is Many, and the Many are One–literally.
- The tendrils of connection and flow pull us like an Invisible Hand guiding us into the paths of a grand Design.
- Harmony, synergy, intelligence, intricacy, and balance make us strong, and small informative nudges move us all.
- GOO's directing, inspiring spark is "in us, of us and more than us" at the same time. It operates through us and we exist through it.
- It is way smarter than any of us could ever be. It is Imminent, pervasive, permeating and omnipresent. It may be Transcendent, existing beyond anything that is and putting reality itself in motion.
- Responding to the pulse of the larger stream within us puts us in consonance with the invisibly ordered flow. To go with this flow is to live in harmony with the laws of Nature and Nature's God.

In short, a Grand Design does lie beneath earthly flux and beyond human ken. It created us and connects us. A Prime Mover exists in our lives and works in unseen ways, despite the fact that we do not know how it works. Indeed, IT is so much more than anything else we know, that it is essentially ineffable: no single set of words can do it justice.

I began to see my own struggle to harmonize my internal scientific/humanistic discord was a microcosm of the larger journey. Like a good fractal, each iota of life (human and non-human) is a co-evolving facet of this Cosmic Mind-Body, working within a nested set of systems within systems, within systems. The Divine Mind-Body seems to be evolving internally by burning off the dross and refining the gold of its parts (including people and civilizations) through the recurrent, fiery trials described above. Humanity is both a natural product of this process and a mirror of the Divine Process co-evolving at all levels.

Realizing how profoundly ordered the entire system is gave the injunction "Know Thyself" new meaning. Whether one calls it God, the Cosmos, or the Divine Ground, the ordering force that made me, apparently made me exactly as I am for a reason. My mix has a role. If nothing else, modern society's scientific/humanistic split and my own are both seeking resolution. My ill-fit drives me to heal, harmonize and integrate that split in me as my service to the larger process. My *raison d' être* is to help facilitate this resolution and communicate it to the world. Doing so heals me.

Thus, the more my dross burns away and my gold emerges, the more I realize that I am an integrator by nature. My particular task is to build a solid, mutually supportive bridge between the scientific synthesis emerging in our time and the social/psychological synthesis also struggling to coalesce. In this synthesis, humanity's own ill-fitting facets— warm, intelligent, strong, practical, spiritual—fit together fully and honorably, instead of simplistically and at odds.

IN SUM

As integral science's view of human and cosmic learning came together, so did the dots of my spiritual journey. What began ostensibly as a quest to expand my intellectual understanding of science led synchronistically to a framework that harmoniously connected the desires of my head, heart, hands, and soul. I have spent the last 20+ years integrating work within and across fields, creating ever clearer, more detailed explanations of why a fully integrated integral science can reconcile such diverse pulls as the need for scientific rigor, economic resilience, empowering education, effective collaborative learning, fairness, equity, compassion, and soul.

The net effect has been like an optical illusion: all the old facts I had learned in school plus a few new ones have re-organized into a radically new, yet remarkably ancient picture of humanity, civilization, and the cosmos that, at least to me, brings striking clarity to the confusion of our times.

I now thank heaven—or the Great Ordering Oneness—for prodding me, often unwillingly, down my path because I now know that, deep within me, there really does exist a "life that feels like my own."

NOTES

1. From, The Gnostic Gospels/The Essene Gospel of Thomas (unknown author).
2. "How Firm a Foundation" verse 3, Hymn by unknown composer, Based on Timothy 2:19, Hebrews 13:5, and Isaiah 43:1,2.
3. Our survival strategy is to pool information, forge productive mental maps and then revise those maps when they prove inadequate or erroneous.
4. Classic works in the energy approach to evolution include Lotka (1922) and Chaisson (2001).
5. The basic pattern can be seen in the process of boiling water. Start with a pot; turn up the heat; little bubbles form, then strings of bubbles, and eventually the whole thing turns to a boil. The energy explanation goes like this: Heat equals an energy build-up. Energy build-ups create pressure that drives the system to move faster. The system (in this case, colliding molecules) does move faster and faster until it reaches the limits of the current pattern of organization. At this point the system becomes unstable. Only two things can happen, the system either: (1) lights upon some naturally occurring diversity that opens a new channel for flow, and form a new pattern of organization; or (2) it explodes or collapses. All organization and developmental progression (evolution) is the result of similar self-organizing processes, operating over and over again, forging new patterns and levels of Being out of old at every scale of existence for billions of years.

REFERENCES

Chaisson, E. 2001. *Cosmic evolution.* New York: Atlantic Monthly Press.

Huxley, A. 1954. Introduction. In *Bhagavad-Gita: The Song of God*, Trans. Prabhavananda, S. and Isherwood, C., 9–23. New York: The Mentor Series, New American Library.

Lotka, A. J. 1922. Contribution to the energetics of evolution. *Proceedings of the National Academy of Science*, 8 (147): 22–35.

Maturana, H., and F. Varela. 1987. *The tree of knowledge.* Boston: Shambhala.

Shiva, S. 2000. *Rumi, the thief of sleep.* New York: Jain.

COMPLEXITY AND TRANSDISCIPLINARITY: REFLECTIONS ON THEORY AND PRACTICE

ALFONSO MONTUORI

California Institute of Integral Studies, San Francisco, California, USA

Systems and complexity theories are transversal approaches that provide a new way of thinking as a response to the traditional reductionist approach that emerged with modernity. Complexity and transdisciplinarity are particularly relevant in an increasingly diverse, networked, uncertain, and fast-changing world. Examples are drawn from personal experience in academia, cross-cultural experiences, and the arts.

> ... our thinking is ruled by a profound and hidden paradigm without our being aware of it. We believe we see what is real; but we see in reality only what this paradigm allows us to see, and we obscure what it requires us not to see.
>
> —Edgar Morin (2008b, 86)

BEGINNINGS

In 1983 I left London and a life in music behind for California to start a Masters degree in International Relations. I was 23. It began as an excuse to leave behind dreary weather and drearier food for a mythical sunshine land. But as soon as I started my studies, to my great surprise I was filled with an excitement that still propels me towards worlds of complexity and transdisciplinarity. After I completed my M.A., a year-long experience teaching management students at Central South University in Changsha, China, inspired even more questions. When I got back to the United States, I looked for a university where I could do my Ph.D., eager to explore questions that were, in hindsight, all related to my own experience. Growing up as a global mutt, never living in the country that issued my passport (Italy), and with my experience as a musician in the turbulent London of the late '70s and early '80s, I was clearly trying to make sense of my life and of the world around me. My immersion in academia opened up a whole world of questions, and even provided some answers along the way.

Finding an appropriate Ph.D. to match my omnivorous nature, on the other hand, was a bit disconcerting. Every time I walked into a department and sat down to speak with the Chair, he or she would mumble something about how interesting my research project was, and then politely add that this was probably not the department for me. I should really try a different department. Psychology would point me to Sociology, Sociology to Political Science, Political Science to Philosophy, Philosophy to Anthropology, and then, ironically, Anthropology would lead me back to Psychology.

Wandering around these departments I could not help but be reminded of an earlier experience. In my late teens and early twenties in London I played in a variety of bands, and eventually started a band myself. What kind of a band? There's the rub. We were pretty good. Our music had been described as "astonishingly well-played" by the British music weekly *Record Mirror*, surely a source of impeccable discernment and stellar credentials. We performed to packed houses, some of them legendary dumps, like the Marquee Club and the Hope and Anchor in London. Everybody had a good time, but nobody could quite label us. In fact, the same publication had presciently written that our music "impertinently side-steps any classification." We would start every set with the theme from the TV show Hawaii 5–0 and then explore reggae, funk, soul, butchered jazz with a psychedelic version of *In the Mood*, all sorts of mutant pop, wandered into the audience with our instruments, and often had a variety of dancers and assorted loonies with burning guitars on stage. But when the record companies would come to hear us they hemmed and hawed about signing us. They really wanted to sign us, but the trouble was, they did not know what record store "bin" to put us in. Was it Rock? Punk? Funk? Comedy? We may have impertinently side-stepped any classification, but it turned out that this added considerable complexity to our so-called musical careers, and so we also impertinently side-stepped a lucrative record deal or any semblance of a career in music. What the hell were we?

As far as I was concerned, the fact that we could not be classified was not a bug but a feature, record companies be damned. And that's probably just as well, because I later realized the wisdom in a famous apocryphal line attributed to Hunter S. Thompson. Something along the lines of, The music business is a cruel and shallow money trench, a long plastic hallway where thieves and pimps run free, and good men die like dogs. There's also a negative side. Rumor has it he was actually referring to the TV business, but his words were "appropriated" and "remixed" over the years to refer to the music business. Now of course there's barely a music business to speak of.

Compounding matters, I am also a "Third Culture Child," a "rootless cosmopolitan," "transcultural," a "mutt" to use President Obama's term. I did not live in the country that issued my passport until my late 40s when I became a (dual) U.S. citizen. At that point I had lived in the United States for over 20 years. Again, the question was—who or what am I? Where do I fit in? Am I Italian? (My first passport, my father was Italian?) Dutch? (I was born in Holland, my mother is Dutch, I support Ajax Amsterdam?) English? (Nothing like high school and undergraduate to build a sense of identity . . .) American? I have lived in the

United States longer than anywhere else. But I do my best swearing in Greek, a language I learned when I lived there as a boy for 8 years, before English, which is my fourth language. Kwame Anthony Appiah's statement that his passport is just a travel document, not a statement about his soul neatly summarizes my feelings about it all (2006).

One of the questions I still regularly get when I give people a hint about my background is, "Yes, but what are you *really*?" In the first pages of one of Lebanese-French novelist Amin Malouf's important books on identity (2001) the same question pops up, followed by the same refusal to accept the frame and that particular way of thinking. It might seem a superficial, impatient, almost natural question, but it's really a deep question in the sense that it speaks of a certain way of understanding the world, identity, of understanding *what is*. Ultimately you have to be *something*, and that something has to be easily classifiable, it has to be what you *really* are, and that has to be one existing category, homogenous, and not some kind of mix, a hybrid. Anything different is ... well, a mutt, in the pejorative sense of the word that is a not-so-distant cousin to "bastard." And there was definitely something vaguely suspicious, something *impure*, about not being clear and distinct, in Descartes's expression (1954).

The underlying issues I was dealing with were similar. With music as with education, I was passionate about something, and there seemed to be some in-dications, even if grudging at times, that I was not completely off the wall. The band was successful, my ideas were not bad, but none of it *fit* anywhere, not into any pre-existing categories. And apparently *I* did not fit anywhere as a person, not in any traditional flag-waving sense, not in any conventional discipline, in any established musical style. I was caught in a headlock by being and knowing, and it was clear that I needed to express my own views about why this complexity was perfectly acceptable, and even desirable, for me, at least.

Not lacking in youthful *hubris*, I naturally assumed there was something wrong with *them*. The university departments, the record companies, the jingoistic na-tionalists. It became painfully apparent, and not just from my own experience, that categories had the ability to deny or at least marginalize the existence of people and things and issues that were patently there. Human beings are very good at creating categories, but we are also good at becoming trapped in them, and we trap others as well as ourselves.

Growing up in a number of different countries it also became clear that what ap-pears real and unquestionable and simply "the way the world is" in one culture may be viewed as bizarre and wrong-headed and even dangerous in a different culture. My experiences made me very aware of the nature and power of categories and per-spectives, of different ways of seeing the world. They instilled a fascination with epistemology at a fairly young age. More specifically, they made me aware that human beings see the world in many different ways and that we typically become habituated to one way of viewing the world. The more time we spend with "our" people, in "our" discipline, "our" country, playing "our" music, the more likely we are to become somewhat ossified, blinkered, and habituated, group-thought out of fresh perception. And a key question was, what are the implications of living across cultures, playing across a number of musical styles, thinking about issues across disciplines? Systems, complexity, and transdisciplinary thinkers seemed to offer a good entry point for my inquiry.

THE CHALLENGE OF SYSTEMS THINKING

I was first exposed to systems theory reading Arthur Koestler and Buckminster Fuller while I was taking my undergraduate degree at the University of London. They were not part of the curriculum. I confess I bought Arthur Koestler's *Ghost in the Machine* (1982) because it had the same title as an album by The Police. When I read Fuller and Koestler, they immediately resonated with me. Looking back on this period of my life, I realize that I really had no idea why their systemic view appealed to me. It just seemed "right," somehow, or at least worthy of further inquiry. It seemed so right, in fact, that one of my main reasons for choosing an "alternative" university for my doctoral degree was the fact that it offered a Ph.D. with an emphasis in systems theory, as well as the possibility of working with one of the leading lights of creativity research, Frank Barron. Arthur Koestler had written a milestone book about creativity, *The Act of Creation*, and had also written extensively on system theory, coining the term *holon* (Koestler 1979, 1982, 1990; Koestler and Smythies 1972).[1] Even when I chose a Ph.D. program I never really spent too much time thinking about why I was driven to pursue these two topics, systems theory and creativity. With youthful passion, I just went ahead and did it, driven by an invisible momentum, and in this case, as with all my other youthful indiscretions, I have no regrets.

Systems theory and creativity were not exactly "hot topics" when I got into them. They were certainly not avenues to bright and lucrative futures in academia or the private sector. When I mentioned I was researching creativity I either got puzzled looks—how can you study creativity? (I still get that one)—slightly sarcastic comments about the trivial nature of such a project, or the inevitable "those who cannot do, teach," followed by a smirk suggesting that the speaker is convinced that his quip was "creative." And yet there was a substantial body of quite significant research on creativity at the time. My interest in systems theory aroused quite aggressive and dismissive comments from my more philosophically inclined colleagues. While for me systems theory seemed to begin to address this problem of disciplinary parochialism, most philosophers at the time dismissed systems theory, as deterministic and scientistic nonsense that involved efforts to dominate, control, and generally oppress people. The following generic description of "the systems theorist" in *50 Key Thinkers* (Lechte 1994, 248) gives an indication of the way systems theory was perceived at the time: "For the systems theorist, human beings are part of a homogeneous, stable, theoretically knowable, and therefore, predictable system. Knowledge is the means of controlling the system. Even if perfect knowledge does not yet exist, the equation: the greater the knowledge the greater the power over the system is, for the systems theorist, irrefutable."

The systems theorist in this excerpt is clearly not a very likable person. And yes, systems theory was for boys: all about control, prediction, and power. Systems theory was portrayed as a way to control, even dominate others, and certainly associated with the colonization of the lifeworld, in other words, a way to instru-mentalize all of life, to make it rational, predictable, controllable, by, of course, the powerful systems theorist who was designing ways to make humans more efficient, productive, and ultimately less human.

Why in God's name would a crazed global nomad musician like myself, hardly known for ice-cold efficiency, rationality, and corporate productivity get into such a nefarious business? Systems theory clearly had a bad reputation, and in all fairness the reputation was not entirely undeserved. Systems theory, cybernetics, and information theory, seemed to form a rather incestuous trio. It was true that in some cases the private sector and the military had seen them as powerful tools to achieve the kind of dreams of world domination associated with Dr. Strangelove (Montuori and Purser 1996). But that critique was based on only one interpretation of systems theory, and a very limited one at that.

My interest in systems theory came from a very different reading of (as well as different readings in) systems theory (and later chaos and complexity theories) than those I saw in most critiques of systems theory. The caricatured description above was in fact exactly the opposite of what I saw in systems and later com-plexity theories, which also says something about the many ways in which these approaches have been developed and interpreted. The work of Gregory Bateson (1972, 2002), Edgar Morin (1985, 1986, 1990, 1991), Gianluca Bocchi and Mauro Ceruti (2002, 2004; Ceruti, 1994, 2008), and the other thinkers I was reading was nuanced, epistemologically sophisticated, explicitly pluralistic and decidedly not oriented towards world domination. I was soon reading works that were not yet translated into English by Morin and Bocchi and Ceruti. The Mediterranean com-plexity thinkers, spear-headed by Edgar Morin, had a very different approach from the more positivistic mainstream of U.S. systems thinking. Ervin Laszlo invited me to translate Mauro Ceruti's classic *Il Vincolo e la Possibilità* from Italian into English, later published as *Constraints and Possibilities* (Ceruti 1994), and I was further swept into a world of epistemology, philosophy of science (interestingly, in France the two terms are used interchangeably), and evolutionary theory. For Ceruti, Darwin and Newton reflected very different ways of thinking, very differ-ent approaches to inquiry, and reading his book a whole world of interrelationships opened up. Ceruti (2008) wrote that

Charles Darwin's work is one of the deepest revolutions in the history of Western science and philosophy because its image of nature was a radical departure from the essentialist way of thinking, and initiated a mutation in our cosmological perspective.

For the pre-Darwinian biologist, the variation found in individuals of the same species were accidents, epiphenomena that did not affect the unitary and im-mutable nature of the species itself. If the variation was noticeably different from the characteristics that were considered normative, this was viewed as a sign of imperfection, and at times, of pathology.

After Darwin, variations came to be considered the most significant aspects of natural history. Their constant appearance, multiplication, and transformation have become signs of a history of nature in the real sense, a history that is deep and creative in which even species are born and die, including all that essentialist thought considered essences or inalterable forms. What today are considered simple varieties of a species could, in the future, become distinct species. In the future, there may emerge reproductive, morphological, and behavioral barriers where now there are only differences in degree. (24)

An entirely different understanding of the world emerges, no longer centered around essences, stasis, homogeneity, and equilibrium but instead changing and pluralistic, interconnected and creative. Ceruti's work does a remarkable job showing how our knowledge of evolution and the evolution of knowledge interweave in a historical dance, and the creativity of this epistemological journey has continued to fascinate me.

WHAT SYSTEMS? WHOSE COMPLEXITY?

In what follows I will draw on the elements of systems and complexity theory, and specific interpretations of them, that have most influenced my own work. Before I do that, a little historical background. System theory, cybernetics, complexity theory, this larger "family" of ideas, movements, and individuals, have, ironically, split off into a plurality of different interpretations, sometimes very different at a basic philosophical level. In some ways, everybody creates their own interpretation based of systems theoretical approaches because they form a bedrock of thinking, as it were. You can be a reductionist in a million different ways, and the same applies to systems and complexity thinking. I became aware of this when I was asked to teach courses on systems theory, and even more when I had to write a (relatively) short encyclopedia entry on systems theory. The original impetus had spun off into multiple interpretations, with very different results.

INQUIRY AND INQUIRER

Perhaps I should begin with the most obvious dimension given the nature of this essay and this volume: the complexity-based approach I draw on integrates the inquirer into the inquiry. In other words, it starts with the basic assumption that every inquiry is conducted by an inquirer, a person with a history, a social and historical context, beliefs, values, biases, blind spots, ways of thinking, and so on. This means that the inquirer is part of the inquiry. In order to understand the subject of my inquiry, I also need to pay attention to *who* is doing this inquiry, and understand myself. Every inquiry is therefore potentially an avenue for self-inquiry. And furthermore, the process of inquiry and the knowledge that is used for, and being generated by, the inquiry is not somehow "external" to the inquirer. The inquirer is not transparent, not a bystander. The reasons for the inquiry, the philosophical and methodological approaches that are brought to bear, these are all brought by the inquirer to the inquiry—by somebody from somewhere. One purpose of this article is to surface why I have been personally drawn to use a systems/complexity perspective in my work. The underlying assumption is that we cannot eliminate the inquirer from the inquiry, as many traditional approaches have attempted to do, but we can make the inquirer more transparent to the reader. This does not mean that now all is subjective, by any means. It does mean that the complex relationship between inquirer and inquiry is being illuminated rather than swept under the carpet. The work of Morin, Bateson, and particularly feminist scholars (Code 1991; Spretnak 2011), who have come to this question from a very different angle, has stressed the importance of not only explicitly acknowledging the inquirer, but really making every inquiry a self-inquiry as well. The implications are enormous, and promise to revolutionize any number of fields, from philosophy to education, because eliminating the inquirer was central to the approach to inquiry of the Machine Age.

OPEN AND CLOSED SYSTEMS

The Newtonian Universe was viewed as being made up of "things" that we would now call closed systems. Closed systems do not require any exchange of matter/energy or information with its environment. A closed system view is extremely problematic when we begin to study living systems, because no living system can be a closed system. Every living system exists within an environment, and has a relationship with that environment.

The father of General Systems Theory, Ludwig von Bertalanffy (1975), wrote:

> Every living organism is a system, characterized by a continuous import and export of substance. In this continuous exchange, breaking down and rebuilding of its components, the organism maintains itself constant, a condition which I termed a steady state. Modern investigations have shown that this continual renewal, this "dying and becoming" within the organism takes place to an extent and at a rate which was hardly suspected earlier. (43–44)

Wilden (1980, xxxi) states that "a closed system is one for which context is effectively irrelevant or defined as such (e.g., the solar system, the cosmos as a whole); an open system, in contrast, is one that depends on its environment for its continuing existence and survival (e.g., an organism, a population, a society)."

One of the key insights provided by the systems approach is that much of social science and management science have thought of individuals and organizations as fundamentally closed systems. Scientific Management wanted to ensure each individual worker was essentially a closed system—performing his or her duty, but having as little other contact as possible with the rest of the organization. In the same way, each department was mostly isolated from every other one. One of the basic precepts of early strategic planning was that the environment was knowable, and had little or no impact on the organization.

Closed and open are relative terms, of course: no living system is either totally open or totally closed. A living system is open to matter/energy and information (in the case of a human being, for air, food, communication with the environment, other people), but also closed in the sense that a human being is not open to everything—having a defined identity also means having boundaries which articulate self- and not-self. So every living system is both open and closed, again one of those paradoxical, both/and relationships. Open systems tend to be far less stable than closed systems, which are by definition systems in equilibrium, with no exchange with their environment. The openness of the system leads to potential disequilibrium. Open systems are stabilized by flow, but their structural stability is only relative because this structure is gradually, and sometimes quite rapidly, transformed by exchanges with the environment.

CONTEXT

The focus on context reminds us that every inquirer is always somebody *some-where*. Not, in other words, a God's eye view from Nowhere. Many forms of inquiry, particularly the ones that modeled themselves on the laboratory models of the natural sciences, stressed the importance of isolating variables and eliminating confounding contextual factors (Polkinghorne 1983). The goal was universal answers that did not depend on the researcher's subjectivity or context. With a lot of different variables in play, it would be difficult to identify exactly what caused what. Isolate a variable, and you have a "clear and distinct" result. X does or does not play a role in Y. This approach works marvelously well for certain things, but when it comes to human issues, it can be problematic. I grew up in different countries, participated in many different subcultures. In London I played in a band, worked as an interpreter for Scotland Yard—the London Metropolitan Police—went to university, lived in the area of London known for embassies and diplomatic residences, and spent most of my time with friends in council houses. I realized that context was of enormous importance.

My suspicion of essentialism and abstraction, in its etymological sense of removing something from its context, is largely due to personal experience seeing myself and others act, and even think, very differently depending on the context, and seeing how politics was greatly influenced by context. Reasoning about war and nuclear issues during the cold war was different in the Soviet Union than in the United States, and it was not all about deception. The assumption that everybody would think alike, "reasonably," about issues was simply preposterous for anybody with a sense of cultural (contextual) differences or understanding of cross-cultural psychology (Fisher 1980, 1997, 1998). In my later research, I saw this in the Romantic understanding of creativity, and specifically of genius, presented an image of "genius without learning," arguing that the genius was so special he did not need to study since all brilliance flowed from his gift. It did not matter where or when the genius was born because no matter what the conditions, genius will prevail. And of course, it was mostly White men who had prevailed, which proved that genius was something found mostly in White men (Montuori and Purser 1995). But things are not quite that romantically easy or exclusive. Context matters.

Bringing up the concept of thinking about thinking is enough to turn most if not all cocktail party guests glassy-eyed and looking for another drink, the front door, or both. Critiques of abstraction, reductionism, and so on can seem very esoteric, and oddly removed from anything real. Interestingly, the criticism I hear most often is that this is all very abstract stuff, very heady, with little or no relevance to real life. And yet it doesn't take a lot to see how a form of reductionism—reducing to *nothing but*—is at the heart of the way we can deprive people of their humanity.

In Zimbardo's classic Stanford Prison experiment (2008) Stanford students were split into two groups, the guards and the prisoners. The experiment had to be stopped early because the guards were out of control and behaving in unexpectedly vicious ways. We later saw this behavior repeated in Abu Ghraib prison. The behavior of the Stanford students was eerily mirrored by the guards at Abu Ghraib. Context, environment, the power of the situation, do matter. Certain conditions will elicit certain behaviors—not deterministically but probabilistically. And our tendency is always to blame a few bad apples, and not take into account how a prison experiment took Stanford's best and brightest and turned them into cruel guards. But the guards were immediately tarnished with the label "White trash," a convenient way to suggest there was something wrong already wrong with them, and no systemic changes were needed, only the elimination of the bad apples.

While reductionism has been very useful in research, it can have a very ugly side if used in extreme ways when thinking about people. To refer to a woman as a "piece of ass," is to shamefully reduce her to a part of her anatomy. What are the implications of this kind of talk? What does it tell us about the way a person is being seen? A waiter can refer to a customer in a café as "the cheese sandwich," and this example, technically "metonymy" (Wilden 1980, 1987), is part of an expedient way to communicate. But it's also clear that taken further, this can easily become deeply problematic. Whenever we reduce somebody to a body part, or any term (alien, thief, sinner, saint, crook) this is a form of depersonalization, stripping a person of their complexity, turning them into a thing, and also making them more likely to be the subject of attack and abuse (Keen 1991; Montuori and Conti 1993).

FROM POLARIZATION TO PARADOX

The pressure toward postmodernism is building from our lack of ability to overcome certain dualisms that are built into modern ways of knowing (Ogilvy 1989, 9)

Along with the dark side of reductionism, there's also the problem of the logic of either/or (Low 2011). We are confronted by either/or choices everyday. Some are mundane and perhaps depressing. The nightmarish (but now fading) choice between chicken or lasagna on an airplane comes to mind. Sometimes we have to turn left or right. But this logic is overused and taken to polarizing extremes. It shows up in extreme cases as "I am right, you are wrong!" and "you're either for us or against us." It shows up in extreme polarizations that are used during wartime, and generally in conflictual situations, reflecting the kind of authoritarian thinking that emerges in individuals who are particularly sensitive to environmental pressures (Adorno et al., 1982; Hetherington and Weiler 2009; Keen 1991; Montuori 2005; Stenner 2005).

The disjunctive, either/or logic involves identifying A in opposition to B, as if these were the only choices available. Once again, this is not some esoteric issue of interest only to the hyper-specialized academic. Traditional gender roles were based on this logic. A boy should not act or feel or think like a girl, and vice versa. Boys and girls identified *in opposition* to each other. In stereotypical cases "hard," silent, and strong men and "soft," emotional and helpless women (Callahan, Eisler, and Loye 1993; Eisler 1987, 1995; Hampden-Turner 1971; Montuori and Conti 1993). Men are from Mars, women from Venus. The sociologist Randall Collins has argued that most intellectual movements emerge in opposition to other movements in a dialectical process (1998). When I was in graduate school, every other book had a title that started with "The Social Construction of . . . " Everything was socially constructed, and any mention of other sources of difference, particularly physiological differences, was met with contempt, dismissed as "scientism," and viewed as a reason to be extremely suspect of the speaker. Today, the few remaining bookstores are brimming with works about the brain, the neuroscience of the formerly socially constructed love, creativity, certainty, gender, you name it. These trends oscillate, back and forth. Gruber sees this dynamic psychology (1999, 690): "The field of psychology presents a puzzling spectacle. The same controversies seem to crop up in every generation, such as the conflict between wholism and atomism, or that between evolution and stasis, or that between sudden intuitive leaps and incremental change."

In the Leadership literature, there were two traditional views of leadership. Thomas Carlyle's "Great Man" theory, which focused exclusively on the individual heroic leader, and the "zeitgeist" theory, identified with Leo Tolstoy, which held that social circumstances were the key factors, with the individual leader simply a product of circumstances (Northouse 2004; Wren 1995). The same dichotomy was found in creativity research, where psychologists focused on individual genius and sociologists on the zeitgeist, suggesting that the individual was simply the outcome of the social factors, trends, ideas that were in the air, and so on (Simonton 1999). The two camps barely communicated, did not reference each other, and generally dismissed the others as naïve at best.

In 1995 my colleague Ron Purser and I wrote an article with the youthfully pretentious title "Deconstructing the Lone Genius Myth: Towards a Contextual View of Creativity" (Montuori and Purser 1995). We argued that the emphasis in creativity research had been almost exclusively on individuals, and that there was almost no research on creative relationships, groups, organizations, the relational dimensions of creativity, the historical and social factors involved, and so on. Even the most isolated genius, we argued, was participating in a discourse, using language, tools, ideas, and was grappling with issues that had been raised by other researchers. Every individual operates in a society, with a history, and so on. We thought we had bent over backwards to explain that we did not propose a "zeitgeist" view, or a collectivist view that rejected the individual. We wanted to expand the scope of the inquiry and bring these views in dialogue, stressing that both had valuable contributions to make to a broader (more contextual) understanding of creativity. We also wanted to propose an open system view of creativity, rather than the existing closed system view, in which the individual was not influenced by his or her environment. Nevertheless, psychologists immediately critiqued us as being sociologists who wanted to deny the importance of the individual. Initially baffled by this response, I realized that the larger "cognitive context" had created two opposing views that did not allow attempts at reconciliation. It was *either* individual genius *or* social forces.

Edgar Morin has referred to this either/or logic as disjunctive thinking, based on Aristotelian logic (2008b). It's either A or B. It cannot be both A *and* B. This kind of thinking is really pervasive, and has marked much of Western thought, although it's beginning to buckle. Deconstruction seeks out these binary oppositions or dualisms that we take for granted, and in the process challenges deeply held assumptions. One area where this kind of oppositional thinking is particularly pernicious is in attempting to understand creativity, where "paradox," meaning terms that are not conventionally thought together, is rife. Creativity offers an opportunity not only to deconstruct, but to see how the two terms are not in a binary hierarchical opposition, but rather mutually interacting.

Summarizing the extensive research on the characteristics of the creative person, Csikszentmihalyi (1996) states that:

1. Creative people have a great deal of physical energy, but they are also often quiet and at rest.
2. Creative people tend to be smart yet naïve at the same time.
3. Creative people combine playfulness and discipline, or responsibility and irresponsibility.
4. Creative people alternative between imagination and fantasy, and a rooted sense of reality.
5. Creative people tend to be both extroverted and introverted.
6. Creative people are humble and proud at the same time.
7. Creative people, to an extent, escape rigid gender role stereotyping.
8. Creative people are both rebellious and conservative.
9. Most creative people are very passionate about their work, yet they can be extremely objective about it as well.
10. Creative people's openness and sensitivity often expose them to suffering and pain, yet also to a great deal of enjoyment.

Traditionally we think of these characteristics as opposed: either humble or proud, open or closed, extroverted or introverted, rebellious or conservative. One of the reasons why creativity has been such an elusive phenomenon, I believe, is precisely because these kinds of paradoxes appear whether we are looking at creative individuals, creative groups or organizations, or the creative process itself (Montuori 2011b). Arthur Koestler's key insight into creativity was the concept of *bisociation*, which involves thinking together terms or concepts that are not usually thought together (Koestler 1990). Creativity is a wonderful example of the need for complex thinking that arises from cybernetics, and recognizes loops, interrelationships, an so on (Hampden-Turner 1999; Montuori 2011b).

LITTLE BOXES ON THE HILLSIDE . . .

In graduate school one of my required texts was Thomas Kuhn's classic *The Structure of Scientific Revolutions* (1996). Kuhn's work added an important element to my thinking. Suddenly the insight that cultural differences created very different ways of seeing the world, and therefore different categories about what is good, beautiful, true, edible, acceptable, clean, polite, and so on, found a parallel in the world of academic inquiry. This was particularly important because it further showed how our understanding of the world and of ourselves involves a historical process of construction, or of *creation* as I prefer to think of it. Eventually we take residence in these constructions for better or worse, and forget that we are the ones who have built them. While so many of us bemoan our lack of creativity, it may well be the case that we are enormously creative and have in fact become trapped in our own creations.

Another required text in graduate school, Graham Allison's *Essence of Decision* (1971), showed three very different ways of framing and understanding the Cuban missile crisis, and it served as a further illustration of the different ways in which we construct perspectives, starting with different fundamental assumptions. Along with a multiplicity of perspectives within disciplines, there was also the problem of water-tight, non-communicating disciplines. Ernest Becker bemoaned disciplinary fragmentation in his underappreciated *The Structure of Evil*, showing how underlying assumptions structured and organized the way we think about the world (1976). These assumptions form the basis for our approach to inquiry, not what we think, but how we think. They are the taken-for-granted (but rarely questioned) starting points for scholars. In his study of scientific revolutions, Kuhn argued that the majority of scientists engage in "normal science," which means they are expanding the research agenda of a certain way of seeing the world, introducing the now popular (and arguably over-used) term "paradigm." Scientific revolutions involved engaging so many anomalies in the dominant paradigm that its very foundations needed to be challenged. Given my background, these ideas fascinated me.

Something clicked when I read Kuhn, particularly because I read it in conjunction with the cultural anthropologists and "radical constructivist" epistemologists like Heinz Von Foerster (1983, 1990), Ernst Von Glasersfeld (1987), and Paul Watzlawick (1977, 1984). Their work spoke directly to my experience of cultural heterogeneity and my experience of "relativism." I hesitate to use the latter term since it has become so tainted by a nihilistic "anything goes" gloss. I mean more broadly knowledge relative to our time and space, our history, culture, traditions, discourse and practices. Everything is said by an observer, Humberto Maturana reminds us, and I should add that the observer is a somebody who is always *somewhere* (1987). Ernst Von Glasersfeld interestingly recounts that his own interest in epistemology also emerged living in several different countries and speaking different languages.

It became clear to me that the material I was studying originated in particular scholarly "cultures." The very way inquiry was organized was a function of a set of underlying assumptions in those cultures and about the organization of knowledge. I had also read Buckminster Fuller (1969), Arthur Koestler (1982), Ervin Laszlo (1969, 1996a, 1996b, 1999), and Fritjof Capra's ambitious *The Turning Point*, in which he discussed at some length the "Newtonian Cartesian" paradigm, and, like Laszlo, Koestler and Fuller, made the case for a systems theoretical way of thinking (1984). In that important book, Capra began to articulate some of the characteristics of a new worldview, drawing extensively on systems theory, and explored the implications for a number of fields, from economics to health. It seemed there was potentially a change afoot, and this change involved new ways of thinking and organizing knowledge. It was becoming clear I was not the only one who felt disciplinary fragmentation and rampant categorization are problematic.

As much as I enjoyed my Californian immersion in scholarly inquiry, I wondered why classes seemed to function as fairly closed compartments. Students were never encouraged to bring material from one class to another class, even if the material seemed obviously relevant. Discussing cross-cultural differences and particularly how the very different experiences of World War II might have influenced U.S.–Soviet negotiations about nuclear weapons and troops in Europe was *verboten* in a course on U.S.–Soviet relations (albeit in the nicest possible way in which a university professor can be dismissive).

The cross-cultural phenomena that fascinated me because of my background seemed to belong only in the course on cross-cultural issues. I found out that this was generally the norm in academia. Water-tight courses, water-tight disciplines, and indeed water-tight sub-disciplines. Mentioning personality psychology in a course on social psychology brought hoots of derision from the teaching assistant (TA). Discussing material from sociology with psychologists studying creativity was also decidedly not a way to win a popularity contest. Wherever I went, it seemed one should only discuss one discipline at a time.

> The emergence of disciplines has often led to the forgetting of their impetus in living human subjects and their crucial role in both the maintenance and transformation of knowledge-producing practices. The results are a special kind of decadence. One such kind is disciplinary decadence. Disciplinary decadence is the ontologizing or reification of a discipline. In such an attitude, we treat our discipline as though it was never born and has always existed and will never change or, in some cases, die. More than immortal, it is eternal. Yet as something comes into being, it lives, in such an attitude, as a monstrosity, as an instance of a human creation that can never die. Such a perspective brings with it a special fallacy. Its assertion as absolute eventually leads to no room for other disciplinary perspectives, the result of which is the rejection of them for not being one's own. Thus, if one's discipline has foreclosed the question of its scope, all that is left for it is a form of "applied" work. Such work militates against thinking. (Gordon 2006, 36)

My passion for transdisciplinarity emerges out of a felt need to go beyond some of the limitations of more traditional disciplinary academic approaches, and certain established ways of thinking (Morin 2008c). Today, these ways of thinking originate in a view of the Universe as a Machine, a view that has had a profound influence on how we understand human beings, Nature, the Universe, and the also the nature of knowledge, thinking, inquiring, and organizing (Capra 1984; Goerner 1999; Russell 1983). As I attempted to understand how our ways of making sense of the way emerged, I also became aware of the importance of history (Bocchi and Ceruti 2002; Ceruti 2008). With the rise of industrialization, fueled by the tremendous developments and successes in science, the machine became the guiding metaphor for life. If God was the watchmaker, the universe was the watch. And we can see that the mechanical metaphor has pervaded much of our thinking on topics ranging from the mind, to the body, to organizations, to education and society. Modernity has even frequently been described as The Machine Age.

With the Machine Age came what we might call Machine Organization (Frederick Taylor's Scientific Management) and Machine Thinking. Machine Thinking was appropriate for dealing with machines. Machines, with all their power and novelty, where naturally the key metaphor of the Industrial Age. How do you begin to understand how a machine is put together? By taking it apart. This same process also works for living systems, but of course when one takes a living system apart, it rapidly tends to lose a key quality. Something was missing. And there's more that is problematic about the machine metaphor.

The more I became interested in inquiry, and drifted toward creativity research, the more I saw that creativity was missing from much of academia. The study of creativity in individuals was fairly established if peripheral in the mainstream of psychology. The types of persons that were being studied were "eminent" individuals, genius and various sub-categories of brilliance (Runco 2007). These were unusual, indeed highly unusual, persons. As I reflected on life in educational systems and organizations, I saw that creativity was barely considered. It certainly was not in any way nurtured or even acknowledged in the educational experiences my peers and I had, with some notable exceptions. It was almost as if creativity emerged despite the educational system.

Educational systems just did not seem designed to foster creativity, and neither did most businesses that I was aware of. The research literature confirmed this (Handy 1994; Purser and Montuori 1999; Robinson 2001). One spoke of creativity in education and organizations in the same way one studied it—yes, there's the occasional genius whiz kid, but they are rare and weird and frankly a pain in the ass. Creativity was equated with genius, and genius did not fundamentally "belong" in education. (It certainly did not belong in students—after all, that could potentially be embarrassing for teachers.) Genius was eldritch, different, radically abnormal. What was most telling for me was that (a) the genius was a total outlier and (b) that creativity did not belong in any system. Educational systems and organizations of all shapes and sizes were not designed to foster creativity in any way shape or form. They were meant to function like well-oiled machines, of course, and the workers, as well as the managers, were supposed to be cogs in the proverbial machine. Creativity was disruptive, subjective, unpredictable, unscientific, artsy and fanciful.

In the Machine Metaphor creativity was always *outside* the machine. The Machine Clockwork Universe was created by God. The organization was started by the great founder, usually with his brilliant product. Education was about the Great Teacher teaching about the Great Men. But creativity was not in or for students or workers. The system was simply not designed for that. It was deeply mechanical and authoritarian. Frederick Taylor's Scientific Management taught us there was One Right Way, and the same principle applied to education (Morgan 2006). When organizations began to ask me to help them with creativity and innovation, I was always puzzled. It seemed like they had their foot firmly planted on brake, and would occasionally glance at the accelerator. It seemed as if they were expecting beautiful plants to grow after throwing a few seeds on cement. It took me a while to realize what this was all about. In the end the best way I can summarize it is by saying that for organizations that are creative, creativity is a central value, as important as any other, and perhaps even more—it becomes the core of the mission. It is intrinsic to their identity, or, more practically put, to their self-definition: this is what we do, who we are. Organizations that view creativity merely as an add-on that needs to be pulled out at specific times will never be as creative. I've never been involved in a musical situation, as a player or producer, where somebody has said, "now we need to be creative" (unless it had to do with money). The same is true for creative organizations. I have never heard anybody in a creative organization, whether a business or a band, say, "let's be creative now." I have heard, "this is great" or "this not good enough." In these contexts, creativity is a given: the creativity of the individuals, of the process, and the product. That was the key difference.

Much of my work has involved showing the limitations of the old Machine view, and the emergence and articulation of a new view in which creativity is central. And as I have shown elsewhere, creativity, complexity, and transdisciplinarity go together hand in glove in a world where creativity is central (Montuori 1989; Montuori and Conti 1993). The implications of complexity and transdisciplinarity go far beyond a set of tools for academic inquiry. They call for a reflection on who we are, how we make sense of the world, and how we might find ways to embody different ways of being, thinking, relating, and acting in the world.

THE ORGANIZATION OF KNOWLEDGE AND KNOWLEDGE OF ORGANIZATION

"In the beginning," of course, there was only Philosophy. Over the years, with the accumulation of more and more knowledge and the development of specialists and specializations, various disciplines had spun off and "gone it alone." Aristotle, the great organizer and classifier, had given his books titles that reflect the names of disciplines, like *Politics*, *Ethics*, *Physics*, *Rhetoric*, and *Meteorology*. But of course, he dealt with them all himself. This was simply not possible in the twentieth century, it was argued, because one would become a classic "jack of all trades and master of none," a superficial generalist, or an "amateur." In the process, disciplinary silos were formed, and it seemed there was little if any interest in communication, let alone integration. The internecine squabbling among disciplines, and the efforts to keep disciplines pure and un-polluted by other disciplinary perspectives, described so carefully and thoughtfully in Bruce Wilshire's *The Moral Collapse of the University: Professionalism, Purity, and Alienation,* didn't seem very "scholarly" let alone "scientific" (1990). As Wilshire pointed out, there were issues of territory, funding, and also the fact that sticking to one discipline or approach allowed one to remain an "expert." The minute material from other disciplines was brought in, narrow experts were not experts anymore, and this could potentially have negative consequences for the experts.

The organization of knowledge paralleled the organization of industry and followed Adam Smith's principle of the division of labor, as disciplines gradually split off from Mother Philosophy (psychology did not cut the cord until the late nineteenth century). Increasing specialization and expertise, with a focus on depth, on drilling deep, rather than the broad but arguably "thin" overview. Buckminster Fuller argued that this was also an organizational principle of divide and rule: only the "bosses" at the top had the "big picture" (Fuller 1969). There is no doubt that this division of labor and specialization has lead to remarkable advances. They're at the heart of Modernity and the Industrial Revolution. But we are increasingly beginning to realize that a lot was lost in the ensuing reductionism, and that the fragmentation of specialization now requires integration.

> Reductionism was the driving force behind much of the twentieth century's scientific research. To comprehend nature, it tells us, we must first decipher its components. The assumption is that once we understand the parts, it will be easy to grasp the whole. Divide and conquer; the devil is in the details. Therefore for decades we have been forced to see the world through its constituents. We have been trained to study atoms and superstrings to understand the universe; molecules to comprehend life; individual genes to understand complex human behavior; prophets to see the origins of fads and religions. ... Now we are as close to knowing everything there know about the pieces. But we are as far as we have ever been to understanding nature as a whole. (Barabasi 2003, 6)

As I began to explore the literature, I was soon attracted to "eccentric" systems/cybernetic thinkers like Gregory Bateson (1972, 2002), Erich Jantsch (1975, 1980), Magoroh Maruyama (1974, 1977, 1994, 2004; Maruyama, Caley, and Sawada 1994), and Edgar Morin (1990, 2007, 2008a, 2008b, 2008c; Morin and Kern 1999). Bateson made contributions to psychiatry, communication, family therapy, cybernetics, anthropology, evolutionary theory, ecology and a number of other disparate fields. Morin has written important books about death, cinema and popular culture, ecology, education, and politics. Maruyama has written about cybernetics, management, cross-cultural differences and futures research. Jantsch wrote remarkable works of synthesis, drawing extensively on the work of Ilya Prigogine, applying them to topics like society and social change, and explicitly addressing spirituality and mystical traditions. What I found particularly compelling about these thinkers was that they explored a wide range of issues, and sought to bring not just a new ideas, but new perspectives to them, new ways of thinking, of approaching the topic. Not just new information, or even frames, but new meta-frames, and efforts at integration, all motivated by the need for application in light of world problems.

Like me, these thinkers never belonged to any particular discipline. In some cases they suffered for it. Bateson was largely forgotten and out of print for a number of years in the United States. His classic *Steps to an Ecology of Mind* was available as an audio book in Italy, which tells us something about the importance of cultural differences in the history of ideas (1972). Jantsch's work was largely ignored although later picked up by equally omnivorous thinkers like Fritjof

Capra and Ken Wilber, both of whom are influential but outside the academic mainstream. Sadly, he is now out of print. Maruyama drifted from department to department in any number of countries, and while his work was published in major journals in many different disciplines—his *The Second Cybernetics* is a citation classic (Maruyama 1963)—he also wrote extensively (and complained privately) about what he called "subunderstanding," or the tendency by scholars to understand works that crossed several disciplines only very partially, typically ignoring or misunderstanding the elements that did not fit in their discipline, reading them through a narrow disciplinary lens (Maruyama 2004). Morin is probably France's most influential living thinker, at this point, celebrated by the prestigious newspaper *Le Monde* with a special magazine issue devoted to his life and work and a regular feature in major newspapers and on television. The day before François Hollande's recent election victory *Le Monde* published a dialogue he had with Morin, and in Latin America and countries like Italy he is viewed as one of the most important contemporary thinkers in the world. But Morin's lack of disciplinary home, not to mention his complete refusal to ride on the coat-tails of so-called postmodernism (which in France is considered an Anglophone creation), in favor of American sources no less, still makes him suspect with many traditional French academics. Until recently he was virtually unknown in the United States. Morin describes himself as an intellectual poacher, and the title of one of several recent biographies is tellingly titled *Edgar Morin, L'Indiscipliné*, or "Edgar Morin, the Undisciplined" (Lemieux 2009).

Morin and the other thinkers I mentioned shared concerns that can be summarized by some key quotes:

> We need a kind of thinking that relinks that which is disjointed and compartmentalized, that respects diversity as it recognizes unity, and that tries to discern interdependencies. We need a radical thinking (which gets to the root of problems), a multidimensional thinking, and an organizational or systemic thinking. (Morin and Kern 1999, 130)

> The reform in thinking is a key anthropological and historical problem. This implies a mental revolution of considerably greater proportions than the Copernican revolution. Never before in the history of humanity have the responsibilities of thinking weighed so crushingly on us. (Morin and Kern 1999, 132)

> The most important task today is, perhaps, to learn to think in the new way. (Bateson 1972, 462)

(Here we find an immediate opportunity for "subunderstanding," because neither of these "thinkers" neatly separates thinking and feeling, for instance—or more generally perhaps, thinking and *being*.)

It is not surprising that Bateson, Jantsch, Maruyama, and Morin have all drawn extensively from General Systems Theory (GST) and Cybernetics. Both GST and Cybernetics emerged as attempts to develop a "transversal" language, a way of thinking that could move across disciplines and re-connect what had been torn asunder in disciplinary fragmentation (M. C. Bateson 2004). Both were supposed to provide a language that could go beyond the barrier of hyper-specialization so that scholars could talk to each other using basic concepts like open system, feedback, etc. Bateson, Maruyama, and Morin have explored the epistemological implications of GST and cybernetics in considerable depth.

These transversal approaches stress the importance of context, and the dangers of decontextualization. If traditional science stressed the importance of the laboratory as the privileged locus for inquiry, to isolate variables, and remove exogenous factors, systems and cybernetic approaches stressed the importance of context and relationship. Reductionist thinking ignores context, and these thinkers saw the implications clearly.

> Without context, words and actions have no meaning at all. This is true not only of human communication in words but also of all communication whatsoever, of all mental process, of all mind, including that which tells the sea anemone how to grow and the amoeba what he should do next. (Bateson 2002, 14)

> There are many catastrophic dangers which have grown out of the Occidental errors of epistemology. I believe that this massive aggregation of threats to man and his ecological systems arises out of errors in our habits of thought at a deep and partly unconscious level (Bateson 1972, 487)

All four thinkers critiqued the dominant way of thinking. The focus on simplicity, inherited from Descartes, meant eliminating complexity. But the complex is that which is woven together, so in the process of simplifying our subject, we unraveled the weave, lost the context. What we got what still extremely useful, but it was partial, and did not provide us with what used to be called "the big picture," Barabasi's "whole," and completely ignored relationships and interconnectedness (Barabasi 2003). We may see the individual threads, but not what Bateson called the pattern that connects (G. Bateson 1972, 2002).

In traditional Machine thinking, reductionism was key. Reductionism holds that the best way to understand a phenomenon is to reduce it to its component parts. One definition of the term analysis, which is one of the most commonly used terms we use when we want to understand a phenomenon, is to reduce something to its component parts. The social sciences wanted to replicate the astonishing successes of the natural sciences, which had led to the Industrial Revolution. They therefore wanted to apply the methods and general principles of physics to study social phenomena (Matson 1964). This has led to some considerable successes, but has also some notable problems. The application of reductionism to the social sciences was challenged by the transversal sciences I mentioned above.

One of the central problems was to apply the method René Descartes had already prefigured in his *Rules for the Direction of Mind*, which we can think of as his manual for clear and effective thinking.

Descartes (1701/1954, 179) wrote that "If we are to understand a problem perfectly, we must free it from any superfluous conceptions, reduce it to the simplest terms, and by process of enumeration, split it up into the smallest possible parts."

The problem here is that in our effort to understand human phenomena, splitting the problem up into simplest terms and finding the smallest significant variable can eliminate precisely what is most human about humanity. To reduce love to hormones, for instance, or brain functions, may provide us with interesting information about hormones and the brain, but ultimately does little to shed light on the wonderful, at times perplexing, often overwhelming, experience that is love. What is even more problematic is the tendency associated with some forms of reductionist approaches to take a "nothing but" approach, whereby, for instance, love is *nothing but* some changes in human neurophysiology, and more broadly that human beings are *nothing but* the function of genes, for instance (Koestler and Smythies 1972).

The "nothing but" we are left with in hyper-reductionist approaches is, in the social sciences, the fundamental unit of analysis. In other words, where do we begin? With the smallest significant unit. This reflects the relationship between reductionism and atomism, which holds that the world can be reduced to basic fundamental atoms, or indivisible "things" that make up the world. Some forms of reductionism can be related to atomism to the extent that the inquirer believes the simplest term or variable is precisely this irreducible atom that is worth studying in any inquiry—what it's *really* all about. This approach considers everything besides the atom "epiphenomenal," meaning secondary phenomena that are not relevant to the inquiry, in the process freeing the problem of any of what Descartes called superfluous conceptions.

In the social sciences in particular, this approach can be very problematic. If one is studying leadership or creativity, for example, one can focus on the individual leaders or creators and ignore their context, the social, political, cultural, and other dimensions. Most psychotherapy has also taken such an approach. The client comes into the therapist's office, and presents his or her issue. The inquiry and proposed solutions (therapies) focus exclusively on the individual's cognitive processes, emotions, and so on, but therapists generally do not address any other aspects of the client's life, let alone interact with them. The therapist never sees where the person lives or works, who s/he spends time with, and other aspects of life that are surely crucial. If she does hear about them, which is not the case in some forms of therapy, it is still only from the client. An alternative to this approach is Family Systems Therapy, which begins to actively look at the broader context (Hoffman 1981, 2001). This approach often involves bringing entire families into the therapist's office, and views the presenting issue not a problem specific to the individual, but the result of certain relational family dynamics, of a larger system of relationships.

One of the key assumptions of a certain kind of popular reductionist approach is that the simplest term or variable is viewed as a "thing." In systems language such an approach is considered to hold that the unit of analysis (the creator, leader, or therapist in my examples) is a *closed system* (von Bertalanffy 1976). Closed systems are technically closed to their environment and do not exchange matter and information with it. Clearly our examples—creators, leaders, and therapy clients—do exchange matter and information with their environment, but viewing them as a fundamentally closed system has been a consistent strategy of inquiry.

One reason for this strategy is that it achieves one of Descartes's aims: simplicity. Including all the other factors is simply a daunting task, requiring knowledge dispersed in a variety of disciplines. It also raises the question of what is and is not significant to the inquiry. This emerges in the search for the unit of analysis. How does one define what is and is not relevant for one's inquiry, and how can one hope to have the background necessary to draw on research that may be unfamiliar to us, or at least not in the core of our own formation?

The open and closed system distinction has very clear implications. If I choose to understand leadership from a closed system perspective, and define my unit of analysis as an individual leader, I might research his or her personality traits, decision-making style, or cognitive processes. But is that enough to understand the complexities of leadership, let alone to provide information that can be useful for leaders? Such an approach can also lead to simply ignoring certain forms of leadership or creativity.

Here we begin to see the connection between a certain way of thinking and its manifestation in the social systems we have constructed. With the printing press and then the scientific and industrial revolutions, there came an enormous proliferation of, and access to, information. Aristotle could write about everything from biology to poetry to ethics, and even in the eighteenth century Immanuel Kant wrote an important work about the Earth's rotation and developed a Nebular hypothesis of the origin of the solar system, as well as the later works he is more known for today on ethics, aesthetics, and the limits to knowledge. But gradually the division of labor set in through specialization and the compartmentalization of knowledge in disciplines.

It's much easier, more manageable, to focus on one specific topic, or a constellation of related topics, than to meander all over the place, crossing into the "territory" of other disciplines, to be a poacher, particularly when it's hard enough to keep up with all the research in our own field. In terms of inquiry, therefore, these are some of the problems of an open system approach.

With disciplinary fragmentation, a number of topics did not "fit" into any discipline. When I first started researching creativity in the mid-1980s it was viewed as individual, personal, the province of the genius and his (and rarely her) personality, imagination, and thinking. Because of this focus, which reflected (once again largely unchallenged and unspoken) cultural and historical assumptions, creativity "lived" in psychology. But this meant that creativity in relationships, groups, and organizations was either ignored because it was simply not "seen" through the lens of (individual) psychology or dismissed as reducible to the process "inside" one individual. And sometimes, alternative views were flatly rejected: creativity is *only* a function of individuals, and there is no such thing as relational creativity—it's always the individual. A camel is a horse designed by a committee. Other people just get in the way. Brainstorming was the only tip of the hat to "collaborative creativity," and tellingly it's a somewhat artificial procedure of dubious value. What about simple dialogue with colleagues, playing with ideas over coffee, arguing over dinner and a bottle of wine, the excitement of sharing ideas with friends late into the night, the more convivial, everyday, unstructured processes? The scholarly models and frames did not seem to reflect the lived experience of people engaging in the improvisational exchanges William Irwin Thompson has called "mind-jazz" (Thompson 1989).

I came to creativity research from my experience as a musician, particularly interested in collective improvisation. But when I reviewed the literature, I found the three Ps of traditional creativity were Person, Process, Product (Barron and Harrington 1981). The very way the topic of creativity was framed could not account for what I was interested in. The "who" of creativity was only the Person. By definition, therefore, not the group, the relationship, the conversation, the friendship, the history. And consequently there was little or no research on musical groups, or any other relational dimensions of creativity, until quite recently (Montuori and Purser 1995). And yet the magic of improvisational music, whether in jazz or in "rock" bands like the Grateful Dead and King Crimson or the world-jazz of Weather Report was an emergent property of the *interaction* between musicians. It was a relational process. This could not be accounted for at the time, and has only recently become the subject of systematic research.

Another troubling issue was that the deeper philosophical assumptions underlying most disciplinary perspectives were mostly ignored. From Plato to Hobbes and Locke, political philosophy was based on well-articulated assumptions about human nature. Some of the early philosophers showed up in histories of several disciplines—Plato and Locke in histories of both political science and psychology, for instance. But if "human nature" was discussed at all in political science and international relations, it was still in the terms outlined by the philosophers, and then mostly through Machiavelli's famous dicta. None of the important research in psychology I was interested in during graduate school—humanistic psychology and the emerging transpersonal field—were addressed. Any "official" reference to psychology or human nature dated back to when the split from philosophy occurred, and no efforts had been made to keep a dialogue going.

Economics was even more dismal. Rational Choice theory may have its place, but leaving out consumer motivations, values, ethics, and psychology in general, not to mention larger social and cultural factors is surely bordering on *reductio ad absurdum*.

How did economists get it so wrong?, asked Paul Krugman rather controversially in a 2009 *New York Times* article, after the recent economic meltdown. Up to that point macro-economists thought they had it all figured out. Apparently not. Economics, allegedly the most "scientific" of the social sciences, was also the most isolated, the discipline least likely to "play well with others." Its reductionist quantophrenia led to an illusion of security, of a solid scientific foundation. Individual disciplines are unable to provide us with the knowledge we need to address the overwhelming complexity of global problems.

> I have taught various branches of behavioral biology and cultural anthropology to American students ranging from college freshmen to psychiatric residents, in various schools and teaching hospitals, and I have encountered a very strange gap in their thinking that springs from a lack of certain *tools* of thought. This lack is rather equally distributed at all levels of education, among students of both sexes and among humanists as well as scientists. Specifically, it is a lack of knowledge

of the presuppositions not only of science but of everyday life. (Bateson 2002, 23)

When I was living on the Monterey Peninsula 1988 I met Riane Eisler and David Loye. David had written brilliant books on a variety of topics, ranging from the brain to future studies to political psychology, and an award winning book on racism and prejudice. I had only just read Riane's *The Chalice and the Blade*, and when I told her about my interest in creativity she asked me to look into the creativity of women (Eisler 1987). Once again a number of doors opened and gave me glimpses into a different world, the emerging literature on the psychology and sociology of women, including Lorraine Code's powerful work on feminist epistemology (Code 1991), and the remarkable fact that much of women's experience was simply not addressed in the literature.

Exploring the creativity of women once again led me to read in a variety of disciplines. Any number of arguments were being made about why women were not represented in lists of eminent creatives, ranging from the essentialist to the insulting. A clear argument could be made that women were for years simply not given access to the very domains in which "eminent" contributions to creativity could be made. But this was a "social" argument that was not part of the general discourse of creativity. A steady interweaving of perspectives followed, and it became clear that it was precisely this process of weaving together, or complexification, that leads to more nuanced perspectives on vexing topics living in fragmented isolation.

I began to see not only the nature of fragmentation, but also the way in which our dualistic thinking, driven by binary oppositions, was profoundly limiting. And the work of Morin and others stressed the need to go beyond these traditional dualisms. For Basarab Nicolescu, a key figure in the development of Transdisciplinarity, "Transdisciplinarity transgresses the duality of opposing binary pairs: subject/object, subjectivity/objectivity, matter/consciousness, nature/divine, simplicity/complexity, reductionism/holism, diversity/unity. The duality is transgressed by the open unity that encompasses both the universe and the human being" (2002, 56). To this we should add, female/male.

MULTIDISCIPLINARY DISCIPLINES

Environmental Studies, Women's Studies, Cultural Studies, Genomics, Robotics, Neuroscience, Artificial Intelligence, and Nanotechnology are some of the most interesting and vital new disciplines. These new disciplines are all mutts, incorporating elements originating in a wide variety of other established disciplines, but now themselves taking on the status of "disciplines." Environmental Studies is an explicitly interdisciplinary field, studying human interactions with the environments, and draws heavily on systems and complexity theories, as my colleague Jennifer Wells has shown. It is informed by ecology as well as ethics, sociology, biology, and economics, among others. Women's studies are also multi- or interdisciplinary, drawing from politics, psychology, sociology, economics, neuroscience, and more. These disciplines arose out of the need to address specific *issues*, such as economic inequality, racism, sexism, and so on, and the underlying assumptions that fueled them.

The curricula of most management programs already draw on a variety of disciplines and research traditions. Students in the Harvard MBA take required courses: Finance, Leadership and Organizational Behavior, Marketing, Technology and Operations Management, Business Government and the International Economy. They can choose electives on Innovation, Negotiation, The Moral Leader in Literature, Film, and Art, area specific courses which include studying specific cultures, and much more. A recent Introduction to the Psychology of Leadership course at Harvard covers topics like Ethics, Charisma, Appreciative Inquiry, Positive Psychology, Slavery, and Mindfulness. Clearly this already provides a multi-disciplinary perspective. We should, therefore, acknowledge the extent to which we are already drawing on other disciplines within some of our established "disciplines." And it is perhaps not surprising that this is mostly happening in what are perhaps the least traditionally "academic" disciplines, the ones that prepare practitioners, because approaching complex practices like leadership from the perspective of one discipline is enormously limiting.

But if our dominant way of thinking is still rooted in the machine view of the world, in analysis, how do we connect all these different sources? How do we go beyond a smorgasbord of courses that simply provide a set of diverse tools? This is a question that is now being addressed out of necessity, because as Bateson (2002) had already seen:

> While so much that universities teach today is new and up-to-date, the presuppositions or premises of thought upon which all our teaching is based are ancient, and, I assert, obsolete. (203)

> The pattern which connects. Why do schools teach almost nothing of the pattern which connects? (7)

The implications of Transdisciplinarity are revolutionary. Fortunately they are beginning to be explored, and on several continents, as McGregor and Volckmann have shown in their book on emerging trends in Transdisciplinarity, *Transversity: Transdisciplinary Approaches in Higher Education* (2011). Lively debates are emerging, and there are ambitious efforts to develop inter- or transdisciplinary curricula. Things are changing, and for me participating in these new dialogues and explorations is tremendously exciting. These debates themselves reflect some of the core issues of transdiscipinarity, namely the larger societal and professional context: how do students with innovative and unusual degrees present themselves in academia and more generally, in professional contexts that are still driven by disciplinary fragmentation?

ALWAYS RETURNING

What emerges is a binocular view of becoming, a sort of perspectival perception of processes and forms. In other words, to develop this perspective, it is necessary to dissolve a problem and learn an art. What needs to be dissolved is the problem of the comprehensive and panoramic synthesis, in other words of a criterion for judgment that is acontextual and definitive, creating a synthesis of competitive points of view, and aims to separate the essential from the inessential, permanent and transitory, primary and secondary. What we can learn is the art of shifting our viewpoint, circulating among points of view, and the expansion of the context in which initial oppositions are located. It is the art of the traveler who, with his own motion lays down a path in walking, or the deciferer of hints who immerses herself in the context and interrogates what she encounters to decide what point of view is most pertinent in that particular moment of her history (Ceruti 2008, 52).

There have been several underlying themes in my own research, and I find that no matter what disciplinary angle or topic I am working with, I am somehow always grappling with the same questions. This is not unusual, I believe, and the philosopher of science Gerald Holton used the term *themata* to refer to the ongoing themes and questions we are always returning to (1988). These days I am particularly keen to take systems thinking, cybernetics, and complex thought out of the realm of the strictly scientific and bring them to bear on the most intimate dimensions of our lives. As one example, I am fascinated by what I am calling complex emotions, those situations when we are feeling both happy and sad, for instance. The Brazilian expression *saudade* captures this mixture of happiness and sadness, usually associated with longing, missing somebody or someplace, and yet being happy that the person or place exists at all (Montuori 2003). There are so many situations that are ambiguous, where we are neither completely happy or completely sad, where we make choices that can very well lead to a positive outcome and yet also lead to the loss of other potentials and opportunities. Immigrants know these feelings when they express gratitude for the benefits of their new country, but also sadness for the home country they have left behind. The complexity lies, of course, in the fact that there are often no easy answers, no black and white, either/or solutions (Chan 2002, 2012; Low 2011).

What I appreciate about complex thought is that, drawing on cybernetics, it does see life not in static, either/or terms, the clear unambiguous demarcation of *this* will make me *absolutely* happy, and *that* will not. While some things may fall into those simply categories, most interesting things, events, and people in life do not. Complexity approaches the world in an arguably more Taoist way, as an ongoing process of navigating the complex options we have, and recognizing that inside every yang there lives a yin, and vice versa. The story of King Midas is a reminder that just because gold (or whatever we desire) is good, that doesn't mean that having more of it or turning everything into gold is necessarily better, or, as Paul Watzlawick writes in his pithy little book *Ultra-solutions, or How to fail most successfu*lly (1988), twice as much is not necessarily twice as good.

A concluding and central theme I'd like to mention is the Scylla and Charybdis of absolutism and relativism. On the global stage, these two terms play themselves out in their most extreme forms as fundamentalism and nihilism. *In practice*, there is no such thing as "absolute relativism," since it would mean completely random behavior. Instead of randomness, what we find is selfishness—reducing everything to the self, to personal power and accumulation, and potentially also descending into hopelessness when the bling doesn't do it thing anymore.

The philosopher Richard Bernstein (1983, 2005) has written eloquently about the phenomenon of Cartesian Anxiety. He describes Cartesian Anxiety as the fear that if there is no absolute foundation to guide our lives, no metanarratives, whether in religion, science, or political ideology. The metanarratives, the big stories that held all the smaller stories together and helped to make sense of them, are gone. There is a fall into an abyss in which anything goes. And indeed we sometimes hear this in discussion when religious believers question whether it is possible to have ethics without God. Their answer is almost inevitably no. My own interest in this topic has undoubtedly emerged through my experiences in a variety of political, cultural, and religious systems, not belonging to any of them, and wanting to give what might once again be a rather self-serving answer based on my experience.

One of the reasons why the complex thought of Morin, and the epistemology of Mauro Ceruti (1994), Gianluca Bocchi (Bocchi and Ceruti 2002, 2004) and others in that Mediterranean complexity tradition appealed to me is because their approach to knowledge involved an exploration of what to do in a context full of uncertainty and ambiguity. In the more traditional epistemological approaches, *certain* knowledge is always the goal. But what if one accepts uncertainty, and acknowledges that our uncertainty and ignorance far outstrip our certainty and our knowledge? What if we accept what Bernstein and pragmatists called *pragmatic fallibilism*, an attitude that accept all knowledge as provisional and open to revision (Bernstein 2005)? If uncertainty and ambiguity are viewed as sources for potential creativity, as well as error and illusion? What to do if we are not guided by absolute principles, but also want to avoid the nihilistic, the self-centered, the dilettante?

I have discussed this issue in a less philosophical way in the context of education (Montuori 2006, 2012). In what I call Reproductive Education (Montuori 2011a) we simply reproduce the absolute knowledge in the words of the wise one, the hierarchy from the teacher to the "great man" or more rarely the "great woman" s/he is talking about, in the same way that classical musicians play the music of the great composer as filtered through the orchestra conductor. The alternative to Reproductive Education is what I call Narcissistic Education, which emerges in opposition to it, and thereby throws out the baby of craft, critical thinking, serious reflection, and immersion in the literature, with the bathwater of oppressive authoritarianism. My alternative draws from musical improvisation (Montuori 2003). Jazz musicians, and also more generally improvising modern musicians, exist within a tradition or set of traditions, a repertoire, a set of instrumental skills, a community of colleagues, and so on. They develop their craft relationally in space and time, learning the history of their music, learning about the people and places and movements, and learning about themselves, their predecessors, their communities, how they are integrating all that has gone before, and how they are moving the music forward. In other words, beyond the Scylla and Charybdis of the absolutist/reproductive approach and the relativist/narcissistic approach, there's the life of Creative Inquiry, of open navigation in a relational network, of questioning the given, learning, developing craft, remaining open, attentive, situating ourselves in an ecology of knowledge, in time and space (Tulku 1987). Rather than viewing uncertainty, ambiguity, and open-endedness as the enemy, as something to be eliminated in favor of certainty, of Descartes's clear and distinct ideas, they become symbols of creativity and entry points into creation and genealogies of creation: How did we get here? What have we created? Where can we hope for? What are "good" futures? How can I embody this good future in the present?

Again, although this discussion takes me into deeply philosophical fields, it emerges out of questions in my own life, and has found applications and articulation in my own teaching. What I am looking for in the process of my inquiry is always returning to its applications and implications for my life, and more broadly for how we, as human beings, make sense of the world, how we live our lives together. Unless it's grounded in experience, and the possibility of making a difference in my life and that of others, it has little interest for me.

CONCLUDING REFLECTIONS

I have devoted much of my life to several of the interrelated topics that have arisen out of my desire to make sense of a complex world in a way that truly reflected its complexity rather than eliminate it or reduce it to simple categories and essences. In academia, I teach in two Transdisciplinary programs, one of which includes a semester-long course entitled *Transdisciplinarity and the Pattern that Connects*. My quest is continually enlivened by the constant challenge of assessing how to make a Transdisciplinarity curriculum exciting, vital, rigorous, relevant, and practical for new generations of students who share a passion for going beyond traditional approaches and have often come from educational experiences with extremely limited and limiting disciplinary perspectives. There are many challenges, and there is much unlearning to do.

In collaboration with my wife, a jazz singer, I continue to play music and produce records that span many musical styles because that's how we hear it, that's what we play, and that's who we are. There is now a much greater openness to musical hybrids. As a member of the National Association of Recording Arts and Sciences I have once again witnessed a debate about the nature of categories and musical styles when the Grammys restructured their awards and eliminated over 30 categories in the process. The dialogue was heated, harsh words were spoken, and law suits filed by musicians from a category that has been eliminated. The questions are still vital, mostly having to do with the difficulty in establishing what musical categories should be represented in what can only be a limited number of awards, and even what actually constitutes a musical category in this age of mash-ups and fusion and remixes. The questions and issues parallel many of the ones explored in the context of Transdisciplinarity.

I continue to be a mutt, and proud of it. But now there are new ways of approaching muttness, and concepts like cosmopolitanism, hybridity and liquid identity are casting a new light on my questions. These new approaches reflect different cultural realities, new demographics, and new ways of thinking. And they provide me with new opportunities to explore not just my own identity, but ways of dialoguing and thinking about identity.

All of which tells me that Transdisciplinarity and Complexity are ideas whose time has come. Exploring and articulating my approach to them will be a passionate endeavor for me and many others, and one of the most exciting adventures in inquiry today. The networked society, with the amazing power of new technology, gives us access to more information than ever before. The problem now is not access to information. It's how to organize that information, turn it into knowledge, and use that knowledge wisely. This is the challenge of Complexity and Transdisciplinarity.

NOTE

1. Barron later wrote a chapter in a book of essays put together for Koestler when he turned 70 (Harris 1976), and I in turn put together a Festschrift for Barron (Montuori 1996).

REFERENCES

Adorno, T. W., E. Frenkel-Brunswik, D. J. Levinson, and R. N. Sanford. 1982. *The authoritarian personality (Abridged edition)*. New York: Norton.

Allison, G. T. 1971. *Essence of decision: Explaining the Cuban missile crisis*. New York: Little, Brown and Company.

Appiah, K. A. 2006. *Cosmopolitanism. Ethics in a world of strangers*. New York: Norton.

Barabasi, A. 2003. *Linked. How everything is connected to everything else and what it means for business, science, and everyday life*. New York: Plume.

Barron, F. and D. Harrington. 1981. Creativity, intelligence, and personality. *Annual Review of Psychology*, 32: 439–476.

Bateson, G. 1972. *Steps to an ecology of mind*. New York: Bantam.

———. 2002. *Mind and nature: A necessary unity*. Cresskill, NJ: Hampton Press.

Bateson, M. C. 2004. *Our own metaphor: A personal account of a conference on the effects of conscious purpose on human adaptation*. Cresskill, NJ: Hampton Press.

Becker, E. 1976. *The structure of evil*. New York: Free Press.

Bernstein, R. 1983. *Beyond objectivism and relativism. Science, hermeneutics, and practice*. Philadelphia: University of Pennsylvania Press.

———. 2005. *The abuse of evil: Politics and religion after 9/11*. Malden, MA: Polity Press.

Bocchi, G. and M. Ceruti. 2002. *The narrative universe*. Cresskill, NJ: Hampton Press.

———. 2004. *Educazione e globalizzazione [Education and globalization]*. Milano: Raffaello Cortina.

Callahan, M., R. Eisler and D. Loye. 1993. *Sex, death, & the angry young man : conversations with Riane Eisler and David Loye*. Ojai, CA: Times Change Press.

Capra, F. 1984. *The turning point: Science, society, and the rising culture*. New York: Bantam.

Ceruti, M. 1994. *Constraints and possibilities. The evolution of knowledge and knowledge of evolution*, Trans. Montuori, A. New York: Gordon & Breach.

———. 2008. *Evolution without foundations*. Cresskill, NJ: Hampton Press.

Chan, K. B. 2002. Both sides, now: Culture contact, hybridization, and cosmopolitanism. In *Conceiving cosmopolitanism*, Eds. Cohen, R. and Vertovec, C., 191–208. Oxford: Oxford University Press.

———. 2012. *Cultural hybridity: Contradictions and Dilemmas*. New York: Taylor & Francis Group.

Code, L. 1991. *What can she know? Feminist theory and the construction of knowledge*. Ithaca, NY: Cornell University Press.

Collins, R. 1998. *The sociology of philosophies: A global history of intellectual change*. Cambridge: MA: Belknap Harvard.

Csikszentmihalyi, M. 1996 The creative person. *Psychology Today* (July–August): 36–40.

Descartes, R. 1954. *Philosophical writings*. London: Open University Press.

Eisler, R. 1987. *The chalice and the blade*. San Francisco: Harper Collins.

———. 1995. *Sacred pleasure: Sex, myth, and the politics of the body*. New York: Harper-Collins.

Fisher, G. 1980. *International negotiation: A cross-cultural perspective*. Chicago: Intercultural Press.

———. 1997. *Mindsets: The role of culture and perception in international relations* (2nd ed.). Yarmouth, ME: Intercultural Press.

———. 1998. *The mindsets factor in ethnic conflict: a cross-cultural agenda*. Yarmouth, ME: Intercultural Press.

Fuller, R. B. 1969. *Operating manual for spaceship earth*. Carbondale: Southern Illinois University Press.

Goerner, S. 1999. *After the clockwork universe*. Edinburgh: Floris Books.

Gordon, L. R. 2006. *Disciplinary decadence. Living thought in trying times*. Boulder: Paradigm.

Gruber, H. E. 1999. Evolving systems approach. In *Encyclopedia of creativity* (Vol. 1), Eds. Runco, M. and Pritzker, S., 689–693. San Diego: Academic Press.

Hampden-Turner, C. 1971. *Radical man. The process of psycho-social development*. Garden City, NY: Anchor Books.

———. 1999. Control, chaos, control: A cybernetic view of creativity. In *Social creativity* (Vol. 2), Eds. Purser, R. and Montuori, A., 17–31. Cresskill, NJ: Hampton Press.

Handy, C. 1994. *The age of paradox*. Boston: Harvard Business School Press.

Harris, H., ed. 1976. *Astride the two cultures: Arthur Koestler at 70* (1st American ed.). New York: Random House.

Hetherington, M. J. and J. D. Weiler. 2009. *Authoritarianism and polarization in American politics*. New York: Cambridge University Press.

Hoffman, L. 1981. *Foundations of family therapy: A conceptual framework for systems change*. New York: Basic.

———. 2001. *Family therapy: An intimate history*. New York: W.W. Norton.

Holton, G. 1988. *Thematic origins of scientific thought. Kepler to Einstein*. Cambridge, MA: Harvard University Press.

Jantsch, E. 1975. *Design for evolution: Self-organization and planning in the life of human systems*. New York: G. Braziller.

———. 1980. *The self-organizing universe: scientific and human implications of the emerging paradigm of evolution* (1st ed.). Oxford: New York: Pergamon Press.

Keen, S. 1991. *Faces of the enemy: Reflections of the hostile imagination*. New York: HarperCollins.

Koestler, A. 1979. *Janus: A summing up*. London: Picador.

———. 1982. *The ghost in the machine* (1st American ed.). New York: Random House.

———. 1990. *The act of creation*. New York: Penguin Books.

Koestler, A. and J. R. Smythies, ed. 1972. *Beyond reductionism, new perspectives in the life sciences: [proceedings of] the Alpbach Symposium [1968]* (New ed.). London: Hutchinson.

Krugman, P. 2009, September 6. How did economists get it so wrong? *New York Times*, p. MM36.

Kuhn, T. 1996. *The structure of scientific revolutions* (3rd ed.). Chicago: University of Chicago Press.

Laszlo, E. 1969. *System, structure, and experience; toward a scientific theory of mind*. New York: Gordon and Breach.

———. 1996a. *Evolution: The general theory*. Cresskill, NJ: Hampton Press.

———. 1996b. *The systems view of the world: A holistic vision for our time*. Cresskill, NJ: Hampton Press.

———. 1999. The "genius hypothesis": Exploratory concepts for a scientific understanding of unusual creativity. In *Social creativity* (Vol. 1), Eds. Montuori, A. and Purser, R., 317–330. Cresskill, NJ: Hampton Press.

Lechte, J. 1994. *50 key thinkers*. New York: Routdlege.

Lemieux, E. 2009. *Edgar Morin l'indiscipliné*. Paris: Seuil.

Low, A. 2011. *I am, therefore I think*. Bloomington, IN: iUniverse.

Maalouf, A. 2001. *In the name of identity: Violence and the need to belong* (1st North American ed.). New York: Arcade: Distributed by Time Warner Trade.

Maruyama, M. 1963. The second cybernetics. Deviation-amplifying mutual causal processes. *American Scientist*, 51(June): 164–179, 250–256.

———. 1974. Paradigmatology and its applications to cross-disciplinary, cross-professional and cross-cultural-communication. *Dialectica* 28:135–196.

———. 1977. Heterogenistics: An epistemological restructuring of biological and social sciences. *Acta Biotheoretica* 26 (1): 120–136.

———. 1994. *Mindscapes in management: Use of individual differences in multicultural management*. Aldershot, Hants, England: Brookfield, VT: Dartmouth Publishing Company.

———. 2004. Polyocular vision or subunderstanding? *Organization* 25 (3): 467–480.

Maruyama, M., M. T. Caley and D. Sawada. 1994. *Mindscapes: The epistemologies of Magoroh Maruyama*. Yverdon, Switzerland: Langhorne Gordon and Breach.

Matson, F. W. 1964. *The broken image; man, science and society*. New York: G. Braziller.

Maturana, H. 1987. Everything is said by an observer. In *Gaia. A way of knowing*, Ed. Thompson, W. I., 65–82. Great Barrington, MA: Lindisfarne Press.

McGregor, S. and R. Volckmann. 2011. *Transversity: Transdisciplinary approaches in higher education*. Tucson, AZ: Integral Publishers.

Montuori, A. 1989. *Evolutionary competence: Creating the future*. Amsterdam: Gieben.

———, ed. 1996. *Unusual associates: A festschrift for Frank Barron*. Cresskill, NJ: Hampton Press.

———. 2003. The complexity of improvisation and the improvisation of complexity. Social science, art, and creativity. *Human Relations* 56 (2): 237–255.

———. 2005. How to make enemies and influence people. Anatomy of totalitarian thinking. *Futures* 37:18–38.

———. 2006. The quest for a new education: From oppositional identities to creative inquiry. *ReVision* 28 (3): 4–20.

———. 2011a. Reproductive learning. In *The encyclopedia of the science of learning*, ed. N. M. Seel (pp. 2838–2840). Heidelberg: Springer.

———. 2011b. Systems approach. In *The encyclopedia of creativity* (Vol. 2), ed. M. Runco and S. Pritzker, 414–421. San Diego: Academic Press.

———. 2012. Creative inquiry: Confronting the challenges of scholarship in the 21st century. *Futures. The Journal of Policy, Planning and Future Studies* 44 (1): 64–70.

Montuori, A. and I. Conti. 1993. *From power to partnership. Creating the future of love, work, and community*. San Francisco: Harper San Francisco.

Montuori, A. and R. Purser. 1995. Deconstructing the lone genius myth: Towards a contextual view of creativity. *Journal of Humanistic Psychology* 35 (3): 69–112.

———. 1996. Ecological futures: Systems theory, postmodernism, and participative learning in an age of uncertainty. In *Postmodernism and organization theory*, Eds. Boje, D., Gephart, D., and Joseph, T., 181–201. Newbury Park, CA: Sage.

Morgan, G. 2006. *Images of organization*. Thousand Oaks, CA: Sage.

Morin, E. 1985. *La Méthode, tome 2. La vie de la vie [Method, volume 2. The life of life]*. Paris: Seuil.

———. 1986. *La conoscenza della conoscenza. [Method, vol. 3. Knowledge of knowledge.]*. Milano: Feltrinelli.

———. 1990. *Science avec conscience [Science with conscience]*. Paris: Seuil.

———. 1991. *Le idee: habitat, vita, organizzazione, usi e costumi [Ideas: Habitat, life, organization, use, and customs.]*. Milano: Feltrinelli.

———. 2007. Restricted complexity, general complexity. In *Worldviews, science, and us: Philosophy and complexity*, Eds. Gershenson, C., Aerts, D., and Edmonds, B., 5–29. New York: World Scientific Publishing Company.

———. 2008a. *California journal*. Brighton: Sussex Academic.

———. 2008b. *On complexity*. Cresskill, NJ: Hampton Press.

———. 2008c. The reform of thought, transdisciplinarity, and the reform of the university. In *Transdisciplinarity. Theory and practice*, Ed. Nicolescu, B., 23–32. Cresskill, NJ: Hampton Press.

Morin, E. and B. Kern. 1999. *Homeland Earth: A manifesto for the new millennium*. Cresskill, NJ: Hampton Press.

Nicolescu, B. 2002. *Manifesto of transdisciplinarity*. Albany: SUNY Press.

Northouse, P. G. 2004. *Leadership. Theory and practice*. Thousand Oaks, CA: Sage.

Ogilvy, J. 1989. This postmodern business. *The Deeper News* 1 (5): 3–23.

Polkinghorne, D. 1983. *Methodology for the human sciences: Systems of inquiry*. Albany: State University of New York Press.

Purser, R. and A. Montuori, ed. 1999. *Social creativity* (Vol. 2). Cresskill, NJ: Hampton Press.

Robinson, K. 2001. *Out of our minds: Learning to be creative*. London: Capstone.

Runco, M. 2007. *Creativity. Theories and themes: Research, development, and practice*. Amsterdam: Elsevier.

Russell, D. W. 1983. *The religion of the machine age*. London: Routledge & Kegan Paul.

Simonton, D. K. 1999. The creative society: Genius vis-a-vis the Zeitgeist. In *Social creativity* (Vol. 1), ed. A. Montuori and R. Purser, 237–264. Cresskill, NJ: Hampton Press.

Spretnak, C. 2011. *Relational reality: New discoveries that are transforming the modern world*. Topsham, ME: Green Horizon Books.

Stenner, K. 2005. *The authoritarian dynamic*. Cambridge: Cambridge University Press.

Thompson, W. I. 1989. *Imaginary landscape. Making worlds of myth and science*. New York: St. Martin's Press.

Tulku, T. 1987. *Love of knowledge*. Oakland: Dharma Publishing.

von Bertalanffy, L. 1975. *Perspective on general systems theory: Scientific-philosophical studies*. New York: G. Brazilier.

———. 1976. *General System Theory: Foundations, development, applications*. New York: George Braziller.

Von Foerster, H. 1983. *Observing systems*. Salinas, CA: Intersystems Publications.

———. 1990. *Ethics and second order cybernetics*. Paper presented at the Paper presented at Systèmes & thérapie familiale. Ethique, Idéologie, Nouvelles Méthodes. Congrès International, Paris, October 4–6.

Von Glasersfeld, E. 1987. *The construction of knowledge*. Salinas, CA: Intersystems Publications.

Watzlawick, P. 1977. *How real is real?* New York: Vintage.

———., ed. 1984. *The invented reality: how do we know what we believe we know? Contributions to constructivism* (1st ed.). New York: Norton.

———. 1988. *Ultra-solutions, or, How to fail most successfully* (1st ed.). New York: Norton.

Wilden, A. 1980. *System and structure. Essays in communication and exchange*. London: Routledge & Kegan.

———. 1987. *Man and woman, war and peace*. New York: Routledge.

Wilshire, B. 1990. *The moral collapse of the university: Professionalism, purity, and alienation*. New York: SUNY Press.

Wren, J. T. 1995. *The leader's companion: Insights on leadership through the ages*. New York: Free Press.

Zimbardo, P. G. 2008. *The Lucifer effect: Understanding how good people turn evil*. New York: Random House Trade Paperbacks.

Index

Abraham, F.D. 24, 26, 80, 81, 126
Abraham, R.H. 24, 26, 79, 81
Abram, D. 35–6
Abrams, N.E. 41
absolutism 14–15, 35, 193–5
Abu Ghraib prison 178
Ackoff, R. 8, 10
Adams, M. 118
Adorno, T.W. 9, 178
advertising 158
Afghanistan 108
Allison, G. 181
allopoiesis 61, 63
ambiguity 194–5; complex emotions 193
ambiguity of me-as-center/me-as-periphery
    135–54; all is One 147–8; classical logic
    148–9, 152; complementarity, principle of
    149–51; condition of internal and external
    unity 154; creativity 141–4, 151–2; dynamic
    center 138, 142; dynamic unity 148, 151,
    152, 153; eyes 138–9, 140, 142; idealism
    136–7, 146, 147, 153; knowing and being
    146–51, 153–4; naive realism 136–7, 146,
    147, 153; product: an idea in a form with a
    demand 143; quantum mechanics 146, 149;
    refutation of solipsism 140; things are
    'empty' 145–7; uniqueness 144
Ames, R.T. 47
Amiden, A. 120–1
Anderson, S. 60
androgyny 19, 24
anthropology 7, 51, 60, 97, 98, 101, 171, 181,
    185
anthropomorphism 52–3
Appiah, K.A. 172
Arbib, M. 75
archeology 106
Aristotle 8, 180, 184, 189
Arnheim, R. 138
Arons, M. 122
arrogant and humble systems theory 4–5;
    arrogant systems theory 5–9; close friends
    make best enemies 9–10; in favor of

arrogance nonetheless 10–12; steering
    course between arrogance and humility 12–
    14; systems theory and ethical pluralism
    14–16
art 35, 52, 84, 87, 124, 125, 138
atomism 128, 188
authentic Self *see* integral science
authoritarianism 105, 131
autogenesis 102
autopoiesis 23, 43, 45, 61, 63, 64, 69, 70, 83,
    84, 86, 88, 89, 102

Bali 55
Banathy, B.A., Sr 126, 130
Banyacya, T. 65
Barabasi, A. 185, 187
Barbour, I.G. 21
Barnes, H.B. 87
Barron, F. 88, 173, 190
Barton, S. 26
Bassui (Zen master) 147
Bateson, G. 6, 7, 8, 10, 19, 20, 22, 23, 24, 28,
    34, 38, 68, 174, 176, 185, 186, 187, 190–1,
    192
Bateson, M.C. 1, 20, 23, 186
Beck, D. 86
Becker, E. 181
behaviorism 73, 89, 115
Bender, H. 125
Bennett, J.G. 141
Bentov, I. 55, 69
Bergson, H. 148
Berman, M. 129–30, 131
Bernstein, L. 150
Bernstein, R. 194
Berry, T. 35, 37, 39, 41, 44, 45
Bett, H. 42
Bianchi, F. 2
Bidell, T.R. 87
bioculturalism 94, 101, 103, 106, 110
bisociation 180
Bocchi, G. 174, 182, 194
Bohm, D. 19, 26, 128